ISAAC ASIMOV

Science-Fiction Writers

ROBERT SCHOLES, GENERAL EDITOR

H. Bruce Franklin: *Robert A. Heinlein: America as Science Fiction*

Frank McConnell: *The Science Fiction of H. G. Wells*

James Gunn: *Isaac Asimov: The Foundations of Science Fiction*

ISAAC ASIMOV
The Foundations of Science Fiction

James E. Gunn

OXFORD UNIVERSITY PRESS
Oxford   New York   Toronto   Melbourne
1982

OXFORD UNIVERSITY PRESS

Oxford   London   Glasgow
New York   Toronto   Melbourne   Wellington
Nairobi   Dar es Salaam   Cape Town
Kuala Lumpur   Singapore   Jakarta   Hong Kong   Tokyo
Delhi   Bombay   Calcutta   Madras   Karachi

Copyright © 1982 by Oxford University Press, Inc.
First published by Oxford University Press, New York, 1982
First issued as an Oxford University Press paperback, 1982

Library of Congress Cataloging in Publication Data

Gunn, James E., 1923–
   Isaac Asimov, the foundations of science
fiction.

   Bibliography: p.
   Includes index.
   1. Asimov, Isaac, 1920–   . 2. Authors,
American—20th century—Biography. I. Title.
PS3551.S5Z62   813′.54   81-19006
ISBN 0-19-503059-1   AACR2
ISBN 0-19-503060-5 (pbk.)

Printing (last digit): 9 8 7 6 5 4 3 2 1

Printed in the United States of America

To ISAAC,
who has dedicated books to so many,
this dedication

EDITOR'S FOREWORD

For the first eight decades of this century critics of fiction have reserved their highest praises for novels and stories that emphasize individual psychology in characterization, unique stylistic nuances in language, and plausibility in the events presented. It is an interesting feature of literary history that during this same period of time a body of fiction has flourished which privileges the type over the individual, the idea over the word, and the unexpected over the plausible event. This body of work, which has come to be called—with only partial appropriateness—"science" fiction, has had some recognition from serious critics but still hovers between genuine acceptance and total dismissal in literary circles.

Schools now offer courses in science fiction—either because one zealous teacher insists upon it or because "the kids read that stuff." But it is rare to hear of works of science fiction integrated into "regular" courses in modern literature. The major reason for this is that as long as the dominant criteria are believed to hold for all fiction, science fiction will be found inferior: deficient in psychological depth, in verbal nuance, and in plausibility of event. What is needed is a criticism serious in its standards and its concern for literary value but willing to take seriously a literature based on ideas, types, and events beyond ordinary experience.

The *Science-Fiction Writers* series of critical volumes is an

attempt to provide that sort of criticism. In designing the series we have selected a number of authors whose body of work
has proved substantial, durable, and influential, and we have
asked an appropriate critic to make a book-length study of the
work of each author selected, taking that author seriously
enough to be critical and critically enough to be serious.

In each volume we will include a general view of the author's life and work, critical interpretations of his or her major
contributions to the field of science fiction, and a biographical
and bibliographical apparatus that will make these volumes
useful as a reference tool. The format of each book will thus
be similar. But because the writers to be considered have had
careers of different shapes, and because our critics are all individuals who have earned the right to their own interpretive
emphases, each book will take its own shape within the limits
of the general format. Above all, each volume will express the
critical views of its author rather than some predetermined
party line.

In the present volume James Gunn discusses a writer who
represents in the clearest possible way the difficulties involved in taking science fiction both seriously and critically.
Isaac Asimov has been enormously influential on the field of
science fiction, but by traditional literary standards he is far
from being a major writer. His most memorable characters are
robots, not people, and his great work, the Foundation Trilogy, can scarcely be said to have a plot, though it is full of
intrigue. Asimov, then, is one of those writers upon whom the
case for science fiction as a field with a different set of values
must rest.

What is the case for Asimov? Is it the case for a scientific
imagination rather than an artistic one? Not exactly: it is the
case for an imagination uniquely poised between the scientific
and the artistic. The "laws of robotics" which he invented are
neither literary nor scientific laws; they are the basis for
thought experiments, for language games that find their most
congenial expression in fictional form. So to, the "psychohistory" of Hari Seldon is not social science but the dream or

perhaps the nightmare of a scientist musing upon the laws of social behavior.

A strong imagination, great energy, combined with literary skills that evolve from the level of apprentice to journeyman but not much farther—that, in a nutshell, is the situation of Isaac Asimov. But we must add to it the fact that Asimov's skills have been sufficient. Rarely more than adequate in the traditional literary qualities of style, plot, and characterization, he has been superior in the qualities peculiar to science fiction: the generation and extrapolation of ideas about the development of science and technology, along with the imagination of the human results of scientific developments. It is because of these powers that he has reached his audience as a science-fiction writer and has had a profound influence on the field. He has been more active as a popularizer of science itself, of course, actually writing much less science fiction than many other writers, both great and small, but he is known for his science fiction, which remains in print, is widely anthologized, taught, and studied. The reasons for this influence and popularity are the subject of James Gunn's book.

Gunn is especially qualified to write on Asimov because he is at home in both the scientific and the literary fields. He is the only person to have been president of both the Science Fiction Writers of America and the academic Science Fiction Research Association. He holds a professorship in English, is a science-fiction writer of serious attainments, and has written an excellent "Illustrated History of Science Fiction" called *Alternate Worlds*. Like everyone in the field, he knows Isaac Asimov personally. Rather than pretend this is not the case and assume the guise of Olympian detachment, Gunn has chosen to acknowledge his acquaintance with Asimov by including an interview with him in this volume. What Matthew Arnold called "the personal estimate" is difficult enough to avoid when dealing with the grateful dead and perhaps impossible in writing about the living. But this has not prevented Gunn from attaining perspective on his subject and generating new insight into the thematic structures of his major works.

January 1982   R.S.

ACKNOWLEDGMENTS

My thanks to the University of Kansas General Research Fund for the grant (allocation #3313-x0-0038) that got me started on my research; to Professor Robert Scholes for his enthusiasm for science fiction and for the persuasiveness that resulted in this series of books being published by Oxford University Press; to John Wright for his cheerful support; to Kim Lewis for her careful copyediting and scrutiny of details that saved me from a number of careless mistakes; to Alexandra Mason and her staff in Special Collections at Spencer Research Library for the unlimited help they were willing to supply; and to Isaac Asimov for taking time out of a busy schedule for an interview and for his repeated suggestions that I should be writing my own fiction rather than writing about his.

Some of the approaches to Asimov's fiction have been drawn from the discussions during the Intensive English Institute on the Teaching of Science Fiction that is offered each summer at the University of Kansas, particularly the discussions of my colleague Steve Goldman, but the opinions and the writing and the errors are all mine.

Lawrence, Kansas   J.G.
December 18, 1981

CONTENTS

ISAAC ASIMOV

1

I, ASIMOV

Writing about the life of Isaac Asimov is like pouring water into the ocean. Asimov has written more about himself than any living author, and generally with frankness and insight. His autobiographical output began in 1962 with the first of his anthologies, *The Hugo Winners*, in which he inserted references to his own life in the introductions. Like many of the events in his life, this happened by accident. In his autobiography, Asimov mentions that he had never edited an anthology, thought it would be fun to try, but was not sure of his judgment in choosing the stories. The stories in *The Hugo Winners* already were chosen (they were the less-than-novel-length stories awarded Hugos by the World Science Fiction Conventions, beginning in 1955), and even the order was evident. All Asimov had to do was to write introductions. Since there was no question about the reason for the stories' inclusion, he decided to deal with the authors, and in a humorous way. The general introduction would be funny too and would deal with the fact that the editor had never won a Hugo. *The Hugo Winners*, indeed, became a highly personal book, as much about Asimov as about the Hugos or their winners. Since then, Asimov has gone on to edit more than a dozen anthologies and added comfortably to his more than two hundred volumes.

The Hugo Winners was a breakthrough for Asimov in an-

other area as well. Up to that point, Asimov says, his attempts
at humor had been well received in person but poorly in print.
Many readers of *The Hugo Winners* wrote to tell him that the
introductions were the best part of the book. After that, collections of his own stories began appearing with introductions,
at first (*The Rest of the Robots,* 1964) with notes about the
stories salted with a few personal comments and later with
full-blown autobiographical detail. This technique reached its
grandest expressions in *Opus 100* (1969), the story of how Asimov came to write one hundred books, with excerpts by cat-
egory; *The Early Asimov* (1972), a kind of autobiography with
illustrations from his early writing; and *Before the Golden Age*
(1974), which carried Asimov back to his earliest memories
and brought his life story up to *The Early Asimov,* illustrated
with his favorite science-fiction stories read between 1931 and
1938.

All of these works were limbering-up exercises for the
massive autobiography in two volumes, the first of which came
out in 1979 as his 200th book (along with *Opus 200,* which
he put together in fairness to Houghton Mifflin, which had
published *Opus 100*). The autobiography offers 1560 pages of
Asimov's life story, complete with photographs, a list of his
two hundred books, and indexes (which, he informs us, he
does not trust anyone else to do).

There have been a great many words about the life of a
man who admits he has "never done anything." They have
largely progressed from "and then I read" to "and then I wrote"
because Asimov's life has been woven from the warp and woof
of reading and writing. The triumph of his writing skill is that
he makes it all so readable.

This kind of obsession with self might be insufferable in a
person who was not at the same time openly amazed at the
good fortune, success, plaudits, renown, and wealth that have
come his way. Asimov has been greatly honored and richly
rewarded for remarkable achievements. Even so, to interpret
everything in terms of one's own reaction to it, including
World War II, may seem excessively egotistical. But Asimov's
attitude of "cheerful self-appreciation," which sometimes
breaks over into "charming Asimovian immodesties" (a phrase

coined by a Doubleday editor in response to a *Time* magazine
article quoting some of Asimov's self-praise), is balanced by
disarming Asimovian self-denigration.

In his autobiographical writings and comments, Asimov
continually invites the reader to share his triumphs, to laugh
at his blunders and lack of sophistication, and to wonder, with
him, at the rise to prominence of a bright Jewish boy brought
to this country from Russia at the age of three and raised in a
succession of Brooklyn candy stores. Asimov is aided too by
the fact that his readers are predisposed to enjoy his success
with him. Some are admirers of his science popularizations
and other non-fiction books and are curious about his earlier
life; others are science-fiction readers and fans, and the
science-fiction community still retains much of the solidarity
and lack of envy of its early ghetto days.

The problem remains: what more can a critic say about
Asimov's life and work that Asimov himself hasn't said already in nearly a million well-chosen words? Asimov's autobiographical writings are both an asset and an intimidation,
revealing priceless information about the circumstances of
creation and publication but also rendering redundant the
critic's job of digging out little-known facts about life and work.
Asimov's life is an open book—in fact, two hundred and more
open books.

Well, the critic can tell the Asimov story more selectively
and send the still curious on to fuller accounts elsewhere, bring
the details of the life into focus in illuminating the work, and
explain the work in terms of a thesis that may be too close to
Asimov for him to perceive. The critic also has an opportunity
to comment on the state of criticism as well as the work and
the author at hand. One reason for undertaking this study was
the conviction that much criticism of science fiction has been
misguided and particularly that critics of Asimov's work have
headed up false trails, trying to bring to the analysis of Asimov's fiction traditional methods and traditional criteria that
are unproductive when applied to Asimov and to much other
science fiction. What I found myself doing as I began writing,
then, was blending biographical, sociological, publishing, and
critical considerations into what I later perceived (perhaps

without sufficient perspective) was something a bit unusual in criticism, perhaps unnatural in normal circumstances, that I eventually thought of calling "criticism in context."

Within the following chapters, for instance, the reader will find a number of plot summaries. These are desirable for several reasons: first, because the reader may be familiar with many Asimov works but certainly not all; second, because the reader may remember the general outlines of stories and novels but not the revealing details; and third (and most important), because what happens is the most important aspect of Asimov's fiction (and most other science fiction) and what happens is revealed in plot.

Other matters that I found important as I got into my consideration of Asimov's work were the conditions under which the fiction was written and the way in which it was published. Asimov himself keeps referring to these matters in his autobiographical writings; he thinks they were important to what he wrote and didn't write, and so do I. In one footnote in his autobiography, he writes:

> In this book I am going to pay considerable attention to the details of the money I received for stories and other things. Perhaps I should be noble enough to rise above such sordid things as money, but the fact is I couldn't and didn't. The money I earned—or didn't earn—has influenced my pathway through life, and I must go into the financial details if the pathway is to make sense.

In the course of the chapters that follow, the reader will find frequent mention of why the fiction was written and how it got into print. The goal of the science-fiction writer was to get published, and the writing done was shaped by what was read in the magazines, what was said by an editor, what was paid for a story, and sometimes how readers responded. More traditional critics may feel that such concerns disqualify the writing from serious literary study. They are wrong: scholars have been trying for centuries to ferret out the same kind of information about Shakespeare's plays.

Asimov's early ambition, for instance, was to sell stories to *Astounding Science Fiction*. Two of his stories were published in *Amazing Stories* before one appeared in *Astound-*

ing; only the *Astounding* story really mattered to him. The relationship between Asimov and John W. Campbell, editor of *Astounding* beginning in 1937, was influential in Asimov's development. Asimov gives Campbell most of the credit for his early science fiction and even his later writing career.

In the analysis of Asimov's fiction that makes up most of this book, then, the reader will find mixed in with the critical comments many details of Asimov's life as they relate to his writing. This is more of his life than one might think: as Asimov himself recognizes, his life was his writing, and his other relationships were either detractions from or contributions to it.

Asimov provides a couple of illustrative anecdotes. When he received copies of his forty-first book from Houghton Mifflin, he mentioned to his wife the possibility of reaching a hundred books before he died. She shook her head and said, "What good will it be if you then regret having spent your life writing books while all the essence of life passes you by?" And Asimov replied, "But for me the essence of life *is* writing. In fact, if I do manage to publish a hundred books, and if I then die, my last words are likely to be, 'Only a hundred!' "

His daughter Robyn asked him to suppose he had to choose between her and—writing. Asimov recalls he said, "Why, I would choose you, dear." And adds, *"But I hesitated*—and she noticed that, too."

Asimov was born January 2, 1920 (as nearly as his parents could calculate; it may have been as early as October 4, 1919) in Petrovichi, U.S.S.R. Petrovichi is a small town about fifty-five miles south of Smolensk and about two hundred fifty miles southwest of Moscow. When Asimov was three, his parents emigrated with him to the United States, at the invitation and sponsorship of his mother's older half-brother. They settled in Brooklyn, where Asimov's father, handicapped by his lack of English and of job experience, bought a candy store in 1926. The candy store, and its successors, became a major part of Asimov's existence. "It was open seven days a week and eighteen hours a day," he reports in his autobiography, "so my father and mother had to take turns running it, and I had to pitch in, too."

The other important fact of Asimov's youth was his pre-
cocity. He had an unusual ability to learn and, as he later discovered, an unusually retentive memory. They were to be major assets in his life and career. He taught himself to read at
the age of five, entered the first grade before he was six (his
mother lied about his age), and became the brightest student
in his class early and continuously, even though he skipped
half a year of kindergarten, half a year of first grade, and half
a year of third grade and changed schools a couple of times.

Asimov's schoolboy practice was to read all his school-
books the first couple of days after he got them and then not
refer to them again. He acquired a reputation as a child prodigy and a sense of his own superiority that he didn't mind
letting other people see. They did not add to his popularity—
he was considered a smart-alecky kid—but he did not have
much association with others anyway. His work in the candy
store kept him busy after school, and the seven-day week meant
that he and his parents never visited anyone or had anyone
visit them.

Asimov recalls that he was orphaned by the candy store
(since he was deprived of his parents' companionship) as well
as protected by it (since he knew where his parents were at all
times). The candy store constricted and shaped his life until
he left home. It also meant that he grew up largely in the company of adults when he was in the store, or in the company of
books when he was not. Both no doubt contributed to his pre-
cocity.

Asimov completed junior high school in two years instead
of three and entered Boys High School of Brooklyn, which at
the time was a selective high school that had an excellent reputation for mathematics. He was twelve and a half upon entering, two and a half years younger than the normal age of fifteen. He continued to be sheltered: he had almost no contact
with girls, as he might have had at a co-educational school.
But in the world encapsulated in his autobiography almost
everything happened for the best—how could it not have happened for the best when he rose so far from such humble beginnings?—and he reasons that though being segregated from
girls may have kept him naïve far into his adolescence, it also

may have protected him from more severe symptoms of rejection, for he was so much younger than his female classmates. Moreover, he had a bad case of acne from twelve to twenty.

High school, however, was the beginning of a series of disillusionments. Asimov discovered limits to his intellectual ability. He was not as good a mathematician as some of the other boys, who may not have been as intelligent but had a special feeling for math. He never made the math team. He discovered as well that other students could study harder and accomplish more; Asimov stuck by his "understanding-at-once-and-remembering-forever" pattern. He had to abandon his illusion of universal brilliance when he discovered, for instance, that he disliked and could never understand economics. And even his attempts at creative writing were ridiculed in a high-school writing class. This bothered him more than anything else because his ambition to write fiction had been growing since the age of eleven, when he had begun writing a series book for boys called *The Greenville Chums at College*, copying it out in longhand in nickel copybooks. When Asimov was fifteen his father had found $10 to buy his son a much-longed-for typewriter, an office-size model.

More disappointments awaited him. His father wanted his elder son (there were two other children, a girl, Marcia, and a boy, Stanley) to become a physician, and the fifteen-year-old Asimov had come to share this ambition. But getting into medical school was not easy; medical schools had quotas (negative, not positive) on the number of Jewish applicants they would accept. For a variety of reasons, Asimov was never to be admitted to the study of medicine. By then his goals had changed, however. After high school, he applied to Columbia College, but was rejected—possibly, he speculates, because he did not make a good showing in interviews. He was asked to change his application to a Brooklyn branch of Columbia University called Seth Low Junior College, where enrollment was heavily Jewish.

Asimov also applied to City College of New York, which had no tuition and accepted him because his grades were excellent. He actually spent three days there before receiving a letter from Seth Low asking why he had not showed up. When his father explained to Seth Low authorities that the family could not afford the tuition, Seth Low came up with a hundred-dollar scholarship and a National Youth Administration job for $15 a month. Asimov switched colleges. His second year, after a summer spent in manual labor to earn enough money, was at the Morningside Heights campus because Seth Low had closed at the end of its tenth year. He was enrolled in Columbia University, not its more prestigious undergraduate college. Asimov was a second-class citizen throughout his undergraduate education, and he never forgot it. When he was graduated, he received a bachelor of science degree in chemistry instead of the bachelor of arts degree, for which University undergraduates were not eligible, he says.

In his second year of college, Asimov's distaste for zoology (he killed a cat and dissected it but never forgave himself) and embryology (he was not good at picking out details through a microscope and even worse at drawing them) led him to drop the biological sciences and switch to chemistry as a major. He liked chemistry and did well at it. After graduation from Columbia he applied (somewhat halfheartedly because of his distaste for biological courses) to a number of medical schools and was rejected by all of them. He went on with the study of chemistry in Columbia's graduate school, but only after some difficulty because he had not taken physical chemistry. He had to spend a troublesome year on probation. As usual, his problem had not been his grades or test scores but his "wise-guy personality."

Asimov obtained his M.A. in 1941 and was working toward his doctorate when the United States entered World War II. A few months later he suspended his studies in order to work as a chemist at the U.S. Navy Yard in Philadelphia, where for the first time he was free of his duties at the candy store and where the steady income gave him the opportunity to marry the woman with whom he had fallen in love, Gertrude Blugerman.

Asimov's autobiography suggests that he was good at the theory of chemistry but not at the practice. He refers to his poor laboratory technique and his difficulties getting the correct results. His talents were probably not those of a research chemist, nor those of a practicing scientist of any kind. But at the end of the war he returned to his doctoral program at Columbia, earned his degree in 1948, did a year of post-doctoral research at Columbia, and finally was offered a position as instructor in biochemistry at the Boston University School of Medicine.

Asimov's discovery of science fiction and his attempts to write it were more important to his final career than his studies. He had come upon *Amazing Stories* in 1928, its second year of publication, when he was eight years old. His father's candy store carried magazines, but the young Asimov was not allowed to read them because his father considered them a waste of time and a corrupting influence. They would turn him into "a bum," his father said. The boy had been reading library books of all kinds, but he longed for the brightly colored pulp magazines with their cover paintings of futuristic machines and planets and alien menaces. Finally, when Hugo Gernsback lost control of *Amazing* and brought out a competitor, *Science Wonder Stories*, the then nine-year-old boy brought the magazine to his father, pointed out the word "Science" in the title, and won his battle. Possibly his father just did not have the spirit to fight because his mother was about to give birth to Asimov's younger brother, Stanley.

The science-fiction magazines filled Asimov's imagination with ideas and dreams. They did not consume all his reading time because there weren't enough of them (only two a month at first, and only three a month in 1930). He kept up his omnivorous reading of other books, mostly library borrowings, but science fiction became what he lived for. Oddly enough, Asimov's early writing efforts did not focus on science fiction. "I had the most exalted notion of the intense skills and vast scientific knowledge required of authors in the field, and I dared not aspire to such things," he remembers.

On his new typewriter, however, he ventured into fantasy and then into science fiction. Like almost every aspiring author, Asimov started many stories and finished none, and what he wrote was derived mostly from what he liked to read. His derivative writing was to persist through several years of his career as a published writer until he finally rid himself of what he called his "pulpishness." He got his inspiration, his plots, even his vocabulary from other science-fiction writers. From them came the blasters and needle guns and force beams that litter his stories and early novels, and even, by an analogous process of invention, such concepts as neuronic whips and psycho-probes, hyperspace and Jumps. When he turned to more unique concepts such as psychohistory and the Foundations, the logical development of robots, a radioactive Earth and the lost origin of man, and particularly human reactions to overcrowded cities, his fiction began to glow with its own fire.

Not long after he got his typewriter, Asimov wrote a letter to *Astounding Stories* that was published in 1935. Two years later, when Campbell had become editor of the magazine and had changed its name to *Astounding Science Fiction*, Asimov began writing letters again, "commenting on the stories, rating them, and, in general, taking on the airs of a critic." Such letters became a monthly event; usually Campbell published them in a letter-to-the-editor section called then, as now, "Brass Tacks."

One Tuesday in May when the new *Astounding* was scheduled to arrive in his father's package of new magazines, it did not show up. The eighteen-year-old Asimov was terrified that it had ceased publication. He called the publisher, Street & Smith, and was assured that the magazine still was being published. But when the new issue had not arrived by the following Tuesday, he ventured off on the subway to the Street & Smith offices in Manhattan, where an executive told him that the publication date had been changed from the second Wednesday to the third Friday of the month. Two days later the magazine arrived.

His panic at the thought that *Astounding* might vanish sent Asimov to the typewriter to finish a story he had been working at for some months titled "Cosmic Corkscrew." He completed the story on June 19, 1938, and took it personally to the editor. Campbell was familiar with Asimov's name from his frequent letters and talked for more than an hour with the aspiring author, read the story overnight, and mailed it back two days later with a polite letter of rejection. That sent Asimov back to his typewriter to work on a story titled "Stowaway." He finished it in eighteen days and took this in person to Campbell. That story came back with a rejection in four days.

A pattern had been established. A rejection would come from Campbell but phrased in ways that would encourage Asimov to turn immediately to a new story. "It didn't matter that he rejected you," Asimov recalled. "There was an enthusiasm about him and an all-encompassing friendliness that was contagious. I always left him eager to write further." "Stowaway," however, did not end up lost for all time with "Cosmic Corkscrew." It eventually found its way into print, in the April 1940 *Astonishing Stories* edited by Frederik Pohl (as youthful an editor as Asimov was a writer), as "The Callistan Menace," though Asimov's third story, "Marooned Off Vesta," had appeared first, in the March 1939 *Amazing Stories*.

Meanwhile, Asimov had discovered other science-fiction readers, and not just readers but fans, fanatics like himself. This led progressively to fanzines, club meetings, and the organizing of the Futurians, a fan group that included many of the later writers and shapers of science fiction, including Pohl, Donald A. Wollheim, Cyril Kornbluth, Robert W. Lowndes, Richard Wilson, and later Damon Knight and James Blish. Asimov attended monthly meetings, became involved in the debates and schisms to which fandom is so susceptible, began meeting other authors, and talked about his writing ambition and finally getting published. All culminated in the first World Science Fiction Convention held in Manhattan on July 2, 1939. Every Futurian but Asimov were excluded by the organizer, Sam Moskowitz, as disruptive influences. Asimov went as an author and has felt guilty about it ever since. But as he became more and more an author, he became less and less a fan.

By the time of the World Convention Asimov was a bona-fide author in his own eyes because *Astounding* had published his tenth story, "Trends," in its issue of July 1939. Almost two years later it published the second of his robot stories (the first, "Robbie," was published in the September 1940 *Super Science Stories* as "Strange Playfellow") and within the next fourteen months two more robot stories, plus "Nightfall," and

"Foundation" and its sequel. Though Asimov didn't know it at the time, "Nightfall" alone made him, in his own words, "a major figure in the field." The stories did not earn that much money, but what they brought in was put to good use, paying for his tuition or accumulating in a bank account. He had three stories published in 1939, seven in 1940, eight in 1941, ten in 1941, only one in 1943, three in 1944, four in 1945, one in 1946, one in 1947, two in 1948, three in 1949, and six in 1950.

It was not a remarkable record of productivity or success; it brought Asimov a total of $7,821.75, which amounted to little more than $710 a year. It was not enough to encourage him to consider a career as a full-time writer, but it did provide a growing feeling of economic security. Finally, Doubleday published his first novel, *Pebble in the Sky*, in 1950. A specialty house called Gnome Press began publishing his robot stories and then his Foundation stories as books. His income from writing slowly began to equal and then to exceed his income from teaching at Boston University School of Medicine, and, after a disagreement with his superior, he turned to the career that had seemed impossible for all those years.

The impression even the casual reader may obtain from Asimov's autobiography is that he has been shaped by his childhood. He refers continually to the way in which the candy store controlled his early life and the way the habits of those years have carried over into his later life. His industry—he still writes seven days a week and ten hours a day, turning out six to ten thousand words on an average day—he traces to the long hours at the candy store, for instance, and to his father's accusations that he was lazy when found in a corner reading.

In a similar way, Asimov traces his ability to eat anything to his mother's hearty, indigestible cuisine, and his habit of eating swiftly to the fact that he and his mother and sister had to eat in a hurry so that his father could be relieved of his duties in the candy store and eat his supper in a more leisurely fashion. He reads while he eats because he loved to read, his father wasn't present, his mother was busy cooking

and serving, and in any case reading was a sign of studious-
ness.

His uneasiness with strangers Asimov traces to the fact that
during his childhood his family visited no one and no one
visited them. The fact that he reads newspapers and magazines so carefully that no one can tell they have been read
started, he believes, when he had to return magazines to his
father's rack looking unopened. As a boy he had to awaken at
6 a.m. to deliver newspapers before school. If he wasn't down
on time, his father would yell at his window from the street
below, and later lecture him about the "deadly spiritual dangers of being a *fulyack* [sluggard]." To this day, Asimov reports, he awakens, without an alarm clock, at 6 a.m.

He describes his infatuation with baseball when he was in
junior high school: he became a Giants fan, which was odd
because Brooklyn had the Dodgers. "By the time I found out
there was a Brooklyn team, it was too late; I was imprinted."
He describes being "imprinted" in other ways as well. He
blames his fear of flying on his mother's oversolicitude about
his health. "My parents . . . trembled over my well-being so
extremely, especially after my babyhood experience with
pneumonia, that I couldn't help but absorb the fact and gain
an exaggerated caution for myself. (That may be why I won't
fly, for instance, and why I do very little else that would involve my knowingly putting myself into peril.)"

His mother's insistence that he keep her informed of his
whereabouts meant that when he was out he had to report in
at frequent intervals by telephone. "I've kept that habit all my
life," he reports. "It is a bad habit. It ties me to the phone, and
if forgetfulness or circumstances get in the way, everyone is
sure something terrible has happened." He traces his avoid-
ance of books on how to write and of college-level courses on
writing to "the ever-present memory of that horrible course in
creative writing in the sixth term of high school."

It may not be surprising that someone who can find so
many habits of the man in the experience of the boy would
imagine a science of predicting human behavior, called "psychohistory," in his Foundation stories. On the other hand, As-

imov can relate anecdotes that seem to demonstrate just the opposite principle of behavior. He recalls his father struggling to balance the books of the candy store every evening, being a dollar over or a dollar under and staying until he had straightened it out. Later in his life, when money was easier, Asimov recalls handing his father five dollars to make up the difference, and his father commenting, "If you gave me a million dollars, that dollar would still have to be found. The books must balance." Asimov never could understand why the books had to balance. Rather than carrying that trait into his own life, he says, "In later life, when I had occasion to balance accounts, I never bothered over trifling discrepancies. I just made arbitrary corrections and let it go. My father did enough searching for both of us in his lifetime."

At the same time, Asimov is capable of seeing his explanations for behavior as "probably simple rationalizations designed to resign me to things as they are." After all, what is an autobiography? It is not so much the finding of the truths in one's existence as a rationalization of how one got from one place to another when there were so many different places at which one could have arrived. Asimov has much to explain, and his autobiography is a search for explanations.

Asimov also is a supreme rationalist, a searcher for explanations in his fiction as well as in his life. The reason for his faith in rationalism and his distrust of emotions may be no easier to come by, however, than any other speculation about his life. Asimov does not rely totally on environment to rationalize his life; some traits are implicit, or genetic, and Asimov simply does not mention them. His intelligence, for instance, and his ability to learn and remember must have been inherited. His habit of counting objects (light bulbs, repeated decorations, holes in soundproofed ceilings) whenever he is bored in public places he traces to his counting automobiles as they passed on Van Siclen Avenue when he was three. He finds no reason for his idiosyncratic fondness for enclosed places. He liked the candy store on Decatur Street because it had a kitchen in the back that had no windows. "Why it should be, I don't know, and psychiatrists may make what they like of it (for I will not ask them, and I will not listen if they try to tell me), but I have always liked enclosed places." He remembers that he thought display rooms in department stores looked better than real rooms and finally realized that it was because they had no windows. He envied the people who ran newsstands in subway stations, "for I imagined that they could board it up whenever they wanted to, put the light on, lie on a cot at the bottom, and read magazines. I used to fantasize doing so, with the warm rumble of the subway trains intermittently passing." Asimov's claustrophilia and agoraphobia will return to the discussion when we examine *The Caves of Steel* and *The Naked Sun.*

A psychiatrist (one of that group to whom Asimov will not listen) might suggest that Asimov's distrust of emotions and faith in rationalism are his responses to "being orphaned" by the candy store at the age of six. Being deprived of his parents' companionship ("never again, after I was six, could I be with him [his father] on a Sunday morning, while he told me stories") came at a difficult time: he was in the middle of second grade. Moreover, his father had admired his son's abilities from an early age. When Asimov taught himself to read at the age of five, his father asked him how he had done it, and Asimov replied that he just figured it out. "That gave my father the idea that there was something strange and remarkable about me; something he clung to for the rest of his life." But the high regard in which Asimov's father held his son's abilities meant that when the schoolboy brought home less than perfect marks from school, he could expect his father's disapproval for not living up to his potential. In his autobiography Asimov recalls many instances of his father's disapproval, few of his approval.

His mother also spent much of her time in the candy store with customers, or with her two younger children. She had a terrible temper, Asimov recalls, and unlike his father "raised her hand to me any time she felt she needed a little exercise. . . ." He also recalls, seemingly without rancor, being beaten with a rope his mother kept in her closet. When he mentioned it to his mother in later life, she did not remember it. His parents, though a devoted couple, were not demonstrative. There were few if any expressions of affection between them, and

Asimov presents the births of three children as the only proof
that there was. Certainly Asimov had reason to distrust emotion and to seek rational explanations for why he was deprived of parental closeness, perhaps even love.

Asimov, nevertheless, always knew that he was his parents' favorite, and his brother knew it as well, apparently
without resentment. Asimov speaks bitterly about the series of
candy stores but remembers his father and mother with great
fondness. The family was always in close touch until the death
first of his father (in 1969, at the age of 72) and then of his
mother (in 1973, at the age of nearly 78), even though Asimov
did not go to see his parents after they moved to Florida a year
before his father's death because of his fear of flying.

In his typical rational way, he looks back upon his childhood as a generally happy period: "I know perfectly well it
was a deprived one in many ways, but the thing was, you see,
I never knew it at the time. No one is deprived unless and
until he thinks he is."

A more general mystery than the origin of Asimov's traits and
neuroses is why certain young people turn to reading, and
sometimes writing, science fiction. Asimov is a case study.
When he began reading science fiction, the number of readers
was small—Damon Knight has called science fiction the mass
medium for the few—but intensely involved. Most had turned
to science fiction out of some kind of youthful frustration with
their lives. A profile of new readers would reveal them to be
mostly boys; mostly brighter than their schoolmates; mostly
social misfits because of personality, appearance, lack of social graces, or inability to find intellectual companionship;
unsophisticated about girls (the study of women readers and
writers still is in its infancy) and ill at ease in their company.
Science fiction was a kind of literature of the outcast that
praised the intellectual aspects of life that its readers enjoyed
and in which they excelled and offered more hope for the future than the present. When those kind of persons discover
others like themselves, fan clubs spring up, sometimes fanzines are published, conventions are organized, and writing
science fiction becomes a virtually universal ambition. When

those kind of persons begin to write, they write science fiction.

Asimov was like that. The Futurians were like that. Damon Knight says that "all we science-fiction writers began as toads." When Robert Silverberg read the first volume of Asimov's autobiography, he wrote for the galley proofs of the second volume because he couldn't wait: there was so much in Asimov's life that paralleled his own that it gave him a sense of *déjà vu*. There are certain curious resemblances between the characters and careers of Asimov and H. G. Wells, who is often called the father of modern science fiction. Both spent their early lives in unsuccessful shops, were precocious students, quick to learn with good memories, and began by writing science fiction but turned to popularizations (Wells's biggest success was his *Outline of History*). Both were selective in what they liked, Wells with biology and evolution, Asimov with chemistry, and both were fond of history. Both became known as pundits, experts in almost everything, and both were attentive to the ladies. . . . The analogy can be carried too far. Wells, for instance, became a serious novelist of contemporary life; Asimov varied his science fiction and non-fiction with detective stories and novels.

Asimov, in spite of his success at other kinds of writing and public speaking, has never thought of himself as anything but a science-fiction writer who sometimes writes other, often easier, things. He introduces himself as a science-fiction writer. Some writers of science fiction have gone on to other kinds of writing and some, like Kurt Vonnegut, Jr., have denied that they ever wrote science fiction. Not Asimov, who always has remained true to his boyhood love. In his autobiography he describes a fancy *World Book* sales meeting at which the board members were introduced with orchestral motifs: to his chagrin, Asimov was introduced as a science writer by "How deep is the ocean? / How high is the sky?" "No matter how various the subject matter I write on," he adds, "I was a science-fiction writer first and it is as a science-fiction writer that I want to be identified."

In an interview in 1979, I said to him that his autobiography revealed a great deal of loyalty to what he was, to the boy he was, and to what science fiction had meant to him when he discovered it. Asimov replied that he had deliberately not abandoned his origins. He had made up his mind when he was quite young, and said it in print, that no matter what happened to him or where he went he would never deny his origins as a science-fiction writer and never break his connection to science fiction, and he never has.

He considers loyalty a prime virtue. In 1976 when he started *Isaac Asimov's Science Fiction Magazine,* he told publisher Joel Davis that he wouldn't give up his *Magazine of Fantasy and Science Fiction* science articles.

> I probably bore everybody with my endless repetition of how much I owe to John Campbell, because I figure I would rather bore them than be disloyal in my own mind. It is the easiest thing in the world to forget the ladder you climb or to be embarrassed at the thought that there was a time when somebody had to help you. The tendency is to minimize this, minimize that, and I'm normal enough and human enough to do the same thing if it were left to itself, but this is a matter of having once made a vow and sticking to it.

He pointed out that it was inconvenient to always have to tell people that Campbell made up the Three Laws of Robotics, and the more important the Three Laws became the more he wanted to be the originator and take the credit, but he couldn't. "Why this is so I never really thought about. I guess I like to think about it only as a matter of virtue. I don't consider myself a particularly virtuous person, but I like to think I have some virtues, of which loyalty is one."

Possibly, however, his insistence on being considered a science-fiction writer is like his relationship to his racial origins. He says he is not a good Jew. Asimov attends no Jewish religious functions, follows no Jewish rituals, obeys no Jewish dietary laws, and yet he never, under any circumstances, leaves any doubt that he is Jewish.

> I really dislike Judaism. . . . It's a form of particularly pernicious nationalism. I don't want humanity divided into these little groups that are firmly convinced, each one, that it is better than the others. Judaism is the prototype of the "I'm better than you" group—we are the ones who invented this

business of the only God. It's not just that we have our God and you have your God, but we have the only God. I feel a deep and abiding historic guilt about that. And every once in a while, when I'm not careful, I think that the reason Jews have been persecuted as much as they have has been to punish them for having invented this pernicious doctrine.

Asimov suggests that because he feels that in some ways he has been a traitor to Judaism ("which I try to make up for by making sure that everyone knows I'm a Jew, so while I'm deprived of the benefits of being part of a group, I make sure that I don't lose any of the disadvantages, because no one should think that I'm denying my Judaism in order to gain certain advantages"), he made up his mind that he was not going to be disloyal in any other way. "I'm not saying I believe this," he concluded, "but this is the sort of thing that people do work up for reasons, and, after all, I'm imaginative enough to think up such reasons, too. . . . I don't guarantee it's correct."

The characteristic that began to appear in Asimov's science fiction, that gave his writing its unique quality and made it so typically Campbellian as well as Asimovian, was its rationality. Asimov agrees with Randall Garrett's assessment that the relationship between Asimov and Campbell was symbiotic. In the interview Asimov commented that he must have been the perfect foil for Campbell.

On the one hand, I was close to him. I lived right in town and I could see him every week. And, for another, I could endure him. I imagine that a great many other writers found him too rich for their blood—at least to sit there and listen to him hour after hour. But I was fortunate in the sense that he was in some ways a lot like my father. I had grown up listening to my father pontificate in much the same way that John did, and so I was quite at home. I suppose if you took all the time that I sat there listening to John and put it all together, it was easily a week's worth—of just listening to him talk. Day and night, 168 hours. And I remember everything he said and how he thought and I did my best—because I desperately wanted to sell stories to him—to incorporate his method of thinking into my stories, which, of course, also had my method of thinking, with the result that somehow I caught the Campbell flavor.

The Campbell flavor was the solution of problems. Much of Asimov's early writing did not quite capture that quality of problem-solving that became characteristic of his later work; those stories were less successful, neither identifiably Asimovian nor distinguished science fiction. His first published story had it, "Marooned Off Vesta," and later it would find its best expression in the robot stories and the Foundation stories, among his early science-fiction successes, and, of course, in the science-fiction mystery novels that came so naturally just before he switched to writing non-fiction, *The Caves of Steel* and *The Naked Sun*.

I made these suggestions to Asimov, and he agreed that they seemed right. "Certainly the stories that really satisfied me and made me feel good about my writing were my robot stories, and the robot stories, of course, virtually every one of them, had a situation in which robots—which couldn't go wrong—did go wrong. And we had to find out what had gone wrong, how to correct it, within the absolute limits of the three laws. This was just the sort of thing I loved to do."

At its most typical, in "Nightfall" for example, Asimov's science fiction demonstrates the triumph of reason, or the struggle of reason to triumph, over various kinds of circumstances, including irrational or emotional responses to situations. If reason is going to prove superior as an approach to life, the mystery is the natural form in which that superiority will be demonstrated.

Asimov has said that his villains generally are as rational as his heroes. "In other words, it's not even a triumph of rationality over irrationality or over emotion, at least not in my favorite stories. It's generally a conflict between rationalities and the superior winning. If it were a western, where everything depends upon the draw of the gun, it would be very unsatisfactory if the hero shot down a person who didn't know how to shoot."

Growing up as he did, excelling at intellectual pursuits but uneasy in personal relationships in which he found himself ignorant of the proper thing to do or uncertain how the other person would respond, Asimov found himself coping in a variety of ways. One way, which he adopted when he was young, was to distance himself from the rest of the world with wit: he still delights in puns and wordplay, which find their most typical expression in personal banter with his friends but also enliven his limericks and verse parodies and display themselves in the titles of and occasional lines in articles and stories. Another way to cope was to demonstrate his greater knowledge or superior mind. His adoption of these two characteristics gave him a reputation as a smart-aleck and a know-it-all with a mission to enlighten everyone around him.

Asimov gives as an example of his behavior the assignment of Leigh Hunt's "Abou Ben Adhem" in his high-school English class. Anticipating the teacher's question about the last line ("And lo! Ben Adhem's name led all the rest"), his hand shot up, and he answered the inevitable question, "Why did Ben Adhem's name lead all the rest?" with "alphabetical order, sir?" He was sent to the principal, but he didn't care.

Asimov finally gave up his mission to educate the masses. He traces his decision to a time when he was in the Army in Hawaii, waiting for the H-bomb tests at Bikini. A couple of soldiers in the barracks were listening to a third explain, inaccurately, how the atom bomb worked.

> Wearily, I put down my book and began to get to my feet so I could go over and assume "the smart man's burden" and educate them.
>
> Halfway to my feet, I thought: Who appointed you their educator? Is it going to hurt them to be wrong about the atom bomb?
>
> And I returned, contentedly, to my book.
>
> This does not mean I turned with knife-edge suddenness and became another man. It's just that I was a generally disliked know-it-all earlier in my life, and I am a generally liked person (I believe) who is genial and a nonpusher later in my life. . . .
>
> Why? I'm not sure I know. Perhaps it was my surrender of the child-prodigy status. Perhaps it was my feeling that I had grown up, I had proved myself, and I no longer had to give everyone a headache convincing them that I was, too, smart.

One other way in which Asimov learned to cope socially was his adoption of a flirtatious attitude toward women—all women—what he calls his "all-embracing suavity," by which he means that he is willing to embrace any female within range and usually does. From a gauche, inexperienced, tentative young man he turned into a good-natured, public Casanova with a "penchant for making gallant suggestions to the ladies." Yet Asimov speculates about his behavior as an adult that "you don't really change much as you get older." The uncertain young man may still be there inside the "all-embracing" older one.

Asimov has denied being anything other than direct and clear in his writing, and that may apply to his personal life as well. Certainly he is open about his life, even on those matters that most people are most closed about: money and sex—and, more important to Asimov, his writing. I asked him in our interview if his disclaimer of knowledge about the craft of writing wasn't a pose. Clearly, he had thought about it, I pointed out. He had criticized other people's stories in his teenage letters-to-the-editor days; he had noticed Clifford Simak's way of leaving space to indicate a break between scenes and, after having had it explained, had adopted it himself; he had even attended the Bread Loaf Writers' Conference, a couple of times as a member of the faculty. Asimov responded that he does not deliberately set up a pose. He really thinks he does not know much about writing, but, as he points out in an afterword to the collection of essays about his work edited by Martin Greenberg and Joseph Olander titled *Asimov*, "without very much in the way of conscious thinking I manage to learn from what I read and what I hear."

As the young Asimov became the older Asimov (still in his late youth, as he would say), what he was became what he is, either conditioned by his early experience or in reaction to it. Asimov recognizes both processes. In one sense he is a rational man in an irrational world, puzzled at humanity's responses to change, unable to understand humanity's inability to see the clear necessity, if it is to survive, to control population and pollution and eliminate war, still assuming "the smart man's burden" to educate the bewilderingly uneducable, even taken aback at times when the people he deals with behave irrationally.

Joseph Patrouch in his *The Science Fiction of Isaac Asimov* (1974) comments that Asimov has not written in his fiction on the subjects about which he is most concerned, the subjects he writes on in his non-fiction and speaks about in his public talks: pollution, overpopulation, and so forth. I asked Asimov about this, saying that in his talks and articles and books he seemed to exhibit a kind of alarm about our world situation that was not in his fiction—a kind of public despair that contrasts with his fictional optimism. In his science writing he tries to persuade by showing the terrible consequences of what will happen if people do not act, and in his science fiction he tries to persuade by showing how the problems can be solved. Asimov agreed.

> In my public statements I have to deal with the world as it is—which is the world in which irrationality is predominant; whereas in my fiction I create a world and in my world, my created worlds, things are rational. Even the villains, the supposed villains, are villainous for rational reasons. . . .
>
> You can see for yourself in my autobiography that I had a great deal of difficulty adjusting to the world when I was young. To a large extent the world was an enemy world. . . . Science fiction in its very nature is intended to appeal a) to people who value reason and b) to people who form a small minority in a world that doesn't value reason. . . . I *am* trying to lead a life of reason in an emotional world.

Asimov, no doubt, still is trying to please his stern father with industry and productivity. Asimov would be the first to admit it. He also would say that it doesn't matter how the past has shaped him. He is satisfied to be what he is: a claustrophile, an acrophobe, a compulsive writer. When he was a teenager, people complained about his eccentricities: his walking home from the library with three books, reading one and holding one under each arm; his love of cemeteries; his constant whistling. Their complaints didn't bother him (though he did, when asked, stop whistling in the cemetery). "I had gathered the notion somewhere that my eccentricities belonged to me and to nobody else and that I had every right to keep them." He added, "And I lived long enough to see these eccentricities and others that I have not mentioned come to be described as 'colorful' facets of my personality."

He has rationalized everything that has happened to him; he is a rational man who knows that the past cannot be

changed, it can only be understood. Moreover, the things that
he is have been rewarded by the world. He has had his many
triumphs. Scientists have applauded his science books: Professor George G. Simpson of Harvard called him "one of our
natural wonders and national resources." He has been guest
of honor and toastmaster at World Science Fiction Conventions. He has won Hugos and Nebulas, and, perhaps best of
all, John Campbell has told him, "You are one of the greatest
science-fiction writers in the world."

As a rational man, Asimov knows that the present must be
accepted, and as a rational man, he knows that what he is is
an excellent thing to be. So the world has said, and so he
agrees. That life of reason found its expression in his fiction
as well as his non-fiction. How it developed and how it expressed itself can be found in the following pages.

2

THE FOUNDATIONS OF SCIENCE FICTION

The foundations of science fiction were constructed in the science-fiction magazines created by various entrepreneurs from the mid-1920s to 1950. Today the influence of those magazines has been diminished by alternative methods of publication: hardcover and paperback books, original anthologies, films and television, comic magazines, even comic strips, which seem to be making a comeback after the original Buck Rogers and Flash Gordon days.

Even contemporary writers who are scornful of the magazines, of the Gernsback ghetto and the Campbell cabal, are writing fiction influenced by the concepts created in the magazines and by the conversations carried on by means of stories and letters and articles that led to a kind of consensus view of the future and the conventions by which it could be described. Reaction has developed, but reaction itself is a kind of tribute to the power of earlier visions.

Science fiction was built on individual works as well: on E. E. "Doc" Smith's galaxy-spanning spaceships and John W. Campbell's mightiest machines, on Murray Leinster's first contacts with the unknown and Robert Heinlein's future history, on A. E. van Vogt's supermen and Isaac Asimov's robots. And on Asimov's Galactic Empire.

The Foundation Trilogy is a basic work upon which a vast structure of stories has been built. Its assumptions provided a solid footing for a whole city of fictional constructions. The way in which it was created, then, and the way in which it came to prominence may be useful examples of the process by which science fiction was shaped in the magazines.

The *Trilogy*, which actually consists of five novelettes and four novellas, has received many tributes to its importance. The 1966 World Science Fiction Convention awarded it a Hugo as "the greatest all-time science fiction series." Donald Wollheim, in his *The Universe Makers*, called it "the point of departure for the full cosmogony of science-fiction future history." Asimov has attributed his success as a writer to it. It continues to be reprinted; it continues to sell well—Asimov does not keep accurate track, but he checked up a few years ago and found that by 1978 it had sold more than two million copies. It may be the best-known science-fiction work of recent times, at least among those works defined as hard-core science fiction.

On the other hand, critics have attacked the *Trilogy* for a variety of reasons. Professor Charles Elkins of Florida International University calls it "seriously flawed," "stylistically . . . a disaster," its characters "undifferentiated and one-dimensional," and Asimov's ear for dialogue "simply atrocious." Its ideas, Elkins concludes, are "vulgar, mechanized, debased . . . Marxism." Although not all the criticism is so savage, Elkins's comments are typical not only of Asimov's critics but of what literary critics commonly say about magazine science fiction as a body of literature.

Asimov himself has described the *Trilogy* as "in the older tradition of the wide-spanning galactic romance." But, strangely, the series contains little action and almost no romance. The stories offer no maidens in need of rescue and no involvement of man and woman in an emotional relationship. What do a couple on a honeymoon talk about? Politics. As for action, all of it takes place off stage, as in Greek drama. The *Foundation* galaxy contains a crumbling empire, decadent emperors, rebellious subject worlds, frontier hardship, and several major space wars that involve the destruction of several planets. But there are only three acts of violence, two of them in the same story.

How to explain the continuing popularity of the *Trilogy*? Why has the *Foundation* become a foundation? The student of science fiction who can understand the appeal and influence of the series may understand much that differentiates science fiction from other kinds of literature, and something about the basic appeal of Campbellian science fiction. The failure to provide adequate answers to these questions is the central problem of scholarship about science fiction. The circumstances of creation, for instance, may provide some measure of understanding, but much contemporary scholarship chooses to ignore such ephemera, preferring to apply to science fiction the same criteria applied to Henry James or William Faulkner or John Updike.

Another view might argue not for lesser standards but for different standards, for more useful standards. How can traditional criticism understand the *Trilogy*, for instance, if it does not take into consideration that it was a series written for one to two cents a word by a part-time writer for the readers of a single science-fiction magazine with a strong-willed editor over a period of years in which the author aged from twenty-one to twenty-eight?

Most traditional criticism consists of textual analysis. In magazine science fiction, textual analysis finds little to work with. The important aspects of science fiction are the characteristics that transcend the text. The first of these is narrative. When the *Trilogy* was being published in *Astounding Science Fiction*, piece by piece, the story was the thing, if not the whole thing, at least the main thing. An entertaining style, a bit of wit, characters who had some resemblance to real people could be added, but those elements were not essential. And sometimes they were handicaps, as in the case of Stanley Weinbaum, whose work, relatively more stylish and with more realistic people then other writers of his time, was more successful after his death than in the brief year and a half in which he tried to sell his stories to the magazines.

Story in *The Foundation Trilogy* is plentiful. Events move on a grand scale, beginning with the approaching dissolution of a galactic empire that has ruled 25 million planets inhabited by humans who spread out from Earth, although they have long forgotten their origin. The Empire has brought 12,000 years of peace, but now, according to the calculations of a psychologist named Hari Seldon, who has used a new science for predicting mass behavior called "psychohistory," the Empire will fall and be followed by 30,000 years of misery and barbarity. Seldon sets up two Foundations, one of physical scientists and a Second Foundation of psychologists (about which nothing more is heard until the last book of the Trilogy), at "opposite ends of the Galaxy" to shorten the oncoming dark ages to only a thousand years. The Foundation Trilogy covers the first four hundred years of that interregnum and tells how the Foundation meets one threat to its existence after another and alone, or with the help of the Second Foundation, preserves Seldon's Plan.

Into this overall pattern fit the individual stories. In Foundation, the first book of the Trilogy, there are five novelettes. The first, "The Psychohistorians," was written specially for the book version that first appeared in 1951. The action takes place on Trantor, the administrative center of the Empire, where 40 million bureaucrats and their families inhabit a world entirely covered with buildings and tunneled a mile deep into the surface. The story is told through the eyes of Gaal Dornick, a young psychohistorian from a distant planet who comes to work with Seldon and is immediately plunged into intrigue that culminates in the trial of Seldon for treason because his calculations predict the fall of the Empire. Seldon defends the accuracy of his prediction and persuades his judges that he and the Empire will be better off if he is allowed to set up his Foundation on the planet Terminus at the edge of the Galaxy in order to compile a great encyclopedia that will contain all human knowledge. At the end, however, Seldon reveals to Dornick that he has manipulated the accusation against him of treason, the trial, and everyone involved in it in order to precipitate the crisis and persuade his 100,000 Encyclopedists and their families to establish his Foundation on Terminus.

The second story, "The Encyclopedists" (called "Foundation" in the magazine version that launched the series in the May 1942 issue of Astounding), takes place fifty years later. Terminus is metal poor but thriving with technology through the efforts of the scientists settled there. Outlying provinces of the Empire are being taken over by ambitious local rulers. One ruler, in a region called Anacreon, has decided to annex Terminus. The Encyclopedists on Terminus are too scholarly and impractical to respond with anything but futile force. They need psychologists, but Seldon had allowed none to emigrate. Mayor Salvor Hardin, who studied psychology briefly, is the next best thing, a politician. He notes that Anacreon and a rival system, Smyrno, no longer have atomic power, because civilization begins decaying first on the frontiers. He takes the entire government of Terminus from the Encyclopedists during Seldon's first filmed appearance in a Time Vault Seldon had prepared so that he could talk to the descendants of the Foundation scientists about the various crises he had been able to predict, but he gives no prior guidance. At this time the long-dead Seldon announces that the Encyclopedia project was a fraud, that he had predicted what was to happen and set up the Terminus colony to influence the course of events without the knowledge of the Encyclopedists. The Encyclopedists' actions had been purposefully limited. Now they no longer have freedom of action, which is the essential condition of a Seldon crisis, a turning point in the Plan he has conceived but never disclosed. Seldon describes their predicament: Terminus is an island of atomic power in an ocean of more primitive energy resources; the solution to the problem is obvious. It is not obvious, however, to anyone but Hardin. The story ends with the Anacreons landing and only Hardin aware that the invaders will be forced to leave Terminus in six months.

In the third story, "The Mayors" (called "Bridle and Saddle" in the June 1942 *Astounding*), which takes place thirty years later, the solution to the Seldon crisis in the previous story is revealed. Hardin played one barbarian kingdom against another by rousing their fears that sole possession of Terminus by any of them would make that kingdom too powerful. The other kingdoms forced the Anacreons to leave. Hardin then sold atomic devices to everyone. But he put atomic science, viewed by barbarians as a kind of magic, within a religious framework of faith and miracles. This has enhanced the military capabilities of the barbarians and conferred religious au-

thority upon their rulers. The Anacreons attack Terminus, but
the Anacreon priests are offended by the blasphemy against
their religious center and lead a rebellion. Seldon appears again
in the Time Vault. His warning this time: beware the spirit of
regionalism (or nationalism) because it is stronger than spiritual power.

In "The Traders" ("The Big and the Little" in *Astounding*
for August 1944) another fifty years have passed. The Foundation on Terminus has absorbed its barbarian neighbors and
rules them with its scientific religion. Basically irreligious
Traders sell Foundation atomic power and gadgets to other
worlds for metals. The Foundation is committed to expansion
through the export of its religion. A Trader named Limmar
Ponyets is sent to Askone, where machines are sacrilegious,
to save another Trader who has been arrested for interfering
in local politics (actually, he was a Foundation agent-mission-
ary). Ponyets works upon Askonian greed for gold by jury-
rigging a transmutation machine to turn base metals into gold,
talks one influential Askonian into accepting the machine, and
then blackmails him, with secret films of his blasphemous association, into introducing Foundation machines.

"The Merchant Princes" (published as "The Wedge" in
Astounding, October 1944) takes place about twenty-five years
later. Religion has rigidified into faith. The Mayor's office has
stultified and even the Traders have grown rich and self-
satisfied. One of them, Hober Mallow, is considered a political
threat by Jorane Sutt, the Mayor's secretary and the real political power. Mallow is sent to investigate the disappearance of
Foundation ships near Korell. When a Foundation missionary
seeks refuge in Mallow's ship from a Korellian mob, Mallow
surrenders him to the Korellians. This leads to an audience
with the Commdor, the hereditary ruler of the "republic," in
which Mallow persuades the Commdor that the atomic devices Mallow has to sell will increase the Commdor's profits.
Mallow dispenses with the religious paraphernalia—"religion," he says, "would cut my profits"—and the Korellian
economy soon is dependent upon Foundation devices and efficiency. Mallow then traces the Spaceship-and-Sun design on

Korellian handguns to Siwenna, where an Empire viceroy wants to carve out a new Empire among the barbarians, and discovers that Siwenna's atomic capabilities have degenerated into ritual. Back on Terminus once more, Mallow is tried for the death of the priest he had turned over to the Korellians but wins his freedom (and is elected mayor) by demonstrating that the so-called priest was an agent of the Korellian secret police. The Korellian republic attacks the Foundation with old Empire atomic cruisers, but the attack slows as Foundation devices on Korell begin to fail. The Korellians rebel in order to regain their prosperity. Mallow predicts future crises in which money power will be as useless as religion.

The second volume of the *Trilogy*, titled *Foundation and Empire*, is made up of two novellas. The first, "The General" (called "Dead Hand" in the April 1945 *Astounding*) takes place about forty years after "The Merchant Princes." The central action is the attempt by Bel Riose, an ambitious and capable young general for the decaying Empire, to conquer the Foundation, whose reputation for trade and science by now has reached Trantor. The Merchant Princes, the only Foundation leaders, are without ideas about how to repel Riose's attack; they send a young trader, Lathan Devers, in a ship to be captured by Riose. The Emperor becomes suspicious of Riose's request for more ships to attack the Foundation and sends his privy secretary, Brodrig, to investigate. But Brodrig joins Riose with the hope of using Foundation technology to conquer the Empire and restore its glory. Riose's authority on the Foundation is Ducem Barr. Barr and Devers escape in Devers's ship to Trantor with a message that implicates Brodrig in a plot with Riose. Though they are unable to break through bureaucratic barriers to reach the Emperor, they learn, as they are leaving Trantor, that Riose and Brodrig are under arrest. The crisis has resolved itself: a weak general was no threat to the Foundation, and the Emperor would not have tolerated a strong general lest he seize the throne. Only the combination of a strong Emperor and a strong general could endanger the Foundation, but a strong Emperor remains strong by permitting no strong subjects. Even a strong Emperor who was also a general could not risk engaging himself in foreign wars for fear of rebellion springing up in his absence. Under any circumstances, the Foundation had to win out.

"The Mule" (*Astounding*, November, December 1945) takes place 105 years after the execution of Riose and Brodrig. Toran, son of a small trader on Haven, and Bayta, a Foundation citizen who is unhappy about the way the wealthy traders have accumulated power, have just been married. They arrive on Haven to learn that Toran's father and uncle are worried about Foundation tax collectors and are speculating about a new and mysterious conqueror of worlds called "The Mule." The worlds have fallen without battle, the most recent of them the pleasure world Kalgan. Toran and Bayta are sent to Kalgan to stir up a war between the Mule and the Foundation; in the conflict the small traders on Kalgan hope to win their freedom. A disturbance on the beach leads Toran to intervene on behalf of the Mule's court Fool, Magnifico, who has fled the Mule's cruelty. Toran and Bayta then flee, accompanied by Magnifico and Han Pritcher, a Foundation spy.

The Mule uses the kidnapping of his Fool as a pretext for an attack on the Foundation. He wins battle after battle until finally, at the very moment a projection of Seldon appears in the Time Vault with comments that reveal he had not foreseen this crisis, the Mule conquers Terminus itself. Toran, Bayta, scientist Ebling Mis, and Magnifico escape to Haven, but it too comes under attack. Before Haven falls, the four are sent to Trantor so that Mis can search the ancient Imperial library for information that might lead to the Second Foundation and then to its help against the Mule. Trantor is in ruins, virtually destroyed by a rebellious general. The four escapees are captured by the heir to what is left of the Empire. Magnifico kills him with the aid of a music-and-image-creating machine called a Visi-Sonor, and they escape to the Library, where an agricultural community has grown up. Mis searches the records, but he is ill and visibly growing weaker. On the verge of death, as he is about to reveal the location of the Second Foundation, Mis is shot and killed by Bayta. Bayta has decided that Magnifico, the Fool, is really the Mule. His mysterious advantage is his ability to adjust people's emotions. Everywhere they have taken him he has sown despair, has adjusted the minds of key leaders to surrender at the crucial moment, and has pushed Mis to discover the location of the Second Foundation so he can remove that threat as well. His critical mistake was to leave Bayta unadjusted. She had been the only person who had liked him without his interference, and he had valued too highly this natural feeling. The novella ends with the Mule's temporary defeat but his continued determination to find the Second Foundation. Whatever his victories, however, they cannot last beyond his death because, like his namesake, the Mule is sterile.

"Search by the Mule" ("Now You See It . . ." in the January 1948 *Astounding*) begins the third volume of the *Trilogy*, titled *Second Foundation*, which consists of two novellas. "Search by the Mule" picks up about five years after "The Mule." The Mule has consolidated his empire while, through an adjusted Han Pritcher, he has continued his search for the Second Foundation. Now he sends Pritcher out again with the capable but unadjusted Bail Channis. For the first time in the *Trilogy*, the Second Foundation psychologists make an appearance, discussing the situation. It had been discovered in old records that the Second Foundation had been established at "Star's End." Channis decides that "Star's End" must refer to a world called Tazenda, which is isolated in space by a dark cloud of interstellar gas. Pritcher and Channis land on Rossem, a poor, cold, agricultural planet in Tazenda's sphere of influence. After some inquiries, Pritcher accuses Channis of treason to the Mule: Channis found the location of the Second Foundation too easily. But the Mule arrives, having traced their ship, and reveals that he has used Channis, whom he suspects of being a Second Foundation agent, to lead him to the Second Foundation. He has destroyed Tazenda, the Mule says, but then Channis admits, under pressure, that Rossem, not Tazenda, is the location of the Second Foundation. The First Speaker, the leading psychologist of the Second Foundation, enters and reveals that Channis was convinced that Rossem was the location but that was false. The Mule has been lured to Rossem; in his absence Second Foundation psychologists can sow rebellion on Kalgan. The Mule realizes how he has been tricked, and in his moment of lowered defenses the

First Speaker enters his mind and reconstructs his memories, eliminating the Mule as a danger.

"Search by the Foundation" (". . . And Now You Don't" in *Astounding*, November, December 1949, January 1950) concludes the *Trilogy*. It opens about seventy years after the end of "Search by the Mule," as a group of conspirators gather in the home of Dr. Toran Darell on Terminus at the instigation of a new arrival named Pelleas Anthor. They believe that people in key positions in the Empire may be under the mental control of the Second Foundation. Such control would show up on encephalographs. To be controlled in this way would be an intolerable limitation of these people's freedom. The conspirators are determined to locate the Second Foundation. One of them, a librarian named Homir Munn, is sent to Kalgan to search the Mule's old palace for information. Unknown to him, he carries a stowaway who had eavesdropped on the conversation, Darell's romantic, fourteen-year-old daughter Arcadia, more familiarly known as Arkady, who is Bayta's granddaughter.

Meanwhile, the First Speaker and an apprentice for speakerhood discuss Seldon's Plan, which contemplated the development of a future civilization based on mental science and led by Second Foundation psychologists. Now that citizens know about the existence of the Second Foundation, they have begun to believe that it will prevent all mishaps. They are failing to exercise normal initiative; the predictions of Seldon's Plan may not work out. Another group is actively fighting the idea of a ruling class of psychologists. The Second Foundation has had to adopt a project with a low probability of success, to preserve the Plan and themselves, by working with individuals rather than large groups. Arkady proves helpful on Kalgan by persuading Lord Stettin's mistress, Lady Callia, that Munn intends to prove that the Second Foundation does not exist and that Lord Stettin, the ruler of Kalgan, is destined to unite the Galaxy instead of the Foundation. Stettin permits Munn's research in the old palace, but also decides to marry Arkady. Callia helps Arkady escape, and Arkady suspects that Callia is a member of the Second Foundation. Arkady is almost captured at the spaceport on Kalgan but is saved by Preem

Palver and his wife, trading representatives of their farm co-operative on Trantor. They take Arkady back to Trantor. Stettin attacks the Foundation and forces its fleets back to its original group of planets. In a final battle, however, Stettin's fleet is wiped out.

The conspirators gather once more in Darell's home, each claiming the solution to the mystery of the Second Foundation. Munn says there is no Second Foundation, but an encephalograph reveals that his mind has been tampered with. Anthor says that the Second Foundation must be on Kalgan, where everything, including the tampering with Munn's mind, has happened. Then Darell reveals a message from Arkady: "A circle has no end." From this he has deduced that the Second Foundation is on Terminus itself. He has invented a device that creates Mental Static and renders helpless minds capable of advanced mental science. Anthor collapses when it is turned on. Other Second Foundation members on Terminus will be sought out and neutralized.

In the final chapter the First Speaker reveals to the apprentice that his plan has worked. Fifty men and women of the Second Foundation have been sacrificed, but the Foundation is convinced that the Second Foundation has been destroyed, and Seldon's Plan has been restored. The Second Foundation is actually located on Trantor, where its psychologists are simple farmers. Why is the Second Foundation described as being at "the opposite end of the Galaxy"? From its periphery, the opposite end of a spiral is its center, and the Galaxy is a double spiral. Moreover, in social terms the opposite end of the extremities is the heart, and Trantor was once the heart of the Empire. What about "Star's End"? An old saying goes: "Stars end at Trantor." The First Speaker is Preem Palver.

Asimov abandoned *The Foundation Trilogy* with "Search by the Foundation" because it had grown too difficult to bring the reader up to date on everything and because he was tired of it. In his autobiography he reveals that while he was writing "Search by the Foundation" (". . . And Now You Don't") he "disliked it intensely and found working on it very difficult." Even Campbell's persistent demand for open endings

that would allow sequels could not persuade Asimov. The future history that had envisioned one thousand years of Seldon's Plan ended after less than four hundred (more than thirty
years later Asimov agreed to write a fourth volume). Nevertheless, Asimov used his concept of a humanly inhabited Galaxy,
of an outward movement of humanity from Earth until Earth
itself was forgotten, and of the rise of an Empire and its eventual fall as the background for half a dozen later novels and
several dozen shorter stories.

Other authors have used the background as well, taking it
not so much directly from the *Trilogy* as from the assumptions
about the future (to which the *Trilogy* contributed) that became the shared property of a generation of science-fiction
writers. What author Jack Williamson called "the central myth
of the future" begins with the expansion of humanity into the
galaxy in the same way that Europe ventured forth in the Age
of Exploration to discover and then to colonize the rest of the
world. The myth was not original with Asimov; it was developed by many writers, particularly by E. E. "Doc" Smith and
Edmond Hamilton in the magazine period. But Asimov said it
best and most completely in his series of stories published in
Astounding between 1942 and 1949. It has since been used by
writers as diverse as Jerry Pournelle and Ursula K. Le Guin.
Moreover, Asimov described a totally human galaxy, partly to
avoid Campbell's prejudice against relationships between humans and aliens in which the humans were inferior. In some
ways readers may have preferred an all-human galaxy.

This, however, does not completely explain the *Trilogy*'s
popularity. The reader must delve into what the series is about
and how its narrative is handled.

One significant aspect of the series is Asimov's invention
of psychohistory, with its implications for determinism and
free will. Psychohistory was put together out of psychology,
sociology, and history—not hard sciences, which Campbell had
a reputation for preferring, but at best soft sciences: a behav-
ioral science, a social science, and a discipline that has difficulty deciding whether to define itself as a social science or a
humanity. Actually, as Asimov pointed out in his 1953 essay
"Social Science Fiction," Campbell had encouraged social sci-

ence fiction from his first days as an editor. Moreover, Campbell had pointed out the logical basis for using the soft sciences for the kind of extrapolation he preferred, in his 1947 essay for Lloyd A. Eschbach's *Of Worlds Beyond*, "The Science of Science Fiction Writing":

> To be science fiction, not fantasy, an honest effort at prophetic extrapolation of the known must be made. Ghosts can enter science fiction—if they're logically explained, but not if they are simply the ghosts of fantasy. Prophetic extrapolation can derive from a number of different sources, and apply in a number of fields. Sociology, psychology, and parapsychology are, today, not true sciences; therefore instead of forecasting future results of applications of sociological science of today, we must forecast the *development of a science* of sociology.

Psychohistory is the art of prediction projected as a science; later it might have been called "futurology" or "futuristics."

The ability to predict or foresee the future has been a persistent notion in science fiction almost from the genre's beginnings. Hundreds of stories have been based on various mechanisms for doing it and the various outcomes of attempts. One might cite as examples Robert Heinlein's first story, "Life-Line," Lewis Padgett's "What You Need," and James Blish's "Beep." What Asimov brought to the concept was the science of probabilities as a mechanism, the element of uncertainty for suspense, and the philosophical question "what is worth predicting?" for depth. His method—statistical probability—prohibited the prediction of any actions smaller than those of large aggregates of population. Four decades earlier, incidentally, H. G. Wells had told the Sociological Society that a science of sociology was impossible because everything in the universe was unique and sociologists could not deal with sufficiently large numbers to handle those things statistically, as physicists did. Asimov could deal with large numbers, and he defines psychohistory, in the epigraph quoted from the *Encyclopedia Galactica*, for Section 4 of "The Psychohistorians," as "that branch of mathematics which deals with the reactions of human conglomerates to fixed social and economic stimuli. . . . Implicit in all these definitions is the assumption that the human conglomerate being dealt with is sufficiently large for valid statistical treatment. . . . A further necessary assumption is that the human conglomerate be itself unaware of psychohistoric analysis in order that its reactions be truly random." Finally, Asimov answers the question "what is worth predicting?" Not individual human lives but a great event whose consequences might be avoided, such as the fall of an empire and the dark ages of barbarism, war, hunger, despair, and death that would follow.

Asimov has been as open about the origins of the Foundation stories as he has been about the other details of his life and writing. One of the charms about the man is his openness. Well, openness may be understatement: since 1962 all of Asimov's anthologies and collections of stories have been strung together like ornaments on the string of his life story, culminating in *Opus 100*, *Opus 200*, and his 640,000-word autobiography.

In his autobiography and a piece he contributed to the *Science Fiction Writers of America Bulletin* in 1967 titled "There's Nothing Like a Good Foundation," Asimov traced the idea for the Foundation stories to a 1941 subway ride when he was going to visit Campbell at his Street & Smith office. Searching for an idea, Asimov looked down at a collection of Gilbert and Sullivan plays he was reading, opened it to *Iolanthe*, and saw a picture of the fairy queen kneeling in front of Private Willis of the Grenadier Guards. His mind wandered to soldiers, to a military society, to feudalism, to the breakup of the Roman Empire. When he reached Campbell's office, he told the editor that he was planning to write a story about the breakup of the Galactic Empire. "He talked and I talked and he talked and I talked and when I left I had the Foundation series in mind."

Exactly what Asimov had in mind may affect the critic's judgment of the work. He had not, for instance, thought out all the different permutations in idea and story; they were built, one on another, as the years passed and the *Trilogy* developed. But he must have discussed with Campbell the implications of prediction. Some critics have tried to explain "psychohistory" on philosophical bases, as "the science that Marxism never became" (Wollheim) or "the vulgar, mechanical, debased version of Marxism promulgated in the Thirties"

(Elkins). Elkins also related the *Trilogy*'s enduring popularity to its fatalism, which "accurately sizes up the modern situation."

People do talk a great deal about determinism in the *Trilogy*. When Bel Riose is informed by Ducem Barr of Seldon's predictions, he says, "Then we stand clasped tightly in the forcing hand of the Goddess of Historical Necessity?" But Barr corrects him: "Of *Psycho*-Historical Necessity." And Riose is defeated, apparently, by what seem like Seldon's inexorable laws.

Psychohistory had its origins not in Marxism (Asimov has called Wollheim's speculation "reading his bent into me," for Asimov has "never read anything about it") but in John Campbell's ideas about symbolic logic. Symbolic logic, if further developed, Campbell told the young Asimov in their first discussion, would so clear up the mysteries of the human mind that human actions would be predictable. Campbell more or less forced Asimov to include some references to symbolic logic in the first story, "Foundation"—"forced," because Asimov knew nothing about symbolic logic and did not believe, as Campbell insisted, that symbolic logic would "unobscure the language and leave everything clear." Asimov made a comparison to the kinetic theory of gases, "where the individual molecules in the gas remain as unpredictable as ever, but the average action is completely predictable."

The spirit of the early stories, however, is determinedly anti-deterministic. If intelligent, courageous, and forceful individuals do not attempt to retrieve the situation, most crises—all but one, perhaps—will not be resolved satisfactorily. Seldon's predictions, like God's will, are hidden from all the characters except the psychologists of the Second Foundation, as they are from the reader. Seldon's prophecies are revealed only after the fact, and even the solutions that he or others say are obvious are obvious only in retrospect, as in all good histories. At the time, they are not obvious to anyone but Salvor Hardin or Hober Mallow; the reader has no feeling that the crises would have been resolved if persons such as Hardin and Mallow had not been there. Moreover, the predictions of psychohistory are expressed as probabilities, and one of the necessary ingredients of Seldon's Plan, discussed in detail in "Search by the Foundation," is the exercise of normal initiative.

As a matter of fact, Asimov has the best of both determinism and free will. Psychohistory and Seldon's Plan provide the framework for diverse episodes about a variety of characters over a period of four hundred years, and those episodes feature a number of strong-minded individuals seeking solutions to a series of problems as they arise. If determinism alone were Asimov's subject, the *Trilogy* would reveal characters continually defeated in their attempts to change events, or manipulated like puppets by godlike prophets, or unable to fight the onrushing current of necessity.

A work in which characters were inexorably defeated by psychohistorical necessity would be so depressing that it would not have remained popular for more than a quarter of a century. Bel Riose is the only character who stares into the face of determinism; only he is frustrated by psychohistorical necessity rather than by the actions of an individual. But in "The General," Bel Riose is not the viewpoint character. The basis of the story is not Riose's predicament but how he is to be stopped, and the resolution does not celebrate the victory of determinism but the survival of the Foundation, even though the efforts of the Foundation are not involved. The reader, whose sympathies are with the Foundation, sees the events as an ally of the Foundation, not as an opponent. The Foundation's unusual power of survival, however, influences both itself and its enemies; it supplies to the Foundation confidence in ultimate victory (which can become overconfidence, and thus a problem), and it discourages the Foundation's attackers (but never enough to eliminate challenges entirely). Asimov seems to be more interested in the psychological impact of Seldon's Plan than in its philosophical implications. Indeed, it is only to those looking from the outside that Seldon's Plan seems like determinism; from within, the Foundation leaders still must find solutions without Seldon's help.

Even in the second half of the *Trilogy*, questions of free will raised by the events of the story relate not to Seldon's Plan but to the psychological manipulation of minds such as that effected by the Mule and the Second Foundation psychologists. Nothing in the story happens unless someone makes it happen; the reader is told on several occasions that "Seldon's laws help those who help themselves."

The Biblical parallel is significant. Psychohistory is no more restrictive of free will than the Judeo-Christian deity. Christians are given free will by an omniscient God; characters in the *Trilogy* receive free will from an omniscient author, as an act of authorial necessity. At the end of *Second Foundation*, Seldon's Plan has been restored, events are back on their ordered course, the rise of a new and better Empire to reunite the Galaxy and the creation of a new civilization based on mental science seem assured. The Second Foundation psychologists have won; that victory, benevolent as it seems, may have ominous undertones, but if we are to accept Asimov as being as benevolent as he is omniscient, the reader can assume that the benefits of mental science will be available to everyone.

Determinism, then, is not what the *Trilogy* is about. The structure of the episodes is anti-deterministic, for the outcome of each critical event is not inevitable. The basic appeal of the stories is problem-solving, an essential replacement for the more customary narrative drives of action and romance. Each episode presents a problem, in a way much like the formal detective story, and challenges the reader to find a solution. In the first published story, "Foundation," the solution is withheld until the next episode, a strategy of Asimov's to ensure a sequel (published in the very next issue) that almost accidentally reinforced the problem-solving quality of the stories. For the reader, the fascination lies in the presentation of clues, the twists of plot, and the final solution that makes sense of it all. In the final episode of *Foundation,* Jorane Sutt says to Hober Mallow, "There is nothing straight about you; no motive that hasn't another behind it; no statement that hasn't three meanings." He might have been speaking of Asimov.

The series of searches for the Second Foundation, the various clues pursued to inconclusive ends, the near revelation by Ebling Mis of its location (though he may have been wrong), and the succession of incorrect solutions shows Asimov imitating methods of the detective novel. In response to Campbell's challenge, he later shaped those kinds of devices more obviously into science-fiction detective novels and stories beginning with *The Caves of Steel* (serialized in 1953). In the final chapter of *Second Foundation,* with its succession of " 'I've got the answer'—'No, I've got the answer' " reversals, Asimov no doubt is parodying the concluding scenes of a thousand formal detective novels.

But even the problem-solving aspect of the *Trilogy* does not account completely for the success of the series. Other aspects, more peripheral to the central structure, might be cited: the characters, for instance, though scorned by some critics, engage the reader's sympathies. They are similar to each other, it is true, mostly by being men and women of action. They do not let events happen to them (as might seem more appropriate if the theme of the *Trilogy* actually was determinism); they make things happen. The *Trilogy,* after all, is a history, and history is about people who have made things happen. The characters may not be strongly differentiated—Salvor Hardin, Limmar Ponyets, Hober Mallow, and Lathan Devers may seem interchangeable—but they may be as differentiated as the personages in most histories. They got into histories by being men and women of action. Clearly Asimov's characters are adequate for the purposes they serve in the *Trilogy.*

Asimov also provides some of his philosophy of history in his storytelling. History fascinates him. He almost took his graduate degree in history instead of chemistry; his customary method of developing both his fiction and his non-fiction is historical; and a number of his non-fiction books are concerned with history. Some of what Asimov says about history comes from his model, Gibbon's *Decline and Fall of the Roman Empire,* little seems to derive from Marxism or whatever impressions of it were in the air when the *Trilogy* was being conceived and created, and a good deal seems to be Asimov's own observations. Government, for instance, never is what it appears to be: in the *Trilogy* figureheads and powers behind the throne proliferate. Every innovation rigidifies into sterile tradition, which must, in turn, be overturned: the grip of the Encyclopedists, for instance, must be broken by Salvor Hardin, and the political power of the Mayor must be broken, in its turn, by Hober Mallow, and the economic power of the Traders must then be modified by the incorporation of the independent traders, and so on. There is, to be sure, a narrative necessity to keep the series going, but the reader cannot ignore the inevitable feeling of continual change, which seems a philosophy: one generation's solution is the next generation's problem. Asimov probably would agree that this is the case in real life.

On top of this, and perhaps the most important aspect of Asimov's writing, is his rationalism. More than any other writer of his time (the Campbell era, as Asimov calls it) or even later, Asimov speaks with the voice of reason. Avoid the emotional, the irrational, the *Trilogy* says. Avoid the obvious military reaction to threats of military attack, says Salvor Hardin. Do not throw the slender military might of the Foundation against the great battleships of the Empire, says Hober Mallow, whose continual retreat before the attacking Korellian forces is considered treason.

Rationality is the one human trait that can always be trusted, the *Trilogy* says, and the reader comes to believe that that is Asimov's conviction as well. Sometimes rational decisions are based on insufficient information and turn out to be wrong, or the person making the decision is not intelligent enough to see the ultimate solution rather than the partial one, but nothing other than reason works at all. Even the antagonists are as rational as the protagonists and therefore cannot legitimately be called villains. In the stories that Asimov likes best, rationality does not triumph over irrationality or emotion but over other rationality, as in the conflict between the Mule and Bayta (though the Mule is betrayed as well by an element of emotion unnatural to him), between the Mule and the First Speaker, and between the Second Foundation and the First Foundation.

Asimov's confidence in rationality must have been comforting to him not only in personal terms but in terms of the times when the stories were written and published. He was only twenty-one when he started writing "Foundation" and had passed through a difficult adolescence. He was still ill at ease with women and society in general, and he was writing largely for maladjusted teenagers who had sublimated their sexual and social frustrations into various kinds of intellectual activity, including the reading of science fiction. The belief that reason could solve problems not only was desirable, it may have been necessary. Moreover, events in the larger world, though they did not encourage a belief in the rationality of human behavior, nourished the hope that rationality would prevail. The United States had just pulled itself out of the incomprehensibility of the Depression to plunge itself into the insanity of war. Just as the theory of psychohistory was for Asimov a way to make Hitler's persistent victories bearable— no matter what initial successes the Nazis managed, the logic of history (psychohistory) would eventually bring about their defeat—so reason had to eventually prove its supremacy. Later, as the Foundation stories began to appear, the success of the Allies, aided by products of scientific laboratories, confirmed that earlier faith.

The *Trilogy* also offers more isolated insights into history, politics, and human behavior. Often these surface in the epigraphs that precede most of the chapters in the form of excerpts from the 116th edition of the *Encyclopedia Galactica* published in 1020 F.E. (Foundational Era) by the Encyclopedia Galactica Publishing Co., Terminus. But Asimov also includes some illuminating concepts within the text of the stories. "It is the chief characteristic of the religion of science that it works," he says in "The Mayors." "Never let your sense of morals prevent you from doing what is right," he has Limmar Ponyets say in "The Traders." "Seldon assumed that human reaction to stimuli would remain constant," Mis comments in "The Mule."

The statement by Mis sums up Asimov's own attitude toward character. His characters have been criticized for being "one-dimensional," and unchanged from contemporary people by the passage of time and the altered conditions in which they live. But this occurs by choice rather than from lack of skill or failure of observation. Asimov divided "social science fiction" into two widely different types of stories: "chess game" and "chess puzzle." The chess game begins with "a fixed number of pieces in a fixed position" and "the pieces change their positions according to a fixed set of rules." In a chess-puzzle story, the fixed set of rules apply but the position varies. The rules by which the pieces move (common to both types) may be equated, Asimov says, "with the motions [emotions?] and impulses of humanity: hate, love, fear, suspicion, passion, hunger, lust and so on. Presumably these will not change while mankind remains Homo sapiens." Basic human characteristics remain the same.

Asimov may not be right, but his choice is defensible against the opposing Marxist view that character will change when society becomes more rational. In addition, the *Trilogy* is concerned not with the revolution, or even the evolution, of character but with the evolution of an idea. There is also a strategic narrative value in the maintenance of contemporary characteristics. The recognizability of characters reflects that the characters accept their world as commonplace. This is the technique that Heinlein perfected as an alternative to the "gee whiz!" school of writing about the future, which introduced a character from the past in order to elicit his wonder at each new future marvel.

A story of the future is not much different than a historical novel, and its problems are similar to those of a translation from a foreign language. The decision a writer must make is not of verisimilitude alone but how much and what kind. Asimov chooses what might be called the verisimilitude of feeling over the verisimilitude of language or of character, just as a historical novelist or a translator might choose the flavor of the original over a literal representation. Science-fiction stories about changes in humanity or its language have been written, but the *Trilogy* is not one of them and does not pretend to be.

Asimov creates a sense of reality in another way: by choosing appropriate but unfamiliar names for characters, objects, and processes. Every name seems foreign yet credible. The science-fiction reader values this above subtle differentiations in character. The non-science-fiction reader often finds it puzzling at best, repulsive at worst. "Psychohistory" has proved so apt a name that it has been picked up as terminology for an academic discipline, though not, to be sure, the discipline Asimov had in mind. The names of characters are subtly altered, by changing the spelling, or dropping or rearranging letters, to suggest evolution within continuity, and the subtlety increases as the series progresses: Hari Seldon leads to Hober Mallow leads to Han Pritcher leads to Bail Channis and eventually to Arkady Darell. Possibly only Heinlein was Asimov's superior in creating future societies, though several other writers have been better with names.

Asimov, however, was the master of the epigraph. Models of imitation, clarity, and dramatization, they offer some preview of his later skill at science popularization. The epigraphs serve as a medium for exposition, which became increasingly burdensome as the series continued—a long essay Arkady writes for school in "Search by the Foundation" serves this function (but also convinced Asimov that the series had to end there)—but which helped Asimov provide essential background information. They also provide a framework that puts events into context and lends to the structure the verisimilitude of a future perspective.

The final virtue of the *Trilogy*, and perhaps the most important to its extended popularity, is its exhaustive treatment of an idea. That idea was not psychohistory or even determinism: it was the Foundations. Each story examined one aspect of the Foundations and their relative positions in the Galaxy and in the events happening around them. In "The Psychohistorians," for instance, the problem for the Foundation is how to persuade the Empire to let the Foundation be set up on Terminus and how to persuade 100,000 Encyclopedists and their families to leave the comfort and security of Trantor for the rigors and uncertainties of the frontier. This problem, of course, is concealed until the conclusion, even until after the resolution. "The Encyclopedists" presents the next problem: how is the Foundation to survive the power of the barbarians that surround Terminus as the Empire slowly begins to lose its control of the periphery? The first solution is to play each group of barbarians against the others; the second, to supply the barbarians with atomic energy within a religious framework centered around Terminus.

In "The Mayors" the problem has become: what will happen to the Foundation when the barbarians are completely equipped with atomic weapons and are restless to use them? The answer: the priests of the scientific religion will not permit an attack on Terminus. In "The Traders" the question has changed to how Foundation hegemony will spread once the religious framework is recognized as a political tool of the Foundation. The answer is: by trade. Economic motivations can succeed where religion fails. Sometimes two problems converge in one story, as in "The Merchant Princes." The political and religious structures have rigidified into useless tradition, and the location of the Foundation has been discovered by the Empire. The solutions to those problems are that the Traders seize political power and that war against the Foundation is clearly linked with economic deprivation.

Each problem solved strengthens the Foundation and its progress toward ultimate reunification of the Galaxy, but each solution contains the seed of a new problem. In "The General," the Foundation faces the problem of its own success, which has made it an attractive prize for the Empire. But it is protected by the essential nature of a decaying Empire—a weak Emperor cannot permit strong generals. In "The Mule" and its sequel, "Search by the Mule," Asimov strikes out in a new direction. With its victory by default over the Empire, the Foundation has no clear challenges to the eventual extension of its power throughout the Galaxy and the final realization of Seldon's Plan. But what about the unexpected, developments that Seldon's psychohistorical equations could not predict because they involve elements of the unique, like the genetic accident that creates the Mule and his unpredictable and Plan-destroying power? The answer: the Second Foundation. Asimov planted mention of the Second Foundation in the first Foundation story, not because he had anticipated the function of the Second Foundation but as a safety measure, a strategic reserve in case something developed in the plot and he needed a way out. In "The Mule," the Second Foundation emerges as a group of psychologists to whom Seldon's Plan was entrusted and who were charged with responsibility for protecting it. Finally, in "Search by the Foundation," two new questions are raised by the revelation of the Second Foundation: what will happen to the Foundation now that it knows of the existence of the Second Foundation and suspects its custody of Seldon's Plan (which destroys one of the basic requirements for the effectiveness of psychohistorical predictions), and what can the Second Foundation do to restore the previous condition and rescue Seldon's Plan? The answer is dual-purpose: the Second Foundation deceives the Foundation into believing that it has located and destroyed the Second Foundation.

In "There's Nothing Like a Good Foundation," Asimov wrote that "in designing each new Foundation story, I found I had to work within an increasingly constricted area, with progressively fewer and fewer degrees of freedom. I was forced to seize whatever way out I could find without worrying about how difficult I might make the next story. Then when I came to the next story, those difficulties arose and beat me over the head." The difficulties are not apparent: each story seems designed to arise out of the earlier ones, and each develops with an air of inevitability appropriate to psychohistory itself. But it is critical folly to assume that the Trilogy is an organic whole, conceived before it was begun, crafted in accordance with some master plan, and produced in full consideration of the contribution of each part to the whole. External and internal evidence demonstrate that Asimov moved from story to story, solving the problems of each as they arose and discovering, on his own or with the help of Campbell, new problems on which to base the next stories. The Trilogy succeeds by its ingenuity, and it is a tribute to Asimov's ingenuity and cool rationality that it seems so complete, so well integrated.

Foundations should be solid. They should leave no important areas uncovered. That The Foundation Trilogy is so solid may be the major reason it has survived and why so many later science-fiction stories have been built upon the "central myth" that it and earlier works pioneered.

3

VARIATIONS UPON A ROBOT

Isaac Asimov's I, Robot has become one of the enduring titles in the developing canon of contemporary science fiction. Asimov's robot stories were the second of the two basic kinds of fiction with which he built his early reputation, the first being *The Foundation Trilogy*. Like the *Trilogy*, I, Robot, has seldom been out of print since its 1950 book publication by Gnome Press. It has sold several million copies in hardcover and paperback and has elicited persistent interest from filmmakers, most recently in the late 1970s with a script by Harlan Ellison that suffered the usual Hollywood complications.

Asimov did not stop writing robot stories after the publication of I, Robot, as he did with the Foundation stories after the publication of the *Trilogy*. Another group of stories was published by Doubleday in 1964 as *The Rest of the Robots*, including three stories that were written early in Asimov's career but published in magazines other than *Astounding*, so Asimov did not think them suitable for inclusion in I, Robot. The remainder of the eight stories in *The Rest of the Robots* had been published after 1950. Since then, Asimov has continued to return to the robots as new ideas have occurred to him or editors have requested new stories.

In all, Asimov has written twenty-nine robot stories. Some are mere finger exercises, but others add significantly to the intellectual and emotional consideration of the robot that As-

imov began in 1939. In fact, considering Doubleday's apparent
determination to bring all of Asimov's fiction back into print,
it may be time for an edition of robot stories that will bring
them all—or at least all the significant stories—under one
cover. It might be called *All Us Robots*.

Asimov's interest in robots and his readers' interest in Asimov's robots provide useful insights into how science fiction
was changing in the 1940s under the influence of the new
editor at *Astounding*, John W. Campbell. The fiction began to
reflect science as it was practiced then and might be practiced
in the future, and scientists as they really were or might become.

In the introduction to *The Rest of the Robots* Asimov wrote:

> . . . one of the stock plots of science fiction was that of the
> invention of a robot—usually pictured as a creature of metal,
> without soul or emotion. Under the influence of the well-
> known deeds and ultimate fate of Frankenstein and Rossum,
> there seemed only one change to be rung on this plot.—Ro-
> bots were created and destroyed their creator; robots were
> created and destroyed their creator; robots were created and
> destroyed their creator—
>   In the 1930s I became a science-fiction reader and I quickly
> grew tired of this dull hundred-times-told tale. As a person
> interested in science, I resented the purely Faustian interpre-
> tation of science.

Asimov went on to point out that nothing is made without
taking into account the dangers involved: knives have hilts,
stairs have banisters, electrical wiring has insulation, pressure
cookers have safety valves. "Sometimes the safety achieved is
insufficient because of limitations imposed by the nature of
the universe or the nature of the human mind. However, the
effort is there." If a robot is considered as another artifact, Asimov reasoned, engineers would have built in safeguards. And
so he began to write robot stories—but of a new variety. "My
robots were machines designed by engineers, not pseudo-men
created by blasphemers. My robots reacted along rational lines
that existed in their 'brains' from the moment of construction."

Asimov's robot stories represent one of the longer continuous considerations of that phenomena, or perhaps of any fic-

tional phenomena: it has stretched from the writing of "Robbie" in 1939 to the publication of "The Bicentennial Man" in 1976, and perhaps it is not over yet. That span has allowed Asimov to think about robots in many different ways and the scholar to study how Asimov's attitudes and ideas have changed, but the manner in which the stories were written also inhibits the scholar from judging, except in the most general sense, the stories as a unified whole. They were created individually, and they must be considered individually. Each builds upon earlier stories and all share certain assumptions, but each was written without thought for its place in any overall scheme. In fact, the best way to think about them may be as variations upon a theme.

The beginning, and the book basic to the entire series of stories, was *I, Robot*. The title represents an initial irony, since it is also the title of a story by Eando Binder (a pseudonym for Earl and Otto Binder, used after 1940 by Otto alone). The publication of Binder's story in *Amazing*, January 1939, and a chance meeting with Otto on May 7 of the same year at the Queens Science Fiction League inspired Asimov's first robot story. In 1950, when Martin Greenberg of Gnome Press was preparing to publish the book, Greenberg dismissed Asimov's suggested title, *Mind and Iron* (a phrase used in the introduction), and suggested *I, Robot*. Asimov said that was impossible because of Binder's earlier story. "F--- Eando Binder," Greenberg said, and *I, Robot* it was. Asimov credits the title with helping to sell the book. As a further irony, the book contains no first-person robot stories—nor did Asimov ever publish any.

The book consists of nine stories united not only by their concern with robots but by the introduction and a continuing narrative between stories, which was constructed, for the book, as an interview by a reporter for *Interplanetary Press* with Susan Calvin when she reaches the age of seventy-five. The linking narrative also functions as an account of the difficulties and successes of United States Robots and Mechanical Men, Inc. (hereafter abbreviated as USR) and a history of robotics itself, since Calvin joined USR as a robopsychologist upon earning her Ph.D. in cybernetics. In the process of bringing the stories together, Asimov provided dates that were missing from the original versions.[1] Out of them I have derived the following chronology of events:

1982   Susan Calvin is born. The same year Lawrence Robertson founds USR.

1996   "Robbie" is constructed as a non-speaking robot and sold to the Weston family as a nursemaid for Gloria.

1998   "Robbie" ("Strange Playfellow"), *Super Science Stories*, September 1940. New York passes curfew law for robots.

2002   Dr. Alfred Lanning demonstrates a mobile, speaking robot (intended for the mines of Mercury) in a psycho-math seminar. Susan Calvin is present.

2003   Calvin earns bachelor's degree.

2003–2007   Use of robots is banned on Earth because of opposition by labor unions and fundamentalist religious groups.

2007   Calvin earns her Ph.D. and joins USR as "the first great practitioner of a new art," robopsychology. Lanning is director of research. USR has hit a financial low point and is forced to turn to the extraterrestrial market. Robots are about twelve feet tall, clumsy, and not much good.

Circa 2007   The First Mercury Expedition. Robots try to help build the mining station there, but the effort fails.

Teens and Twenties   Gregory Powell and Michael Donovan handle most of the difficult robotics cases.

2015   "Runaround," *Astounding*, March 1942. The Second Mercury Expedition. USR has developed a new type of robot, SPD-13 ("Speedy").

2015½   "Reason," *Astounding*, April 1941. USR has developed a new kind of robot, QT-1 ("Cutie"),

1. Some confusion in dates remains: the Introduction says that Susan Calvin joined USR in 2008; she says, in the lead-in to "Runaround," that it was 2007. "Runaround" also refers to *fifty*-year-old antique mounts (robots).

to direct energy beams from Sun to Earth from solar stations.

2016 "Catch That Rabbit," *Astounding*, February 1944. USR has developed a master robot, DV-5 ("Davie"), which controls six sub-robots, for asteroid mining.

2021 "Liar!," *Astounding*, May 1941. USR creates a robot, RB-34 ("Herbie"), which has the accidental ability to read minds.

2029 "Little Lost Robot," *Astounding*, March 1947. Work is progressing (in a station situated in the asteroid belt) on a hyperatomic drive for interstellar travel. USR creates an experimental group of robots, NS-2 ("Nestors"), some of which are not impressioned with the entire First Law of Robotics so that they can work with scientists who are involved in dangerous research.

2029 or 2030 "Escape" ("Paradoxical Escape"), *Astounding*, August 1945. "The Brain," a larger positronic robot brain installed as a computer, makes possible interstellar travel by suppressing its anxiety about the temporary death of human passengers in the "hyperspace" Jump.

2032 "Evidence," *Astounding*, September 1946. Humanoid robots are possible and may have been constructed.

2052 "The Evitable Conflict," *Astounding*, June 1950. The world is unified under a "World Coordinator," and the world's economy is entirely under the control of giant computers called "The Machines."

2064 Susan Calvin dies.

Little more information than that sketched above is provided about the world in which *I, Robot* exists because little more is necessary for the understanding of the basic narrative. That narrative is about robots and the problems people have with them in spite of the precautions engineers have taken in constructing them. The most important precaution, and probably the single most important contribution to the success of the robot stories, is the Three Laws of Robotics.[2]

Asimov was not the first to write about robots. As he points out in *The Rest of the Robots,* Homer, in the *Iliad,* describes Hephaestus being served by maidens he has created from gold as mechanical, thinking creatures. There were other robot predecessors: Talos, the bull-headed man made of bronze, who guarded Crete for King Minos; a Golem, molded of clay by various medieval rabbis[3] and animated by a "shem" or name of God; Roger Bacon's talking brazen head; Mary Shelley's Frankenstein's monster (1818); and Karel Capek's robots in his 1921 play *R.U.R.* (Rossum's Universal Robots), which introduced the Czech word for worker, "robot," into the language. But every robot up to Asimov's time, virtually without exception, turned against its creator, and it was this tradition against which Asimov was rebelling.

The trend had begun to turn, however, even before Asimov's first robot story. Lester del Rey's "Helen O'Loy," published in *Astounding* in December 1938, described a robot created as so much like a person that she falls in love and eventually makes an ideal wife for her creator. Binder's robot, Adam Link, was a noble creature moved by a strong sense of honor and love. His brain was constructed of "iridium sponge," those of Asimov's robots, "a spongy globe of platinumiridium." And Binder's Adam Link stories—a total of ten of them—continued to appear in *Amazing* throughout 1939, 1940, 1941, and 1942 (seven of them were collected in *Adam Link—Robot,* published by Paperback Library in 1965). In "Adam Link's Vengeance," published in February 1940, the robot

2. The word "robotics" was invented by Asimov, although he didn't realize it at the time. He has said that if he is to be remembered at all in future years it will be for the Three Laws of Robotics.

3. In 1970 Professor Marvin Minsky (in "The Bicentennial Man" there is a robopsychologist named Merton Mansky) of the M.I.T. project on artificial intelligence spoke at the SFWA Nebula Award banquet about his work and the help that writers such as Asimov and Arthur C. Clarke had provided in laying out the chain of development from the golem to the provision of teleological goals. Asimov got up and responded that the thought that had been running through his mind was, "What kind of goals would a Golem have if a Golem could have goals?"

thinks, "A robot must never kill a human, of his own free will."

No doubt there are other robot predecessors and even other stories in which resemblances to *I, Robot* are clear. My purpose in citing them, however, is not to detract from Asimov's accomplishments but to point out debts that he himself is quick to acknowledge (though he may not realize the full extent of them; a magnificent memory may not always be an asset, and Asimov occasionally has discovered, to his horror in the case of "Green Patches," that he was reworking someone else's idea). When Asimov showed "Robbie" to his friend and fellow Futurian, Frederik Pohl, the young Pohl, already an agent, told him that Campbell would reject it because it was too reminiscent of "Helen O'Loy." *Amazing* rejected it as well because it was too similar to "I, Robot," which they had published just six months before (and they must have had Binder's "The Trial of Adam Link" already in type for the July issue). Eventually, Pohl himself published "Robbie" in *Super Science Stories*.

"Robbie" set up many of the conflicts that later pervaded *I, Robot* and even the entire series of robot stories. In the story, the Westons have bought Robbie as a nursemaid for their daughter Gloria because, as her mother says, "It was a novelty; it took a load off me, and—and it was a fashionable thing to do." Two years later, however, Mrs. Weston wants to sell the robot back to the company. "She [Gloria] won't play with anyone else"; "I won't have my daughter entrusted to a machine—and I don't care how clever it is. It has no soul, and no one knows what it may be thinking. A child just isn't made to be guarded by a thing of metal"; and ". . . something might go wrong. . . . Some little jigger will come loose and the awful thing will go berserk. . . ." George Weston protests: "A robot is infinitely more to be trusted than a human nursemaid. . . . Robbie was constructed for only one purpose really—to be the companion of a little child. His entire 'mentality' has been created for the purpose. He just can't help being faithful and loving and kind. He's a machine—*made so*. That's more than you can say for humans." Nevertheless, George surrenders to his wife's persistence, only to reunite the inconsolable Gloria with Robbie at the end.

Other problems besides unreasoning opposition to robots run through the robot series: 1) human resentment of robots (Asimov calls it "the Frankenstein complex") and the difficulties of introducing robots on Earth; 2) determining what is good for people; 3) the difficulties of giving a robot unambiguous instructions; 4) the distinctions among robots and between robots and people, and the difficulties in telling robots and people apart; 5) the superiority of robots to people; and also 6) the superiority of people to robots.

Asimov rearranged the order of the stories when they were published in *I, Robot.* He also made some small editorial changes for consistency. "Reason," for instance, is placed third in the book, although it was written and published second, before the codification of the Three Laws.

Pleased by the appearance of "Strange Playfellow" ("Robbie") in print, Asimov decided to "press Campbell's buttons" by using a religious motif in a robot story. Campbell responded as Asimov had hoped, asking Asimov to write the story for him and buying it immediately. It was the first Asimov robot story to appear in *Astounding.* "Reason" incorporated two of Campbell's editorial preferences: a philosophic concern with religion—Cutie deduces by "pure reason" that he could not have been constructed by such inferior beings as Donovan and Powell but must have been created by the most powerful thing around, the energy convertor, which he therefore reasons to be a god—and a pragmatic conclusion. When Cutie handles the energy beam perfectly, even through an "electron" storm, the two engineers decide to leave him with his delusion and even to ship other QT models to the station to be indoctrinated with the religious belief that works so well.

"Liar!," the third robot story written by Asimov, incorporated the Three Laws of Robotics for the first time.[4] Campbell had suggested the Three Laws during a discussion that preceded the writing of the story, and Asimov codified them:

1. A robot may not injure a human being or, through inaction, allow a human being to come to harm.

4. The mention of the First Law in "Robbie" and of the Three Laws in "Reason" clearly are interpolations for the 1950 book, as is the mention of Susan Calvin in "Robbie" and "Runaround."

2. A robot must obey the orders given it by human beings except where such orders would conflict with the First Law.
3. A robot must protect its own existence as long as such protection does not conflict with the First or Second Laws.

Typically, Asimov has always insisted that Campbell originated the laws, and Campbell always said that they were implicit in Asimov's stories and discussions. Whatever the exact truth of origin, the Three Laws, as Asimov noted in his autobiography, "revolutionized science fiction":

> Once they were established in a series of stories, they made so much sense and proved so popular with the readers that other writers began to use them. They couldn't quote them directly, of course, but they could simply assume their existence, knowing well that the readers would be acquainted with the Laws and would understand the assumption.

Campbell may have worked more intuitively than through conscious theory, but what he wanted was: a rational inspection of all premises; a movement away from traditional responses, primarily emotional and irrational, toward pragmatism; and the construction of new and more logical systems of operation. Campbell, as a writer, also may have perceived the fictional opportunities the Laws of Robotics would provide. As Asimov noted in *The Rest of the Robots*, "There was just enough ambiguity in the Three Laws to provide the conflicts and uncertainties required for new stories, and, to my great relief, it seemed always to be possible to think up a new angle out of the sixty-one words of the Three Laws."

The Asimov robot stories as a whole may respond best to an analysis based on that ambiguity and on the ways in which Asimov played twenty-nine variations upon a theme. The importance to the evolution of science fiction, at least in the period between 1940 and 1950, was that this was an intellectual development. The emotional response—the fear of the machine, the fear of the creature turning on its creator—was derided. In the robot stories, such responses are characteristic of foolish, unthinking people, religious fanatics, short-sighted labor unions. The Frankenstein complex may be observably true in human nature (and this, along with its appeal to human fears of change and the unknown, may explain its persistence in literature), but it is false to humanity's intellectual aspirations to be rational and to build rationally. Blind emotion, sentimentality, prejudice, faith in the impossible, unwillingness to accept observable truth, failure to use one's intellectual capacities or the resources for discovering the truth that are available, these were the evils that Campbell and Asimov saw as the sources of human misery. They could be dispelled, they thought, by exposure to ridicule and the clear, cool voice of reason, though always with difficulty and never completely.

"Robbie," for instance, considers the question of unreasoning opposition to robots: Grace Weston's concern about Robbie, the villagers' fear of him, New York's curfew for robots. Mrs. Weston, who herself has an unreasoning determination to get rid of Robbie, says, "People aren't reasonable about these things." The climax of the story, in which Robbie moves swiftly to save Gloria from being run down by a tractor, makes clear the advantages of the robot's single-minded concern for its function and its instantaneous response to a crisis that paralyzes Gloria's parents for vital split seconds.

"Runaround" is an exercise in the conflict between two of the Three Laws. Speedy, a valuable new robot designed for use in the mines of Mercury, has been ordered to get silenium from a pool. But he is found circling the pool acting drunk, and it turns out that carbon monoxide released by volcanic activity in the area can combine with iron to form volatile iron carbonyl. At a certain distance from the pool Speedy's instinct for self-preservation (the Third Law) exactly balances the necessity to obey orders (the Second Law). Powell is able to break Speedy out of his deadly circle only by placing himself in danger so that Speedy must rescue him (the First Law).

Many of the stories develop from unforeseen consequences of the creation of new robots (sometimes complicated by inaccurate or unspecific orders, as in "Runaround"); others come about through accident. Both stem naturally from Asimov's premise that unforeseen consequences or accidents are eventualities that rational persons cannot guard against.

"Catch That Rabbit" concerns a master robot with six sub-robots who is created for asteroid mining but occasionally malfunctions when not watched and cannot remember why. It turns out that six sub-robots are too many for Davie to handle in an emergency. When Donovan and Powell discover this, partly by accident, they are able to pinpoint the affected part of Davie's positronic brain, the part that is stressed by a six-way order.

"Liar!" begins with the accidental creation of a telepathic robot, Herbie. Herbie is asked to tell each of the characters what he has learned from reading other characters' minds, and because he cannot "harm" them, according to the First Law, he tells them what they want to hear. In particular, he tells plain, spinsterish Susan Calvin that the man she loves, Milton Ashe, is in love with her. When they all discover that Herbie has been lying to them, Susan drives Herbie insane by forcing on him the dilemma that no matter what he does he will be hurting someone.

"Little Lost Robot" brings in a search for a hyperatomic (interstellar) drive at a base in the asteroids. A new kind of robot, the Nestor series, has been created to work with scientists in dangerous situations from which ordinary robots would pull the scientists to safety. Some Nestors have not been impressioned, therefore, with the entire First Law, and one of them is told by an irritated scientist to get lost. The variation Asimov used here was the conditions under which the First Law would have to be relaxed, those conditions being when robots had to discriminate between dangers. When the Nestor hides among identical robots and refuses to reveal itself, Susan Calvin attempts to force it into the open by placing a man in danger. At first, all the robots spring to save the man. In a second, slightly different experiment, they all remain seated, having been convinced by the hiding Nestor that any attempt to save the man could not succeed and they would only destroy themselves. In a final test, Susan places herself in danger. The malfunctioning Nestor reveals itself by recognizing that harmless infrared rays rather than dangerous gamma rays are involved and by forgetting, in its feeling of superiority, that the other robots have not been trained, as it has, to tell the difference.

"Escape" involves computers rather than robots, but the problems are the same: in this case, how can a robot (computer) be forced to solve a problem if the solution might involve the death of a human being? Such a conflict with the First Law has, apparently, burned out the computer of a competitor, Consolidated Robots,[5] which approaches USR to hire its computer to solve a problem, probably concerning the development of an interstellar hyperatomic or space-warp drive. USR's computer, called "The Brain," incorporates USR's patented emotional brain paths and operates on a childlike, "idiot-savant" level. The ship that it builds turns out to "kill" the occupants (Donovan and Powell) but only temporarily while they are in the space-warp. The computer's emotional imbalance during the drive, however, turns The Brain into a practical joker.

"Evidence" presents another problem in discrimination. In "Little Lost Robot" the question was how to detect the one in a group of identical robots that has been instructed in the strongest terms to get lost. In "Evidence" the question is how to tell a humanoid robot from a human when the individual in question stands on his rights as a presumptive human. Stephen Byerley, accused by political opponents of being a robot, is running for mayor. The evidence is presented: no one has seen Byerley sleep or eat. But this is not proof that he does not. He refuses to be searched or X-rayed and wears a device that protects him against X rays attempted by subterfuge. He practices as a district attorney but does not actually condemn convicted criminals to death. The Asimovian touch is contained in the fact that he is a good district attorney, a good man, and would make a good mayor. When asked if robots are so mentally different from men, Susan Calvin says, "Worlds different. Robots are essentially decent." At the climactic mo-

5. This is the only mention of competition in the robot business.

ment of the campaign, Byerley strikes a heckler, something a robot would be unable to do. But after the election, Susan Calvin notes that it would have been possible for him to strike a robot made up to look human.

"The Evitable Conflict," the final story in *I, Robot*, concludes the saga of the robots—for their first decade at least—by dealing with the question of robot superiority and the ambiguity in the First Law about what constitutes harm—or good. The Machines, which have become too complex for humans to understand, have taken over the operation of the world's economy. For the first time in human history the economy is running smoothly, except for a few small problems here and there. These problems, however, should not occur, and they worry Stephen Byerley, who has now become World Coordinator. He tells Susan Calvin about his investigation. One by one, he and Susan discard hypotheses that the Machines are being given wrong data or that their instructions are being ignored. Wrong data or sabotage (by the anti-robot Society for Humanity) simply become part of the data for the next problem and are taken into account by the Machines. The small inefficiencies, they finally decide, have been caused by the Machines themselves as they shake loose those few persons who cling to the side of the boat for purposes the Machines consider harmful to humanity. The Machines are acting for the ultimate good of the human species, which only the Machines know or can know. Mankind has lost any voice in its own future, but then, if one considers the uncontrolled swings of the economy when it was in the hands of humans and the seemingly inevitable conflicts that accompanied them, humanity never had any control. For all time now, all conflicts are finally evitable. Only the Machines are inevitable.

One might contrast this attitude toward the omniscient and omnipotent machine with Jack Williamson's treatment of the same theme in "With Folded Hands," which appeared three years before "The Evitable Conflict" and may have been on Asimov's mind. Indeed, the title of Asimov's story might refer to Williamson's conclusion about his "humanoids," who do everything for humanity and leave mankind with nothing to do but sit with folded hands. There are two major differences between "The Evitable Conflict" and "With Folded Hands," however: Asimov's Machines not only control human affairs better than humans but humanity never has been "free," and the Machines do not let humanity know it no longer is in control.

This account of the stories that make up *I, Robot* gives only a hint of the qualities that make the stories, and the book, persistently appealing. Except for "Liar!" and "Evidence," these are not stories in which character plays a significant part. Virtually all plot develops through conversation with little if any action. Nor is there a great deal of local color or description of any kind. The dialogue is functional at best, and the style, at best, transparent.

At times, as in the climactic moment in which Susan Calvin torments Herbie into insanity with a dilemma, Asimov's unadorned language rises to the demands placed upon it by the narrative. But mostly it lies passively and unambiguously between the reader and the story. While it seldom adds much to enjoyment of the story, it seldom detracts from it either— unless the reader demands something that Asimov and the story are unprepared to give.

The robot stories and almost all Asimov fiction play themselves on a relatively bare stage. The reader perceives only those stage properties that are essential to the plot, and those only in general details. Mercury, the closest planet to the sun and the scene of "Runaround," could have called forth descriptions of the unique qualities of that unusual planet (and has in stories by other authors), but it is presented only in terms of heat and brightness: "The sunlight came down in a white-hot wash and played liquidly around them." The reader is denied even a description of the silenium pool, whatever *that* might be. Solar Station #5, in "Reason," exists only in terms such as "officer's room," "control room," and "engine later in his juveniles, Lucky Starr and Bigman.

The characters in the robot stories fill the requirements for what they must do and little more. Gloria's attachment to Robbie and Robbie's faithful dedication to Gloria make them a pleasantly sentimental pair, but Gloria's parents are stock parents: the foolish but determined mother and the sympathetic but susceptible father. Unless readers pay close attention in the Powell and Donovan stories, they may find it difficult to remember that Powell is English and logical, Donovan is Irish and impulsive. The use of such pairs (as well as larger groupings of friends and colleagues) had become conventional in science fiction by then. Asimov used an almost identical pair later in his juveniles, Lucky Starr and Bigman.

The antagonists, where such exist, are seldom characterized at all. The employees of USR, however, begin to assume greater life: Robertson, Lanning, Bogert, and finally Susan Calvin herself. The closer the characters work with robots the more interesting characteristics they accumulate. Susan Calvin clearly became a favorite of Asimov. "As time went on," he wrote in *The Rest of the Robots*, "I fell in love with Dr. Calvin." She is plain, stiff, forbidding, unemotional, logical— "much more like the popular conception of a robot than any of my positronic creations," Asimov continued. She is a character much like Mr. Spock in *Star Trek*, who became, accidentally one would assume, the catalyst for the popularity of that series. The reader comes to love Susan Calvin too.

It is the robots who display the "infinite variety" that Shakespeare praised in Cleopatra: Robbie with his more than doglike devotion; the drunken Speedy, caught between imperatives; the arrogant Cutie, blinded by the brilliance of his own logic; the puzzled Davie; the tender Herbie; the Machiavellian Nestor; the childlike Brain; the coolly competent Stephen Byerley; and, in a lesser way because they never appear directly, the omniscient Machines. They all have names (again, excluding the Machines), and this is a concession not only to the human characteristic of naming vehicles and machines but to the humanization of the robots. They capture our interest more than the people—as they should. *I, Robot,* though never in the first person, is always about robots, and the characters' reactions to the problems that the robots bring with them create the stories.

Asimov never identifies with his robots, however. He gives them self-awareness and human characteristics so that the characters (and the readers) can better deal with the problems they present. Readers read the robot stories incorrectly when they begin to care more about what happens to the robots than what happens to the people—at least in the Asimovian universe. Asimov is a rational man, and rationally the robots are still machines: humans should no more become fixated on their endearing characteristics than they should fear their rebellion.

All of this, including the lack of action and the conversational mode by which the stories proceed ("The Evitable Conflict" consists entirely of a conversation between Byerley and Susan Calvin), is less important than that each story exists as a puzzle to be solved. The delight of the reader is in the ingenuity with which Asimov's characters solve the puzzle. The robots exist to present the puzzle in their behavior; the characters exist to solve the puzzle.

This view of Asimov's fiction may explain much of his style. His dialogue, for instance, is a vehicle for describing and then analyzing the problem, and clarity is its most important attribute (robots may have problems understanding human statements, but other humans do not, unless information is deliberately withheld, as in "Risk," a story included in *The Rest of the Robots*). An emphasis on setting would imply a relevance of setting to the outcome that would be misleading; a presentation of human variation would suggest that human differences are the main subject, instead of robot differences. In spite of the fact that "Liar!" and "Evidence" (the stories in which character plays a more important part) are clearly the most effective stories in the book, they are equally clearly most effective because of the more-or-less accidental coming together of the Asimov method with a suitable subject. Susan Calvin's human reaction to Herbie's lies *is* the means by which the problem is solved and the question of Herbie disposed of. Stephen Byerley's ambiguous presence *is* the problem of robot superiority that must meet the test of human fear.

The other stories are less successful as fiction because Asimov does not find a humanly involving method for expressing them. "Liar!" and "Evidence" would be unsuccessful if it were not for the ingenuity of the solutions to the problems they present; the human problems solve the robot predicament. It is always so in the robot stories: Weston not only must get Robbie and Gloria back together again but must do so in a way that demonstrates Robbie's superiority as a nursemaid; Powell must get Speedy back but in a way exploiting the Three Laws. If readers do not involve themselves in solving the problems, they will find little else to enjoy in *I, Robot*.

As in *The Foundation Trilogy*, Asimov discovered, or learned from Campbell, the method that best suited his rational temperament and that best developed the kind of ideas he wished to explore: the mystery. As a rational person in an irrational world, Asimov had a compulsion that fit perfectly with what Campbell thought science fiction ought to do: that is, to show rationality prevailing over fear, prejudice, sentimentality, short-sightedness, and all the other irrational forces in the world. Thus the mystery, the puzzle, the success of the logical, unemotional Susan Calvin over all the other less logical, more emotional characters in the stories. "Robbie" was less successful (and less acceptable to Campbell, perhaps) partly because it was not a puzzle, not a mystery. "Reason" was Campbell's kind of story, and Asimov's too, because it presented the puzzle of Cutie's obsession and how to solve it, and the ending was a neat twist that had not been foreseen.

The puzzle and the ingenious solution were what sold Asimov's robot stories to Campbell and to his readers. But those were not the stories' only virtues. The concern with the Three Laws also had relevance to human behavior, sometimes stated, more often not. This does not mean simply the overt references to such matters as the Frankenstein complex: the fear of robots and the banning of their use on Earth has more fictional value than philosophic validity. Although clearly motivated by Asimov's dislike for the archetype and enabling him to deal with contrasts in attitudes and behavior, the terrestrial antipathy toward the robots seems less convincing than desirable for reasons of plot. Robot computers are not banned, nor are other non-humanoid robots. The banning of the robots and apprehension concerning them, however, provides many conflicts in a series that has little inevitable conflict built into it. Asimov is able to get around the bans when he desires, particularly in the robot stories published after 1950.

More important are the philosophic implications of the

Three Laws. In "Runaround," for instance, Speedy is in the position of a human who has been ordered to perform an important task but who discovers that doing it will endanger his life. A human might not exhibit his conflict in a fashion so cleverly balanced between a command that must be obeyed and a danger that must be avoided, but the circle he enscribes around the selenium pool shows an understanding of human nature that a soldier cowering in a shell hole might not. Cutie has the characteristics of many prophets, finding his certitude in Platonic introspection rather than scientific evidence; and his analysis suggests to the reader, in passing, how improbable are the universe and the life itself that we take for granted.

By the time Asimov reached the writing of "Evidence," the comparisons between robots and humans had become overt. Susan Calvin points out:

> ". . . if you stop to think about it, the three Rules of Robotics are the essential guiding principles of a good many of the world's ethical systems. Of course, every human being is supposed to have the instinct of self-preservation. That's Rule Three to a robot. Also every 'good' human being, with a social conscience and a sense of responsibility, is supposed to defer to proper authority; to listen to his doctor, his boss, his government, his psychiatrist, his fellow man; to obey laws, to follow rules, to conform to custom—even when they interfere with his comfort or his safety. That's Rule Two to a robot. Also, every 'good' human being is supposed to love others as himself, protect his fellow man, risk his life to save another. That's Rule One to a robot. To put it simply—if Byerley follows all the Rules of Robotics, he may be a robot, and may simply be a very good man."

Clearly, as she herself states in the same story, Susan Calvin likes robots considerably better than human beings. By the end of the book, so may the reader.

The story of the robots does not end here. Asimov continued his exploration of the theme with three stories published in magazines other than *Astounding* in the 1940–50 period, and eighteen more scattered over the following quarter century, some of them mere throwaways, others better than most if not all the stories in *I, Robot*. The first group of eight was published in *The Rest of the Robots* in 1964.

"Robot AL-76 Goes Astray," *Amazing*, February 1942, presents a confused robot. It was built to work in the mines of the airless moon with a disintegrator (called a Disinto). Somehow it gets lost on Earth and makes a Disinto out of scrap and two flashlight batteries, only to be told by a frightened human to destroy it and forget about it completely. AL-76 is confused, but it is not as confused as the people who are afraid of him.

"Victory Unintentional," *Super Science Stories*, August 1942, is a sequel to "Not Final," an *Astounding* story that presented the threat of a teeming, xenophobic civilization on Jupiter. In "Victory Unintentional" a robot expedition lands on Jupiter. The robots are taken by the Jovians to be humans and prove so superior to the Jovians that the Jovian superiority complex crumbles.

"First Law," *Fantastic Universe*, October 1946, is a casual short-short and a tall tale about a robot (of the MA series) that breaks the First Law because it is a mother, and mother love supersedes every other law.

"Let's Get Together," *Infinity*, February 1957, describes a stalemate between East and West that is unbalanced by a report that the East has developed a superior ability to manufacture humanoid robots. Ten of them reportedly are in the U.S. carrying fragments of a TC (total conversion) bomb. A big scientific conference is to consider the problem, but as the scientists are gathering, the Chief of the Bureau of Robotics decides that the meeting is the means for bringing the humanoids together and wiping out the scientific minds of the West.

"Satisfaction Guaranteed," *Amazing*, April 1951, is a story that might have qualified for *I, Robot*. In an attempt to make robots acceptable on Earth (and in the home), USR makes TN-3 ("Tony"), "a tall and darkly handsome" humanoid. It turns out to be a perfect household servant, not only helpful but creative, redecorating the house and the mistress of the house. By seeming to fall in love with her, Tony also restores her sense of adequacy. Susan Calvin comments that "machines can't fall in love, but—even when it's hopeless and horrifying—women can."

"Risk," *Astounding*, May 1955, returns to the scene of "Little Lost Robot," Hyper Base, where the search for a hyperspace interstellar drive has achieved success—except that animals come back mindless. A robot is placed in an experimental ship, but at the appointed time nothing happens. Over strenuous objections, Susan Calvin sends a man to investigate rather than a robot. He discovers that the robot, instructed only to pull the control bar *firmly* toward him, pulled it with robot strength and bent it. The point of the story, however, is that a man was sent rather than a robot, not because human life is valued less but because a robot can't be useful unless it can be given precise orders. It can't be asked to "find out what's wrong."

"Lenny," *Infinity*, January 1958, begins with a child accidentally inserting random programming into a new LNE ("Lenny") model. Lenny turns out to behave like an infant. Susan Calvin says that Lenny has great promise because it is teachable, but it raises First Law fears when it breaks an employee's arm—trying to ward off a blow, as it turns out. Susan protects Lenny, pointing out that the robot did not know its own strength and could not yet differentiate between good and evil. Moreover, it will help to solve the problem of getting young people interested in robotics by adding the spice of danger. Perhaps more important, she feels motherly "toward the only kind of baby she could ever have or love."

"Galley Slave," *Galaxy*, December 1957, takes up the problem of mental drudgery. USR introduces a proofreading robot, EZ-27 ("Easy"). A few months later Professor Simon Ninheimer, opposed to the idea of leasing Easy at the beginning, sues USR because Easy inserted embarrassing mistakes into Ninheimer's new book. Easy has a block against talking about the problem. The robot is brought into the courtroom as Ninheimer is describing how badly his reputation has been injured by Easy's action, and Easy rises to speak. Ninheimer shouts that it has been told to remain silent. Easy was about to take all the blame upon itself. Ninheimer's motivation was not simply hatred of robots but an effort to keep creative scholarship from being taken over by robots.

The remainder of the robot stories are scattered throughout five different collections of short stories. All were written and published after 1956. Two of them, in which robots play a less central role than in any of the previous stories, were reprinted in Asimov's collection of stories *Earth Is Room Enough* in 1957.

"Jokester," *Infinity,* December 1956, deals with Multivac, Asimov's all-purpose computer (named, by analogy, after the early computer called Univac). Grand Masters, the only persons capable of comprehending the functions of the giant computer and of asking the meaningful questions, the scarcity of which had created a bottleneck in dealing with Multivac, are permitted great latitude. One of them, Meyerhoff, who has a reputation as a jokester, begins telling jokes to Multivac in an effort to discover who originates such jokes. Multivac ultimately reveals that jokes are placed in selected human minds by extraterrestrials who use them to study human psychology. Once the origin of jokes is known, the method will become useless as an objective technique. Humanity loses its sense of humor; there will be no more jokes, no more laughter.

"Someday," *Infinity,* August 1956, tells the story of a couple of children who pull out of storage a robot storyteller called Bard and try to get it to tell more modern stories. It ends up kicked, abused, and deserted, telling itself a story about a poor little storytelling robot named Bard who will be appreciated someday.

Here, as elsewhere, is a playfulness in Asimov, an occasional lack of seriousness that results in stories tossed off casually. Some critics might consider this grounds for disqualifying Asimov from literary consideration, but Asimov does not consider himself a literary man. He is a writer, and he writes anything that appeals to him. Some stories are inconsequential, but there are Asimov stories that ask the reader to take them seriously. The playfulness should be assessed at its own level, like Asimov's limericks and love of puns.

Two more robot stories appear in *Nine Tomorrows,* an Asimov collection published in 1959. They, too, deal with Multivac.

"All the Troubles of the World," *Super-Science Fiction,* April 1958, describes a world fifty years after the creation of Multivac, when it tries to destroy itself because it has been loaded with all of humanity's troubles and it "wants to die."

"The Last Question," Science Fiction Quarterly, November 1956, has been called, by Asimov himself, "the best science fiction short story ever written." It has also been the basis for several planetarium shows. It begins on May 21, 2061, when two technicians ask Multivac if entropy can be reversed. As humanity spreads outward through the galaxy and then the universe, people ask the same question of increasingly more complex computers and always get the same response: "Insufficient data for meaningful answer." The universe winds down into the heat death called entropy, and humanity fuses its mind with Cosmic AC, which exists in hyperspace. Finally, AC learns how to reverse entropy and says, "Let there be light." "And there was light."

Three robot stories are contained in Asimov's Nightfall and Other Stories, published in 1969.

"Insert Knob A in Hole B," Fantasy and Science Fiction, December 1957, is a minor short-short about two spacemen on a space station who cannot get equipment to work properly because it is all shipped unassembled with inadequate instructions. Finally, they are shipped a robot programmed to put everything together. But it arrives unassembled.

"The Machine That Won the War," Fantasy and Science Fiction, October 1961, is another Multivac story. Multivac has been given credit for winning the war with aliens from the star Deneb. But in the last few months of the war, the man who was feeding Multivac the data began to fudge it because the data was unreliable, the man who was reading the results began to fudge them because he knew Multivac was unreliable, and the man who had to make the decision relied on flipping a coin.

"Segregationist," Abbottempo, Book 4, 1967, describes a world in which humans are getting metal replacement parts that make them increasingly like robots, and robots are getting fibroid replacement parts that make them increasingly like humans. The surgeon is old-fashioned and prefers to be all one thing—robot.

The Best of Isaac Asimov, published in 1973, contains, in addition to a reprint of "The Last Question," a robot story involving Elijah ("Lije") Baley and R. Daneel Olivaw, the principal characters in Asimov's two robot detective novels, *The Caves of Steel* and *The Naked Sun*. "Mirror Image," *Analog*, May 1972, presents a problem in which two robots confirm identically opposite stories of their masters, each of whom claims to have discovered an important mathematical technique and to have confided it to the other. Olivaw brings the problem to Baley. Baley questions the robots and comes up, finally, with an asymmetrical response that he interprets as proving the older mathematician's robot is lying. At the end, Baley reveals that the response could have meant just the opposite, but he already had decided that the older mathematician would never have confided in a younger man.

A final (though with Asimov nothing is certainly final) five stories are included in *The Bicentennial Man and Other Stories*, an Asimov collection published in 1976.

"Feminine Intuition," *Fantasy and Science Fiction*, October 1969, introduced a feminine robot for the first time (other than the throwaway MA series in "First Law"). JN-5 ("Jane") is developed to be intuitive and to produce useful guesses about which suns are likely to have habitable planets. But she is destroyed in an airplane accident along with her creator. Apparently, however, she had come up with the names of three stars within eighty light-years that probably have habitable planets. Though someone may have heard her reveal the names, a search turns up no one. Finally, the eighty-year-old Susan Calvin is recalled from retirement and from the evidence comes up with the answer: Jane had spoken before she boarded the plane and was overheard by a truck driver, someone nobody would have thought of.

"That Thou Art Mindful of Him" was commissioned for an anthology entitled *Final Stage*, published in 1974, which was intended to contain the ultimate stories on a variety of themes. Asimov's, of course, was robots. The story also was published in *Fantasy and Science Fiction*, May 1974. It returns to the Second Law: how can a robot judge whether or not to obey an order, i.e., what is a human being? In space the question is not as important, since most humans in space are responsible. But if robots are to be introduced on Earth, a diverse group of uninformed humans will be able to give them orders, and robots must be able to discriminate. JG ("George") models are created to make that judgment; they will begin by obeying all orders and then learn discrimination. George Ten persuades his creator to allow him to discuss the matter with George Nine. They come up with one solution to the introduction of robots on Earth: USR can make simple robots such as robot birds, bugs, and worms, that can handle ecological problems, and do not need the Three Laws because they are limited to simple actions. These robots will begin the process of accustoming humanity to robots. Meanwhile, George Ten and Nine come to the conclusion that only they are human. Eventually, they will take over. It seems the Frankenstein complex has proved not so illogical after all. With "That Thou Art Mindful of Him," Asimov appeared to have written himself out of the positronic robot series. But he was above such petty inconsistencies.

"The Life and Times of Multivac," *New York Times Magazine*, January 5, 1975, returns to the theme of the omniscient, omnipotent computer. In "The Evitable Conflict," the Machines had taken over control of everything because they knew what was good for humanity, but they kept their omniscience and omnipotence to themselves. In "That Thou Art Mindful of Him" the Machines, it was revealed, had phased themselves out, perhaps unwisely(!), after they perceived their job was done. In the present story, a few people have begun to perceive a similar takeover by Multivac as slavery. Ronald Bakst gains the confidence of Multivac and supplies it with a problem in his field of mathematical games that he says could lead to human genetic changes that would create a humanity more likely to accept Multivac's direction. Bakst is viewed as a traitor to humanity but uses Multivac's distraction to uncouple a joint at a key spot and burn out the computer. At the end, as the other rebels stare at him, Bakst asks uncertainly, "Isn't that what you want?" Such ambiguity is unusual in Asimov.

"The Tercentennary Incident," *Ellery Queen's Mystery Magazine*, August 1976, offers a new look at the question of the robot as political leader. At a Fourth of July celebration around the Washington Monument in 2076, the President of the United States, which now is a part of a planetary Federation, is disintegrated. But he then appears upon the platform to announce that what had happened had been the breakdown of a robot made to serve certain presidential functions. President Winkler becomes a great President. But a Secret Service agent named Edwards, who had seen the incident, believes that the real President had been disintegrated by a new and secret weapon and replaced by a robot. Edwards tries to convince the President's personal secretary and urges him to observe the President closely and, if he discovers sufficient evidence, to persuade him to resign. But the secretary turns out to have been part of the scheme from the beginning and now must do away with Edwards. Asimov noted in an afterword that this story was a return to the theme developed in "Evidence" thirty years previously and suggested that he had come up with a better story—and perhaps a better answer to the question of robots and political power.

"The Bicentennial Man," *Stellar Science Fiction* No. 2, February 1976, provides a kind of closing counterpart to "Robbie." Like Robbie, NDR ("Andrew") is a loyal and loving servant. He loves and serves the Martins. Unlike Robbie, Andrew not only can talk but, by some strange combination of brain pathways, can also create art and learn. The Martin family benefits by selling his art but also deposits half the income in a bank for Andrew's benefit and sees that he is provided every robot improvement. Finally, Andrew asks to buy his freedom, begins to wear clothes, writes a history of robots, obtains legal rights for robots, has his brain put in an organic body, and becomes a robobiologist. While USR develops ways of making robots with more precise positronic pathways (to avoid a repetition of Andrew) and then of making robots controlled by a central brain (as in "With Folded Hands"), Andrew develops a system for gaining energy for his new body from the combustion of hydrocarbons. He also learns to reason that what seems like cruelty might, in the long run, be kindness. When asked where all this is leading, Andrew says, "My body is a canvas on which I intend to draw—" A roboticist completes the sentence: "A man?" For his accomplishments Andrew is honored as the Sesquicentennial Robot on the 150th anniversary of his construction. He then wants to be declared a man by the World Legislature. After twenty-six years of defeat, Andrew recognizes that human antipathy toward him is rooted in his immortality, and he arranges for the potential to be drained slowly from his brain so that he will die within a year. On his 200th anniversary, the World President signs the act and declares the dying Andrew "a Bicentennial Man." Andrew's last thoughts are of the child to which he was nursemaid.

"The Bicentennial Man" is a fitting conclusion to the robot saga. At last Asimov had arrived at the essential question: what is the difference between robots and humans? He first asked the question in "Evidence." He brought up and dismissed external evidence; even actions might only demonstrate that Byerley is an extremely good man. In "Victory Unintentional," the robots are believed to be humans and a superior race by the Jovians because the robots never say they are not. In "Let's Get Together," the question of distinguishing humanoids from humans is short-circuited by induction. In "Risk," we learn that the difference between robots and humans is that humans can be given general orders; in "Lenny," that humans, and only unusual kinds of robots, can learn. "That Thou Art Mindful of Him" speculates that, given the opportunity to make a judgment, robots will decide on the basis of their superiority that only they are human. "The Tercentenary Incident" distinguishes robot from human only by superior performance.

In "The Bicentennial Man," Asimov follows the question to its final answer. Andrew's first human attribute is his artistic ability, but this is not enough, nor is his bank account. The distinguishing characteristic seems to be freedom, but that is not enough. Andrew continues to explore the differences between humans and robots in an effort to discover the definitive answer: humans wear clothes and robots do not; humans have rights and robots do not; humans have biological bodies and robots have metal bodies; humans gain energy from the combustion of hydrocarbons, robots from atomic energy; humans can discriminate between short-term cruelty and long-term kindness and robots cannot; humans die and robots are immortal. But perhaps the final distinction is Andrew's sentimental and hard-to-rationalize desire to be human when he is so clearly superior to humans in every way. The sentimentality that threatens the story is essential to the argument: robots are always rational and humans are not. Humans act for emotional reasons, and, ultimately, so does Andrew. Andrew, indeed, has become human.

In the process of writing twenty-nine stories about robots over a period of thirty-one years, Asimov let various inconsistencies creep in. This is apparent not simply in the problem of chronology, which has various minor glitches, but in that of incompatibility: if some of the events took place, others could not. Some inconsistencies, as those in "The Evitable Conflict," Asimov disposes of by declaring in a later story that the Machines phased themselves out when they thought their job was done (in "That Thou Art Mindful of Him"). Others he simply ignores, such as the fact that the Machines and the Multivac of "The Life and Times of Multivac" could not coexist, nor if Multivac was destroyed could it be "The Machine That Won the War" nor the computer that answered "The Last Question." And if the robots take over some time after the end of "That Thou Art Mindful of Him," some of the subsequent stories would be not only redundant but impossible. In other cases, as in "Lenny," the invention of the teachable robot is made and then forgotten. "Segregationist" suggests the coexistence and even equality of humans and robots; robots are introduced and reintroduced on Earth, as in "Satisfaction Guaranteed," "Galley Slave," "That Thou Art Mindful of Him," and "The Bicentennial Man," as if none of the other attempts had ever led to anything.

Asimov is eclectic. He never set out to write a consistent future history of the robots, even though the publication and the surprising success of *I, Robot*, with its parts glued together, made it seem as if he had. A certain number of common elements and cross-references has tended to reinforce the illusion. But it would be a mistake to judge the robot stories on this basis. *I, Robot* is the only self-sufficient and almost self-consistent work and should be adequate for the critic who desires unity.

The robot stories are a body of literature, much like the Scandinavian sagas or the Greek legends, that focuses on the question of how one should respond to the reality of the particular universe in which these groups of stories exist from a cluster of viewpoints. The greatest value of the robot stories is not in internal consistency but in multiplicity of consideration. In these stories Asimov provided readers with the unique excitement of an inquiring and artistic mind returning again and again to a single question and discovering not only new variations but sometimes different answers.

4
THE SHORT STORIES

Asimov's two great literary inventions—the Foundation galaxy with its future history and psychohistory, and the realistic, production-model robot—should not obscure his creation of an even more substantial body of individual stories and novels that are not linked by common characters or common themes, even though most of them fit into the same future history as *The Foundation Trilogy*. In this chapter and in Chapter 6, I discuss Asimov's non-series stories and novels. To do that I must return to the beginning of his science-fiction career.

Asimov had been writing science fiction for three years and seeing his stories published for two when, on March 17, 1941, he entered the office of the editor of *Astounding Science Fiction* as he had done many times before. As usual he had an idea for a story to discuss with Campbell, but this time Campbell brushed it aside. Campbell had his own idea to present. As Asimov recalled in his autobiography:

> He had come across a quotation from an eight-chapter work by Ralph Waldo Emerson called *Nature*. In the first chapter, Emerson said: "If the stars should appear one night in a thousand years, how would men believe and adore; and preserve for many generations the remembrance of the city of God."
>
> Campbell asked me to read it and said, "What do you think would happen, Asimov, if men were to see the stars for the first time in a thousand years?"

I thought, and drew a blank. I said, "I don't know."
Campbell said, "I think they would go mad. I want you to write a story about that."

After discussing the idea with Campbell and providing answers to such Campbell questions as "why should the stars be
invisible at other times?," Asimov went home to write the
story. He started it the next evening.

It was a critical time in Asimov's development as a writer,
although he was not to recognize that fact until much later.
Up to that time he had written thirty-one stories and sold sev-
enteen. Of the ones he had sold, only three measured up to
his own standards of passability—the three positronic robot
stories, "Robbie," "Reason," and "Liar!"—and only one of
these, "Liar!," would meet most objective critical standards.
"My status on that evening of March 18," he wrote in his autobiography, "was as nothing more than a steady and (perhaps) hopeful third-rater. What's more, that's all that I considered myself at that time."

Despite Asimov's initial concern, the story developed with
unprecedented ease. By April 8 it was finished, 13,300 words
entitled "Nightfall." It was published in *Astounding* for September 1941. The magazine's cover painting illustrated the
climactic scene of the novelette. Over it were the words:

NIGHTFALL

by Isaac Asimov

Almost thirty years later, the story came out at the top of the
voting by the Science Fiction Writers of America for stories
that had appeared before 1965—the year of the first Nebula
Awards and the first Nebula Award volume honoring the best
science fiction of the year—to be published in *The Science
Fiction Hall of Fame.*

After the publication of "Nightfall," Asimov recalled, "I
was no longer a minor writer, hovering about the fringes of
science-fiction fame. Finally, after three years of trying, I was
accepted as a major figure in the field—and I was still only

twenty-one." To the detriment of his peace of mind but the benefit of his career, Asimov didn't realize that anything had changed. He kept struggling.

The story that marked such a turning point in Asimov's literary career is not exceptional in many ways (Asimov himself does not consider it either the best story of all time or even his own best story). The plot develops much more mechanically than in some of his better stories, even in some earlier ones such as "Liar!," the characters are barely functional, and the language is little more than that. Why do readers, even fellow writers, rate it so high? The answer reflects the situation of science fiction in 1941. John W. Campbell, Jr., was consolidating his position of leadership in science fiction, and what was appearing in *Astounding* was becoming, for most science-fiction readers, the definition of science fiction.

The most important element of "Nightfall" was subject. It had a big one: the relationship of people to the universe. This was to become the most significant theme Campbellian science fiction would explore. It asked: what is humanity? how does humanity understand itself and its situation? what can humanity do about it?

The story's second element, the reversal, was another Campbell favorite. On the planet where "Nightfall" takes place, the situation is almost the reverse of the situation on Earth. Lagash experiences eternal day rather than the alternation of day and night. How this affects people's behavior becomes the subject of "Nightfall."

The third element was a clear-cut test of scientific investigation as opposed to other routes to "knowledge." Emerson's poetic vision was just the starting place. "Nightfall" begins with the Emerson quotation as an epigraph. The answer to Campbell's question—"why should the stars be invisible at other times?"—was Lagash, a planet that is part of a complex solar phenomenon that places three pairs of suns in the sky. Alpha, around which Lagash orbits, has a small red-dwarf companion named Beta. There are two more distant pairs. One pair is named Gamma and Delta; the other pair is not called by name (logically they would be Epsilon and Zeta, but the nomenclature is only figurative anyway). The result is that La-

gash is virtually never in darkness, for one or more of the suns
is always in the sky. But once every two thousand and forty-
nine years, a large moon, neither seen nor suspected until just
before the story begins, eclipses Beta when that sun alone is
in the sky. The eclipse covers all of Lagash and lasts more
than half a day.

This, improbable and unstable an astronomical configura-
tion though it is, sets up Emerson's world of if. It is not an
exact replica, perhaps because Asimov felt that a one-thou-
sand-year cycle of savagery to civilization would be implau-
sible, perhaps because the longer time span would be approx-
imately the length of time between the height of the Roman
Empire and the present, or between Athenian democracy and
Newton. A more likely reason is that an exact parallel would
seem contrived and the point of the story would be seen as a
simple attack on Emersonian romanticism.

Four hundred years before the story opens, a scientist
named Genovi 41 (the Lagashian Galileo) discovered that Lagash rotated around Alpha rather than vice versa. Since then,
astronomers have recorded and analyzed the complex motions
of the six suns. Twenty years before the story begins, the Law
of Universal Gravitation was discovered (by the Lagashian
Newton) and used to explain the orbital motions of the six
suns. In the last decade, the motions of Lagash have been
studied; the Law could not explain them, however, until a satellite of Lagash was postulated. Two months before the story
begins, the scientists at Saro University calculated the orbit of
the suspected satellite and came up with the prediction of
Beta's eclipse. This had been matched with archeological evidence that nine or more previous civilizations on Lagash had
reached levels comparable to the present one and then had
been mysteriously destroyed by fire.

Further evidence is provided by a cult built around a leg-
end that every two thousand and fifty years Lagash enters a
huge cave, all the suns disappear, total darkness comes over
all the world, and things called Stars appear, rob men of their
souls, and leave them unreasoning brutes who destroy their
own civilization. In the two months following the prediction
of Beta's eclipse, Saro University scientists have built a Hide-

out where some three hundred people, mostly women and children, will be shut away from the eclipse and the predicted madness, with food, weapons, and all printed records except the photographs to be taken of the eclipse and the Stars, whatever they are, at the Observatory.

The story develops mostly through lectures by the Director of the University, Aton 77, and a psychologist, Sheerin 501, to Theremon 762, a newspaper reporter who has been ridiculing their predictions in his newspaper column. A Cultist, Latimer 25, also appears with the intention of destroying the astronomical cameras set up to record the Stars; he thinks photographs will damage the Stars' religious significance. At the end, the eclipse begins. A mob, incited by the Cultists, gathers in the city to storm the Observatory. Its attack is held off until totality occurs and the Stars appear. Everyone goes insane, and Saro City begins to burn as the crazed citizens try to create light.

The story succeeds partly because it is a mystery to be solved, a puzzle to be worked out. Asimov is feeling his way toward his method and recapitulating the way in which he too was forced to solve the question that Campbell posed to him: under what conditions might Emerson's world of if become reality, and what would happen if it did? The reader begins by struggling with the meaning of "nightfall," a word that does not occur in the body of the story and for good reason. The Lagashians have no experience with that period of darkness we call night. (The word "night" is used only at the end, in a metaphorical sense in the final sentence, "The long night had come again.") What is this experience of nightfall that Aton describes in such terrible terms on the second page? "In just under four hours civilization, as we know it, comes to an end. It will do so because, as you see, Beta is the only sun in the sky." The rest of the story, largely lecture though it is, is the explication of that mystery and the establishment of psychological credibility for the final scene.

A major part of the story's appeal, certainly for Campbell and no doubt for his readers as well, was the alignment of forces: the rational people, the scientists, opposed by the irrational, the mobs and the Cultists. The mobs reject the warnings of the scientists because ordinary people place their faith in everyday experience continuing as it always has and will not believe in such abstractions as theories of gravitation and calculations about an invisible satellite. The Cultists, on the other hand, have preserved unique information about earlier catastrophes, but they interpret that information according to their desires rather than their intellects. They reject scientific "facts" in favor of religious "knowledge." They are right about events but for the wrong reasons, and thus their responses are also irrational.

Against these forces Asimov places the scientists, who may be passionate enough in pursuit of their goals (Aton blusters at Theremon, and another astronomer, Beenay, attacks Latimer), but they are willing to accept whatever "truth" best explains the facts. In earlier stories ("Black Friar of the Flame," which was written early in 1939, "Half-Breed," "The Secret Sense," etc.), Asimov had sometimes allowed emotion to become a motivating force. In "Nightfall" he established the position that he was to maintain throughout most of the rest of his work: rationality must struggle to prevail in a world made difficult not only by the mysteries and hard truths of the universe but by people unable or unwilling to think clearly. The subject of "Nightfall" is ignorance; ignorance of the laws that govern the universe, ignorance of phenomena such as "night" and "stars," which makes the Lagashians, even the scientists, victims of their fears.

Asimov's style suited his subjects and his method. The mystery and the puzzle are story types in which only rationality can prevail, and Asimov's direct, clear prose, as unlyrical and unmetaphorical as possible, persuaded readers that they were being presented all the facts upon which to draw their own conclusions. Asimov, in fact, objected to a paragraph that Campbell inserted near the end of the story:

> Not Earth's feeble thirty-six hundred Stars visible to the eye; Lagash was in the center of a giant cluster. Thirty thousand mighty suns shone down in a soul-searing splendor that was more frighteningly cold in its awful indifference than the bitter wind that shivered across the cold, horribly bleak world.

In his autobiography Asimov complained that this

> simply wasn't me. It has been praised as proof that I could
> write "poetically," which gravels me, since I don't want to
> write poetically; I only want to write clearly. Worst of all,
> Campbell thoughtlessly mentioned Earth in his paragraph. I
> had carefully refrained from doing so all through the story,
> since Earth did not exist within the context of the story. Its
> mention was a serious literary flaw.

Earth, of course, could not exist within the context of the story
because if Lagash were aware of Earth, the psychological fear
of darkness and the Stars would be irreparably weakened. The
entire paragraph is an intrusion, literally, of the "editorial"
voice.

A few other rewards for the science-fiction reader emerge
from the story, such as the application of the meaning derived
from the unique situation of Lagash and its outcome to the
situation of Earth: if Lagashians are psychological victims of
their environment, how does Earth's environment in a similar
way affect us psychologically, religiously? The reader enjoys
knowledge greater than that of the characters. Beenay, for instance, speculates about the incredible possibility of the Stars
being distant suns, maybe as many as two dozen suns in a
universe eight light-years across, and about the question of
how simple the law of gravitation would be in a one-sun system. The former speculation makes us smile at Beenay's na-
ïveté; the latter gives us momentary pause. The law of gravitation was not that simple for humanity—Newton came up
with his law at a moment in Western civilization roughly
comparable to that in Lagash's development. Beenay also
comments that life would be impossible on a planet with only
one sun, since life is fundamentally dependent on light, and
that planet would have none half the time. From this the reader
realizes the difficulty of imagining an existence basically alien. Sheerin also praises the torch as a "really efficient artifi-
cial-light mechanism," providing the reader with more com-
parative speculation. And Beenay urges the astronomers, just
before totality, not to waste time trying to get two Stars at a
time in the scope field—"one is enough."

The final impact of the story comes from the size of its

concept and the image with which the story concludes—civilization burning, even the rational astronomers themselves maddened by the sight of the Stars—in a pair of passages that are not without their own poetry:

> For this was the Dark—the Dark and the Cold and the Doom. The bright walls of the universe were shattered and their awful black fragments were falling down to crush and squeeze and obliterate him [Theremon]. . . .
>
> Aton, somewhere, was crying, whimpering horribly like a terribly frightened child. "Stars—all the Stars—we didn't know at all. We didn't know anything. We thought six stars in a universe is something the Stars didn't notice is Darkness forever and ever and ever and the walls are breaking in and we didn't know we couldn't know and anything—"
>
> Someone clawed at the torch, and it fell and snuffed out. In the instant, the awful splendor of the indifferent Stars leaped nearer to them. . . .

Only the thought of the three hundred possible survivors, tucked away from all the madness in the Hideout and representing a possible break with the terrible consequences of ignorance, remains to sustain the reader.

Asimov's own three favorite short stories that he considers better than "Nightfall" are "The Last Question" (1956), "The Bicentennial Man" (1976), and "The Ugly Little Boy" (1958). (There may be others.) All were written much later than "Nightfall," with greater craft and in more skillful prose. Readers still may have reasons to prefer "Nightfall." "The Last Question," for instance, deals with a subject even larger than "Nightfall"—the death and creation of the universe—but it contains virtually no characters. Readers may marvel at its cleverness but are unlikely to be moved by it. "The Bicentennial Man" and "The Ugly Little Boy" are Asimovian anomalies. They are sentimental stories of character in which people change rather than solve puzzles (although there is some puzzle-solving in "The Bicentennial Man"). Their implications are personal rather than general of the species; they deal with individuals rather than civilizations or humanity itself.

Before "Nightfall," Asimov's stories, with a few exceptions, had been imitative and relatively undistinguished. He says as much (in *The Early Asimov*) when he describes "Half-Breed" (*Astounding*, February 1940), in which he placed an intelligent race on Mars, one that was sufficiently like Earthmen to make interbreeding possible. "I just accepted science fictional clichés. Eventually I stopped doing that." This, of course, is how most writers begin. They are directed toward writing by a love of reading, and they re-create what they love. Eventually, if they have talent, they find their own subjects and their own ways of dealing with them.

Asimov's first published story, "Marooned Off Vesta," interestingly enough, held at its heart the Asimovian subject—the rational mind presented with problems by the universe, by accident, or sometimes by the irrational elements in humanity—and the Asimovian method—the characters are faced with a puzzle or a mystery and work toward a solution. In the story, a spaceship accident maroons a group of survivors three hundred miles from the asteroid Vesta, where help is available. They must find a way to propel the wreckage toward the asteroid. One of them finally rigs a method of releasing water retained in the wreck as a jet of steam; even at the low temperature of space, water boils in a vacuum.

"The Callistan Menace," the first story Asimov wrote, also was a puzzle but not much of one. Originally, it had been titled "Stowaway" because a space-struck boy of about thirteen stows away aboard a ship heading for the mystery world Callisto, a satellite of Jupiter. Crewmen are in danger of being killed by giant Callistan magnet worms when the boy emerges in a non-metallic rubber spacesuit to rescue them.

Asimov's tenth story and his first in *Astounding*, "Trends," was not a puzzle story and seems comparatively weaker for that reason. It was about the first steps toward spaceflight, and its chief claim to significance was its prediction of resistance to space exploration. Campbell may have liked it not only for its social theme but for the fact that the resistance to spaceflight was led by an evangelical religious group and its charismatic leader.

Over the next year Asimov wrote nine more stories and sold about half of them. He was published in *Amazing*, *Astonishing*, *Cosmic*, *Future*, *Super Science*, and *Planet* but not in

Astounding again until he wrote his nineteenth story, "Homo Sol" (September 1940). The story is important in that it is in some ways prefatory to the Foundation stories, as is the earlier-written but later-published "Black Friar of the Flames" (*Planet,* Spring 1942). "Homo Sol" inspired in Asimov a resolution not to deal with aliens and thus to avoid Campbell's biases and his own futile arguments. That resolution may have led to Asimov's all-human Galaxy, which is a striking aspect of the Foundation stories.

July 29, 1940, Asimov notes in *The Early Asimov,* was a turning point in his publishing career. Up to that day he had written twenty-two stories in twenty-five months. Of these he had sold (or was to sell) thirteen; nine never sold and no longer exist. After this day, except for two short-short stories, he never again wrote a science-fiction story that he could not sell.

"Not Final!" (*Astounding,* October 1941) is the first non-robot, non-Foundation story after "Nightfall" that hints at Asimov's future capabilities. Like "Nightfall," the theme of "Not Final!" has magnitude. Human spaceships have achieved interplanetary flight. Inhabitants of Jupiter have been contacted by radio, but once they learn that humans are not Jovians they send a final message that humans are vermin and will be destroyed. With all the resources of mighty Jupiter and a technology equal to that of Earth, the Jovians cannot be stopped. There is one small catch: no kind of matter known can withstand the pressure of Jupiter without smashing, and no Jovian spaceship can leave Jupiter without exploding. In the final episode, however, a human inventor develops a spaceship hull made incredibly strong by a force field that can be maintained because it flicks on and off, stroboscopically, eight hundred thousand times a second. "Victory Unintentional," the sequel to "Not Final!," is summarized in Chapter 3.

At this point in his writing career, Asimov's robot stories were well established and his Foundation stories were beginning to be published. "Nightfall" had given him a cover on *Astounding,* and he was being published in that magazine with some regularity. He had no reason to believe that he could make a living as a writer, but this writing was a great help to his bank account—he was paying his tuition as well as some other expenses although still living at home. In 1942, while he was continuing his graduate work in chemistry at Columbia (having passed on the second try his qualifying examinations to undertake research) he experienced his first dry spell. It was fourteen months before he returned to his typewriter and then only on a limited basis.

He had good reasons for his temporary abandonment of what had seemed like unimaginable success a year or two before: his research toward his Ph.D. consumed time and energy, he met and fell in love with Gertrude Blugerman whom five months later he persuaded to marry him, and he applied for and accepted a job at the Naval Air Experimental Station of the U.S. Navy Yard in Philadelphia, where Robert Heinlein and L. Sprague de Camp already were at work. After "Author! Author!," which was sold to *Astounding*'s companion fantasy magazine, *Unknown,* but not published until 1964 in an anthology of *Unknown* stories because of the magazine's untimely death, and "Death Sentence" (*Astounding*, November 1943), Asimov wrote only one story during the rest of the war years that was not a Foundation story or a robot story.

That story was "Blind Alley" (*Astounding*, March 1945), and, in spite of Asimov's resolve to stay away from areas of dispute with Campbell, it was about aliens. Two aspects of the story, however, must have pleased Campbell: the aliens were non-threatening, a dying race that had specialized in the biological sciences as well as psychology and psychiatry, and once they came into contact with humans (in the period of the thriving Galactic Empire), all the humans' efforts could not keep them from eliminating themselves by voluntarily having no offspring. The other pleasing aspect was the solution to the problem: an opportunity for the aliens to speed off to the Magellanic Clouds and a galaxy of their own was created by a clever bureaucrat who used the turgid bureaucratic channels of communication and methods of operation for his own purposes. That must have appealed to Campbell's conviction that "it's all a matter of knowing how."

Asimov was busy through the rest of 1944, 1945, 1946 with robot and Foundation stories. In addition, he was drafted into the Army in September 1945, and released a year later. This period saw him produce "The Mule," "Evidence," "Little Lost Robot," and "Now You See It . . . ." Then he wrote another non-robot, non-Foundation story, "No Connection." It too was about aliens, in this case intelligent bears who have succeeded to the mastery of North America after humanity wiped itself out in atomic wars. But in Europe anthropoids have evolved into a new kind of humanoid civilization and pose a threat, including even atomic warfare, to the peaceful, cooperative ursine civilization. An ursine archeologist, investigating radioactive ruins, finds evidence of a previous human civilization, which he calls "Primate Primeval," but he rejects the notion that any connection would exist between the sordid present of neutron bombardments and the glorious, mysterious past.

Both "Blind Alley" and "No Connection" were problem stories and were modestly successful insofar as they represented effective problem-solving. After Asimov's first non-fiction article, a research spoof, "The Endochronic Properties of Resublimated Thiotimoline" (Astounding, March 1948), which was important to his future career, Asimov took a gamble on a novella, "Grow Old with Me," for Startling Stories, partly to prove to himself that he was not a one-editor author. Its rejection by Startling and Astounding was a blow to his writing ambitions. He stopped writing for a year while he completed work on his Ph.D. and accepted a job to do post-doctoral research on anti-malarial drugs.

Asimov then produced a time-travel paradox story titled "The Red Queen's Race" (Astounding, January 1949), in which a crazed researcher attempts to send back to Hellenistic times a chemical textbook translated into Greek so that the Greeks can build a stronger civilization that will withstand barbarian attacks. After a long effort to undo the action, the assistant professor of philosophy who translated the textbook tells investigators not to worry. The textbook was sent back to this world.

All the non-series stories mentioned so far, with the exceptions of "Nightfall" and "Marooned Off Vesta," were reprinted by Asimov in his collection The Early Asimov. The last story in that collection is "Mother Earth" (Astounding,

May 1949). It is important largely for its premonitions of the robot novels. The Terrestrian Empire is in the process of falling; its fall has been predictable from the introduction of positronic robots into the Sirian sector colony Aurora and from the establishment of an immigration quota against Earth by the Outer Worlds. A possible war by the Outer Worlds against Earth will be the final blow for the Empire. But a former terrestrian ambassador sets up Earth to lose a quick war in order to prepare for a second Terrestrian Empire in which the citizens of the Outer Worlds will have deteriorated because of the alien chemistry of their planets and revolted against Outer Planet genetic policies or will have produced different varieties of humanity on all fifty Outer Worlds. Variety will be the norm, and they will no longer be united against Earth.

By the time "Mother Earth" was published, Asimov's career had taken several new directions. He finished the last of the Foundation stories, ". . . And Now You Don't," Doubleday had asked him to expand the unsuccessful novella "Grow Old with Me" to 70,000 words in order to publish it as a book, and he had accepted a teaching job at the Boston University School of Medicine for $5,000 a year. He still had no way of knowing he could make a living as a freelance writer. As he reported in The Early Asimov, his total earnings for eleven years of writing had not reached $8,000.

By 1952, as his books began to be published with remarkable regularity—two a year beginning in 1950—Asimov's income from writing began to exceed his salary. By 1957 he discovered that he was primarily a writer and was making considerably more money by writing than as a professor, When a new dean began to pressure him to devote more time to research and would not be convinced that Asimov's writing was his research, Asimov resigned everything except his title—by that time he had been promoted to associate professor—and turned to full-time writing for the first time. Unfortunately for science fiction, he decided to devote his time to non-fiction.

In the years between 1949 and 1958, however, Asimov had produced his best science-fiction novels and some of his best stories. He was particularly inspired by the creation in 1950 of *Galaxy Science Fiction*, edited by Horace L. Gold. *The Magazine of Fantasy and Science Fiction*, founded a year earlier under the editorship of Anthony Boucher and J. Francis McComas, was more of an inspiration to others than to Asimov. *F&SF* specialized in fantasy and literary stories; Asimov, in technology and problem-solving. To *F&SF* Asimov sold humorous science-fiction verse based on literary models, mostly Gilbert and Sullivan, as well as, beginning in 1958, monthly science articles, which he subsequently was to collect in many of his books. *Galaxy*, through Gold's requests, ideas, and goading and through the three cents a word, escalating with the fourth story to three and a half cents on up that the magazine offered, helped Asimov to produce some of his best fiction.

As Asimov mentions in his autobiography, he had grown beyond Campbell:

> In part it was because he [Campbell] had taken a wrong turning. He had moved into dianetics and from there into a series of other follies, and there was no way in which I could follow him. Furthermore, he could not separate his personal views from the magazine, but strove to incorporate those views into the stories he elicited from the authors, and many authors were only too delighted to comply and to "press Campbell's buttons." I could not do it any more than I could comply with his penchant for human superiority over extraterrestrials in earlier years.
>
> Second, there were new markets opening up, and I wanted to branch out. . . .

Six of the first eight issues of *Galaxy* included works by Asimov: two short stories, a novelette, and a three-part serial. The first story, in the first issue of *Galaxy* (October 1950), was "Darwinian Pool Room." It consisted of a conversation containing speculation about the possibility of the evolutionary process coming up with something to supersede man and ending with the joking suggestion that man's successor might be the thinking machine, which was being developed at the same time as the means for eliminating humanity, the hydrogen bomb.

Asimov felt better about the publication of his second *Galaxy* story (second issue, November 1950), since Gold had been under no first-issue pressure to accept it. Asimov titled it "Potent Stuff," Gold changed the title to "Misbegotten Missionary." Asimov changed it to "Green Patches" when he reprinted it in his own collection, *Nightfall and Other Stories*. It involved an apparently pleasant planet on which a telepathic life form that could take any shape and could take over any living creature had united all living things into one biological entity. It revealed itself on any entity it took over only through two tiny patches of green fur. An expedition to the planet had destroyed itself and its ship when it had realized it was being assimilated. A new expedition realizes just as it is about to dock back on Earth that it may be carrying "green patches." The Captain must decide whether to destroy his ship. But he can find no evidence of live "green patches." Ironically, the live creature had been camouflaged as a piece of wiring. That wiring carried current only when the airlock door was opened, and the creature was electrocuted when the ship docked.

It was ironic, also, that Asimov realized halfway through the story that he was creating "an infinitely inferior 'Who Goes There?' " He called Campbell and told him about it. Campbell told him not to worry, that no two stories are exactly the same when by a competent writer. Asimov continued the story, trying to make it as different as possible from Campbell's "Who Goes There?," but with a broken spirit. To add a final irony, Asimov sent the story to Gold, who had requested it. As Asimov later reported in the collection, the story's acceptance ended "a more-than-seven-year agony of self-doubt."

Further proof of Asimov's new independence came with *Galaxy*'s serialization of Asimov's new novel, commissioned by Doubleday after the success of *Pebble in the Sky*, the novel that had begun life as "Grow Old with Me." The new novel was *The Stars, Like Dust*, which Gold, as was his frequent and not always appreciated practice, retitled *Tyrann* (January, February, March 1951).

"Hostess," Asimov's next story in *Galaxy* (May 1951) also involved editing problems. Asimov had attended a meeting of the Eastern Science Fiction Association in Newark, New Jersey, and discovered that Ted Sturgeon's upcoming story in

Galaxy (perhaps "Rule of Three") shared not only a gimmick
with the story that Asimov already had sent to Gold but similar names for the main characters. Eventually, Asimov rewrote
the story in Gold's living room, and Gold later changed the
name of the woman character. Asimov restored the story to its
original form (except for the woman's name) in *Nightfall and
Other Stories.*

"Hostess" is a novelette of more than usual interest. It was
also the first story Asimov experimented with by dictating it
to a machine for his wife to type. The novelette retains the
Asimovian stamp of problem-solving. It develops as a series
of puzzles: 1) Rose Smollett, a fellow in biology at a presti-
gious research institute, is at age thirty-five a bride of less than
a year and wonders sometimes why her husband, Drake, a
member of the World Security Board, married her; 2) Drake
opposes welcoming into their home a cyanide-breathing alien,
Harg Tholan, whose herbivorous race developed from cowlike
creatures and who is on Earth ostensibly for biological research; and 3) Tholan raises the delicate question of the Inhibition Death that has begun to affect the four other intelligent
races in the Galaxy, stopping their growth and bringing about
their deaths within a year. Only Earthmen, it seems, stop growing when they reach maturity, and only they are carnivores.

The story contains some fascinating details about the evolutionary development of a herbivore and speculation about
how this might affect psychological and social adaptations.
The underlying tension between cyanide-breathers and
oxygen-breathers, between herbivores and carnivores, erupts
in a grisly scene in which Tholan is deprived of his cyanide
by Drake and forced to talk. Tholan reveals a theory that he
has not yet shared with anyone else: only Earthmen are im-
mune to the Inhibition Death. He thinks the Inhibition Death
is caused by a parasitic kind of life native to Earth that kills
when it is spread to aliens who are not adapted to it. He thinks
the parasite is spread by young men who disappear into space,
but that it must return to Earth to reproduce by using some
intermediate host. Drake restores Tholan's cyanide and then
kills him.

When Rose questions him, Drake reveals that Tholan was

right, but he insists that the parasite has become symbiotic and is indispensable to humanity's existence, that the absence of the parasite is called cancer. To get rid of the parasite, extraterrestrials would have to eliminate all human life. Drake leaves with Tholan's body, and Rose realizes that he has lied to her, perhaps to avoid killing her. Cancer could not be the absence of the parasite, since it is present in many other kinds of living things. And she realizes too that young men who disappear into space usually do so in the first year of marriage, that the parasite must require close and continuous association with another parasite in order to reproduce, that Drake will not be returning, and that she has been a hostess. She also knows now why Drake married her.

The story differs from earlier Asimov stories, and from most later ones, for several reasons. One is its complexity; it is difficult to summarize. Second, its primary motivation is not so much the solution of a physical puzzle but the answer to the question of why Drake is behaving so strangely. Its development is one in which a character changes: Rose moves from puzzled happiness to misery. Knowledge, which usually brings satisfaction if not always success in the Asimov story, is no consolation for Rose. And third, the conclusion is ambiguous. Asimov seldom leaves the reader in doubt about the outcome of the situation, but in this story many threads are left dangling. If Drake lied to Rose, what is the truth about the parasite and the Inhibition Death? Will other aliens deduce the truth and descend upon Earth to wipe out the Terran hosts? Will Rose be able to convince her colleagues at the Institute about the parasite, will they launch a research program, and can the parasite be isolated and destroyed? Is the parasite capable of directing human activities, and did it direct Drake's? And so forth. What the story loses in clarity, however, it gains in human resonances. Asimov does not write this kind of story often.

Astounding published the next Asimov story, "Breeds There a Man . . . ?" (June 1951), which is somewhat related to "Hostess" in its lack of a definitive ending. A scientific genius working on a force field that could prevent the civilization-destroying effects of an atomic war fears that he will kill himself. He blames this urge to commit suicide on extraterrestrials who are using Earthmen for an experiment and do not want humanity to advance too far. Eventually, at the cost of his health and then his life, the scientist perfects the force shield, leaving unanswered the question of whether his ideas about extraterrestrial manipulation were correct.

Asimov's next story in *Galaxy*, "C-Chute" (October 1951), was a response to the Korean War, as was the previous story. Both dealt with alien threats to humanity. "C-Chute" also was a bit different from the usual Asimov story, focusing more on character, in this case a group of non-combatant strays in a spaceship captured by aliens. The Earthmen quarrel about how to behave toward their captors and about the proper action to take in their circumstances. Finally, the least likely of the group, a precise, mild-mannered bookkeeper for a paper-box company, puts on a spacesuit and makes his way through the C-chute (used to dispose of battle casualties). He goes back through the steam cylinders that control the ship's attitude and into the chlorine-filled alien atmosphere in order to kill the two aliens and reclaim the ship.

"In a Good Cause—," which Asimov wrote for the first anthology of original science fiction, Raymond J. Healy's *New Tales of Space and Time* (1951), is cited by Asimov as an example of how an author can sometimes write stories that advocate positions the author does not share. Two friends, Richard Altmayer and Geoffrey Stock, take different routes to meet a challenge of competition from herbivorous, communal aliens. Because the aliens have horns and exhale hydrogen sulfide, Earthmen have named them Diaboli. (Asimov's use of the Diaboli illustrates the dangers of influence-tracing. A scholar noting the similarity of the Diaboli to Arthur C. Clarke's Overlords in *Childhood's End* might conclude that Clarke was inspired by Asimov. The Overlords, however, were presented first in a story entitled "Guardian Angel" published in 1950. Both stories, as a matter of fact, may owe a debt to John W. Campbell's 1934 *Astounding* serial, *The Mightiest Machine*.) Altmayer becomes a draft resister, later a radical leader. Stock becomes a soldier and then a leading politician. In a series of scattered incidents, Stock uses Altmayer to achieve just the opposite of what Altmayer himself intended to achieve. But each incident prepares the way for the time when at last Earth attacks the Diaboli and defeats them by preventing the other human-settled planets from taking their side. Humanity can expand into the galaxy. In a final irony, Altmayer is released from prison to represent Earth in a United Worlds organization. Altmayer will have a statue raised to him; Stock will be forgotten.

It seems likely that Asimov did not so much object to the irony in the evaluation of history as to the Machiavellian way in which Stock used Altmayer to achieve his ends and the way in which he slaughters the Diaboli in the name of human expansion. Asimov's fiction usually follows his convictions, but sometimes, as he points out in his autobiography, a story would take the bit in its mouth.

"The Martian Way" (*Galaxy*, November 1952) is quintessential Asimov. It survived a request for extensive revision by Gold (Asimov held Gold's changes to the insertion of a woman character) to become one of the twenty-two novellas included in *The Science Fiction Hall of Fame Volume II*. The inspiration for the story came out of the Joseph McCarthy era. "It dealt," Asimov wrote in his autobiography, "with Martian colonists with a problem, who were victimized out of a solution by a McCarthy-style politician and who were in this way forced to find a still better solution." When it appeared, Asimov "thought that the story would elicit a mass of mail denouncing my own portrayal of McCarthyism, or supporting it, but I got nothing either one way or the other. It may be that my satire of McCarthy was so subtle that everyone missed it."

The satire was not that subtle. The "McCarthy-style politician," named John Hilder, is making political capital on Earth out of opposition to space travel, which is costing a great deal of money, he says, for a small return. In particular, he rouses the rabble against letting Martian colonists take Earth's water, which is used mostly for reaction mass. (The situation of Asimov's first *Astounding* story, "Trends," has progressed both in stage of development and sophistication: spaceflight has moved into the colonization stage and opposition to spaceflight has moved from fundamental religious groups to politicians.) The amount of water used by the colonists is re-latively small, but Hilder's campaign succeeds in getting even that closed off. One Martian colonist, Rioz, suggests that the Martians simply take the water, stealthily or by force, from Earth's oceans. But another, Long, says that this is Earth way, the Grounder way, "trying to hold on to the umbilical cord that binds Mars to Earth." The Martian way is to look farther out, where ninety-nine percent of the rest of the matter in the solar system is to be found, including vast amounts of water. Eventually, despite great difficulties, a group of rocket pilots from Mars, whose normal job is reclaiming the metal "shells" or stages left in orbit by ships that have used up their reaction masses, fits a gigantic iceberg from the rings of Saturn with rocket jets and brings it back to Mars.

As the mountain of ice is lowered to the surface of Mars, the committee from Earth led by John Hilder is faced with the humiliation of the Martian colonists offering to sell water to Earth. Hilder sees his own political future turning to water along with the campaign rhetoric of his political party, the anti-Wasters. The Martian way is to accept spaceflight as nat-ural, even to consider planets as a kind of spaceship. (Asimov previsions in this story not only "spaceship Earth" but also a later proposal to tow icebergs from the Antarctic to provide supplies of fresh water.) Eventually, "it will be Martians, not planet-bound Earthmen, who will colonize the Galaxy." That too is the Martian way.

"Sucker Bait" (*Astounding*, February, March 1954) is a novella about the failure of a colony on a pleasant, Earth-type planet called Junior. A ship is sent to discover what went wrong. One member of the expedition is temperamental Mark Annuncio of the Mnemonic Service, a young man whose abil-ity to remember everything he has ever read makes him an invaluable resource in a galaxy with nearly 100,000 inhabited planets, where all sorts of information can be lost. He also has hunches based on the correlation of information he has mem-orized. One correlation leads him to a violent course of action that forces the crew off the planet in a hurry. Annuncio and the man nominally responsible for him, Oswald Mayer Shef-field, are placed on shipboard trial for mutiny and are almost railroaded into a death sentence. Finally, Sheffield persuades the crew to hear Annuncio's testimony. Annuncio reveals that the danger on Junior is in the dust: it contains beryllium that kills by deranging enzymatic reactions. The crew might all be doomed.

"Dreaming Is a Private Thing" (*Fantasy and Science Fiction*, December 1955) describes a new art form, the creation of dreamies by means of a dream recorder that picks up thoughts, which then can be distributed to consumers. The story proceeds as a day in the life of the manager of Dream, Inc. The manager tests a ten-year-old boy as a potential dreamer and tries to persuade the boy's parents to allow him to be trained. He talks to an agent of the Department of Arts and Sciences (a prevision of the National Endowment for the Arts?) about pornographic dreamies, discusses competition with another company, Luster-Think, that has opened up dream palaces for public dreaming, and deals with a dreamer who wants to quit. It is a quiet, well-modulated story that suggests many of the possibilities implicit in a world where dreams become a commodity. It is presented as a series of small human problems rather than a mystery or puzzle.

"The Dead Past" (*Astounding*, April 1956) deals with a new science, chronoscopy—time-viewing by means of an invention called the chronoscope. T. L. Sherred's "E for Effort" (*Astounding*, May 1947) had been the definitive statement on the discovery of a method for viewing the past. In that story a couple of poor inventors first use their cameralike device to film documentaries, then historical spectaculars, and finally attempt to bring peace to the world. They are stopped by a sudden government attack when it becomes apparent that nothing can be kept secret now that not only any time but any place can be viewed; without secrets all government is endangered.

Asimov returned to that concept in "The Dead Past," in the best tradition of the science-fiction dialogue, suggesting that chronoscopy would be so expensive that only the government could afford it; use of the machines would be rationed. A history professor, who is refused the opportunity to view Carthage, urges a young colleague to invent his own chronoscope. The young man does, but there are problems. (The well-written science-fiction story never presents an invention without accompanying problems, a dramatic principle that H. G. Wells popularized in *The Invisible Man*.) In the first place, viewing becomes impossibly fuzzy after a century and a quarter back because of loss of detail. In the second place, people like the history professor's wife, whose baby was killed in a fire that the professor accidentally may have started, would spend their time reliving the past. In the third and final place, if chronoscopes became cheap enough for everyone to own one, people would be able to spy on their neighbors and anyone else they might choose to watch. Privacy would become a thing of the past. The story ends with a government spokesman, who has been considered a villain, unable to suppress the broad release of the invention.

The depiction of a government acting responsibly to suppress an invention with major social implications must have appealed to Campbell. The government agent says, ". . . you all just took it for granted that the government was stupidly bureaucratic, vicious, tyrannical, given to suppressing research for the hell of it. It never occurred to any of you that we were trying to protect mankind as best we could." The story no doubt appealed to Asimov too, as an example of how social considerations should influence scientific decisions.

"Profession" (*Astounding*, July 1957) considers a future Earth where skills are imprinted electronically on the brain. A society has grown up to prepare young people for this event, which will be important to Earth, the mother planet of a group of more prosperous and more powerful colonies. Earth specializes in the production of education tapes, which it sells to the other planets, and also exports tape-imprinted skilled workers. The process helps to keep the Galactic culture unified. George Platen, the protagonist of the story, is told that his "mind is not suited to receiving a superimposed knowledge of any sort." He struggles against his fate as he becomes a ward of the planet and is sent to be with others of his kind in a place which he is told finally is "A House for the Feeble-Minded." After escaping and trying to make a place for himself in the world of the educable, however, Platen discovers that he is one of the elite, one of the few who have the capacity for original thought, who invent the new instrument models and make the educational tapes. The system used to deceive him is defended as necessary both to protect the majority from considering themselves failures and to identify the creative minority who refuse to accept what they have been told. "It is much safer," one character explains, "to wait for a man to say, 'I can create, and I will do so whether you wish it or not.' " But the situation remains shaky; it seems more like Campbell's idea than Asimov's.

Finally came one of Asimov's best-known and, by many, best-loved stories, "The Ugly Little Boy" (*Galaxy*, September 1958). The work illustrates the two basic kinds of story development: one presents the protagonist with a problem or a series of problems that he or she must solve, the other introduces a character and places that character under a stress that changes him or her. Asimov seldom wrote the second kind of story. In an interview, he said, "I don't know that I have the kind of literary power that is required for that sort of thing. I can deal with rational action, but I'm not sure that I can deal with the inner recesses of being." Asimov restricts himself almost entirely to the problem-solving story, though his variations often end with the identification of a problem rather than its solution, as in "The Dead Past" or "Profession." To identify the problem, according to the logic of Asimov's fiction and perhaps his personal beliefs, is to perceive its solution, or to perceive that it is incapable of solution and must be lived with, as in "Nightfall." But even in "Nightfall," it is better to know, for with knowledge comes some kind of reward, even triumph.

"The Ugly Little Boy" is different. It is the story of a character whose problem cannot be solved. With the resolution of the situation comes not triumph or acceptance but a personal statement, ineffectual and even tragic though it may be. Edith Fellowes, a nurse hired to tend a Neanderthal boy brought from the past to the high-energy laboratory of Stasis, Inc., to be studied, begins her job with skepticism and cold efficiency. Gradually, she becomes attached to the Neanderthal boy whom she calls Timmie. When he must be returned, she cannot pre-

vail upon her coldly scientific supervisors to let him stay—it
is impossible and she recognizes it—so she returns with the
now seven-year-old boy to his own time. It is a solution that
solves nothing. Miss Fellowes will have not much more chance
of surviving in the Pleistocene than Timmie himself, perhaps
not as much. Her return with him will comfort her a bit for a
short time. Reason tells the reader that it will be, in Thomas
Hobbes's words, "poor, nasty, brutish, and short" but not, for
the moment at least, "solitary." As a consequence, the resolution seems sentimental and un-Asimovian. The reason many
readers like the story—"People say that they've read [it] and it
made them cry at the end, and I answer that I am pleased
because it made me cry when I wrote it," Asimov has said—
is the reason it is not effective as science fiction. The action
Miss Fellowes takes is irrational, and it can be accepted only
if we assume that it is better for her to die comforting Timmie
in the Pleistocene than to survive to lead a lonely and unre-
warding life.

During this writing period, Asimov was beginning to lead
a gregarious and successful existence. No longer was he the
eager and respectful apprentice science-fiction writer sitting
at John Campbell's feet or even the published author still eager to please editors and readers. He was a successful novelist
and author of science articles and non-fiction books who was
beginning to be sought after by magazines and publishers. His
career no longer depended upon the reception of any one story,
and the spirit of playfulness that had sometimes manifested
itself in his fiction was released more often. Many stories often
were produced casually between other assignments or projects: "What If—" (Fantastic, Summer 1952), "Flies" (Fantasy
and Science Fiction, June 1953), "Nobody Here But—" (Star
Science Fiction, 1953), "It's Such a Beautiful Day" (Star Science Fiction No. 3, 1954), "Strikebreaker" ("Male Strikebreaker," The Original Science Fiction Stories, January 1957),
"I'm in Marsport Without Hilda" (Venture Science Fiction,
November 1957), "The Up-to-Date Sorceror" (Fantasy and Science Fiction, July 1958), "Unto the Fourth Generation" (Fantasy and Science Fiction, April 1959), "What Is This Thing
Called Love?" ("Playboy and the Slime God," Amazing Sto-

ries, March 1961), "My Son, the Physicist" (*Scientific American*, February 1962), and *"Eyes Do More Than See"* (*Fantasy and Science Fiction*, April 1965), as well as others.

There is room to speculate on why no Asimov story of substance, with the possible exception of "Dreaming Is a Private Thing," appeared in *Fantasy and Science Fiction*. Possibly Campbell and later Gold challenged Asimov at a level closer to his basic interests or pushed him to greater effort. Possibly the emphasis of *Fantasy and Science Fiction* on more stylish and literary stories resulted in Asimov trivializing his ideas. Perhaps *Fantasy and Science Fiction* simply was uninterested in Campbellian science fiction, where Asimov's sources of creative energy still resided.

The stories listed above and the Asimov mysteries—both the science-fiction and the more traditional ones—that were collected in *Asimov's Mysteries* (1968), *Tales of the Black Widowers* (1974), *More Tales of the Black Widowers* (1976), and *The Key Word and Other Mysteries* (1977) were entertaining, though some were no more than one-liners. They represent the casual and uncommitted Asimov. During the early part of the 1950s, Asimov's energies were going into his novels (particularly the robot novels), into the occasional robot story, into the first of his science texts and popularizations, and then, after 1958, when he gave up his full-time teaching at Boston University School of Medicine, almost totally into non-fiction of all kinds. In his science fiction after 1958 the younger Asimov occasionally appeared with several of the robot stories, including "The Bicentennial Man" and such stories as "Founding Father."

"Founding Father" (*Galaxy*, August 1965) was written at the request of Frederik Pohl. Pohl, now editor of *Galaxy*, sent Asimov a cover painting showing, as Asimov recalled in *Buy Jupiter and Other Stories*, "a large, sad space-helmeted face, with several crude crosses in the background and with a space helmet balanced on each cross." Stories commissioned to fit a cover were common in science fiction, since many magazines bought the cover art first. Most such stories were eminently forgettable, but a surprising number of memorable ones did emerge.

One of them was "Founding Father," which relates the story of five men, members of the Galactic Corps, who are stranded by a series of accidents on a planet they had come to explore. They are forced to live in the wreckage of their spaceship while they try to reverse the ammonia-chlorophyll-protein cycle on the planet by inducing Earth plants to grow. Nothing seems to work, however, as one by one the crew members die from ammonia poisoning or from some microorganism. Petersen, the final survivor, buries the others in the garden. As he too goes out to die amid the helmeted crosses, he sees that the Earth plants, nourished by the bodies of his comrades, are looking healthy. He dies knowing that this alien planet one day will be capable of supporting human life because of their sacrifice.

Perhaps the most meaningful aspect of this story is the way in which it illustrates the species orientation of science fiction. The final physical defeat of the exploratory crew is usually occasion in more traditional fiction for an awareness of tragedy or a realization of the futility of human efforts to prevail against the unforgiving environment, or even an example of the universe or God punishing the hubris of a species that dares to pit its understanding and its tools against the vast unknown. The ultimate success of the crew would be a kind of ironic comment about the workings of fate. In Asimov's story the ending becomes a victory for the human species, a triumph of the human spirit over the stubborn but not unmovable resistance of the outer world, a joyous celebration of the humanization of one more corner of a universe that was not created for humanity but might, if humans are intelligent enough or brave enough, be understood and made sweet.

The 1965 publication date of "Founding Father" also is significant for the future of Asimov's science-fiction writing. New Worlds, a British publication, had failed the year before. Michael Moorcock had been named editor of the new New Worlds the same year and had begun its conversion into the flagship of revolution in science-fiction writing that would soon be called "the New Wave." New Wave writers opposed much of what had gone before, both in letter and in spirit, particularly the letter and spirit of Campbellian science fiction. The spirit of the New Wave was iconoclastic, nihilistic, and pessimistic: no victories for the human spirit, no celebration of the capacity of the human mind to comprehend the alien universe, no triumphs over incredible difficulties. The works were impressionistic, experimental, subjective renderings of individuals trapped in incomprehensible worlds, against which struggle and even attempts to understand are useless and man's best choice is simply to accept his fate.

The view of humanity's role in the universe that Campbell espoused and Asimov found congenial, replicated as it was in his own rise in the world, continued to be expressed by others in a variety of stories published throughout the 1960s and 1970s. But the dominant impression, perhaps because it came with revolutionary fervor, was that the New Wave had captured the mood of the times, if not the magazines. Stories and novels that Asimov must not have liked and must have felt were not part of the science fiction he had helped to shape were winning acclaim and awards. He also must have felt that science fiction no longer needed him. His science-fiction writing, now only a change of pace from his profitable and satisfying non-fiction production that accounted for the majority of his two hundred plus books, became even more desultory and casual.

Asimov's return to serious writing in 1971 with *The Gods Themselves* (when much of the debate about the New Wave had dissipated) was an act of courage, perhaps even bravado. After being out of the mainstream of science fiction for more than a dozen years, Asimov might well have wondered if this new novel would be greeted with scorn or laughter. The fact that the book won both Nebula and Hugo awards was confirmation that Asimov belonged in the post-Campbell world of contemporary science fiction after all. More Asimov stories appeared. Some of them, like "Take a Match" (*New Dimensions II*, 1972) and "That Thou Art Mindful of Him" (*Final Stage*, 1974) read like the old Asimov. Some, like "The Bicentennial Man" (*Stellar Two*, 1976), which also won Nebula and Hugo awards, demonstrated insights and skills that the old Asimov had not displayed.

5

THE ROBOT NOVELS

In the period after the publication of Asimov's first novel in 1950 and his leaving his teaching position at Boston University in 1958 for the full-time writing of non-fiction, his science-fiction writing reached a high point of skill and significance that culminated in *The Caves of Steel* and *The Naked Sun*. These two novels form another series that deserves separate consideration from that of the unconnected novels in Chapter 6.

The Caves of Steel was serialized in *Galaxy* in 1953, published in hardcover by Doubleday in 1954, and published in paperback by New American Library in 1955; *The Naked Sun* was serialized in *Astounding* in 1956, published in hardcover by Doubleday in 1957, and published in paperback by Bantam Books in 1958. They were brought together in the hardcover edition with *The Rest of the Robots* published by Doubleday in 1964. In 1972 they were published by Doubleday in one volume under the title by which they are better known, *The Robot Novels*. Asimov, however, calls them "science fiction mysteries." Whatever they are called, they represent Asimov at the peak of his science-fiction powers.

Asimov agreed with that judgment, in almost those exact terms, when he discussed *The Caves of Steel* in Chapter 55 of Part I of his autobiography, *In Memory Yet Green*. Chapter 55 itself is titled "Science Fiction at Its Peak," and Asimov writes:

I was very proud of the stories I was writing now [1953]. It seemed to me that they were much more deftly written than my stories of the 1940s. I think so to this day.

It seems to me that most people associate me with the 1940s and think of the positronic robot stories, the Foundation series, and, of course, "Nightfall," as the stories of my peak period. I think they're all wrong. I think my peak period came later—in 1953 and the years immediately following.

By now, after all, the pulpishness in my writing had completely disappeared. That had been taking place all along, through the 1940s, but between what Walter Bradbury taught me and what I had learned at Breadloaf, the change accelerated under my own deliberate prodding.

My writing became ever more direct and spare, and I think it was The Caves of Steel that lifted me a notch higher in my own estimation. I used it as a model for myself thereafter, and it was to be decades before I surpassed that book in my own eyes.

What had brought Asimov's capabilities to fruition? Partly, one can guess, experience. Asimov had been writing science fiction for fifteen years and getting it published for fourteen when he began work on The Caves of Steel. Some writers, such as Edgar Rice Burroughs and A. E. van Vogt, begin writing at the top of their form and never do it much differently; others, like Robert A. Heinlein and Theodore Sturgeon, continue to improve until they attain full command of their writing skills and creative drives. For writers like the latter, the process seems to take about ten years, depending perhaps upon the age at which the writer begins to publish and the amount of writing done. Heinlein, for instance, started writing in 1939 at the age of thirty-two and came into his mature period in 1949. The first adult novel in which he demonstrated his integrated abilities, The Puppet Masters, was published in 1952 (the year before The Caves of Steel). Asimov, who was only eighteen when he went to see John Campbell for the first time and nineteen when his first story was published, was thirty-three when he began writing The Caves of Steel.

Asimov also was gaining confidence as he matured. He had become a successful author in many ways. Instead of creeping "pallid and frightened" into Campbell's office, he now was able to breeze into the office of any science-fiction editor in

New York and "expect to be treated as a celebrity." His science fiction was beginning to appear in books with regularity, and he had some assurance that every novel he wrote would be published as a book. *I, Robot* and *Pebble in the Sky* had been published in 1950; *Foundation* and *The Stars, Like Dust,* in 1951; *Foundation and Empire* and *The Currents of Space,* in 1952—two books a year, alternating between Doubleday and Gnome Press. And his Lucky Starr juvenile novels, written under the pseudonym Paul French, were beginning to appear from Doubleday, *David Starr: Space Ranger* in 1952. *Second Foundation* and *Lucky Starr and the Pirates of the Asteroids* were in the works for 1953. His first scientific book, *Biochemistry and Human Metabolism,* which was neither particularly satisfying (because it was a collaboration) nor particularly successful (but which showed the way to the future), had been published by Williams & Wilkins in 1952. Asimov also had completed a non-fiction book on his own, first called *The Puzzle of Life* and then *The Chemistry of Life.* Two publishers had rejected it, but he knew now that he could write non-fiction, and another publisher had approached him to do a book about science for teenagers.

Asimov had gained confidence in worldly ways as well. He had been promoted to assistant professor at the Boston University School of Medicine at the end of 1951, and he was beginning to think of himself as a writer rather than the research chemist he had considered himself for the last dozen years. He had earned $1,695 from his writing in 1949, more than $4,700 in 1950, $3,625 in 1951, and "an astonishing" $8,550 in 1952, the last amount being half again as large as his university salary, now $5,500. He had $16,000 in the bank; he owned his own car; and he and his wife were thinking about buying a house. They now had a son, two years old.

He had matured in other ways. His social insecurity, particularly with women, had eased with success, and he had adopted a Rabelaisian approach to all women of all ages. He had even enjoyed his first extra-marital encounter and had acquitted himself well.

What novel was the focus of all these maturing influences?

The Caves of Steel is placed in a time about three thou-

sand years in the future. Earth is a homogenous society of eight
billion people who live in Cities of twenty million or more in
population. The open country outside the Cities is given over
to agriculture and mining, done entirely by robots. Earthmen,
as Asimov calls them, have worked out efficient systems of
living and supplying the necessities of life and accommodat-
ing themselves to the pressures of everyday existence. On fifty
other inhabited planets, however, live the Spacers, once settlers from Earth but now quite different: they can live for up
to 350 years, are free from infectious diseases, control their
births not only in quantity but in quality, and though few in
number are militarily powerful because they have many machines and robots and depend upon interstellar travel. Upon
previous occasions they have sent down their "gleaming
cruisers from outer space" into Washington, New York, and
Moscow to collect what they claimed was theirs. They have
constructed a "Spacetown" adjacent to New York. In Spacetown, a Spacer has been murdered. The plot revolves around
the investigation of that murder by Elijah ("Lije") Baley, a C-
5 rating detective on the New York City police force, who is
forced by the Spacers to accept as a partner a humanoid robot,
R. Daneel Olivaw.

The novel was based on an idea suggested by Horace Gold.
Gold had serialized *The Stars, Like Dust* (*Tyrann*) beginning
in the fourth issue of *Galaxy*. Campbell, however, had published *The Currents of Space*, Asimov's subsequent novel, in
part at least because Asimov felt guilty about the fact that six
of the first eight issues of *Galaxy* had contained Asimov fiction. Gold wanted Asimov's next novel. He suggested a robot
novel. At first, Asimov didn't want to do it; he didn't know if
he could carry a whole novel based on the robot idea. Gold
suggested an overpopulated world in which robots are taking
over human jobs. Asimov thought that was too depressing and
was not sure he wanted to handle a heavy sociological story.
Finally, in view of Asimov's liking for mysteries, Gold suggested that "he put a murder in such a world and have a
detective solve it with a robot partner. If the detective doesn't
solve it, the robot will replace him."

In his autobiography Asimov recalled that "when I wrote

it [*The Caves of Steel*], I did my best to ignore this business of robots replacing human beings." Fear of such replacement had been ridiculed in *I, Robot,* where the difficulties of introducing robots on Earth was caused by fundamentalist religious groups and labor unions, and prejudices against robots were voiced by silly, ignorant, or malicious people. Asimov's resistance to the concept was understandable. If the novel was to work, however, much of the philosophic, even historical, development of the robot in *I, Robot* had to yield to new imperatives. Every person, even sensible persons such as Baley, had to be anti-robot, and yet robots had to be common enough on Earth for Earthpeople to fear their takeover of human jobs. After "Robbie" in *I, Robot,* Asimov had never allowed robots openly on Earth. This may explain, in part, why *The Caves of Steel* is set so far in the future. Asimov further rationalized the use of robots on Earth by placing responsibility for their increasing presence on Spacer pressure. As for robots replacing human workers, "that was typically Gold and not at all Asimov," Asimov said, "—but Horace kept pushing, and in the end, some of it was forced in, but not nearly as much as Horace wanted."

Gold was at least as good with ideas as Campbell. He gave Frederik Pohl the idea for "The Midas Plague" and Alfred Bester the idea for *The Demolished Man,* which became a turning point in Bester's science-fiction career. Now he gave Asimov the idea for what may, with some justice, be called Asimov's best science-fiction novel. What pleased Asimov most about it, however, "was that it was a pure murder mystery set against a science fiction background. As far as I was concerned it was a perfect fusion of the two genre, and the first such perfect fusion. A number of people agreed with me in this."

The Demolished Man, which is a murder mystery and, in a sense, a detective story, had appeared in *Galaxy* eighteen months before *The Caves of Steel,* but it was not a formal mystery. Other murder mysteries had been published in which science fiction played a part: Anthony Boucher's *Rocket to the Morgue* (1942), for instance, or Mack Reynolds's *The Case of the Little Green Men* (1951). Scientific detectives were common earlier in the century, such as R. Austin Freeman's Dr.

Thorndyke. Sam Moskowitz devoted a section of his *Science Fiction by Gaslight* to "Scientific Crime and Detection," including stories such as L. T. Meade and Robert Eustace's "When the Air Quivered" from *The Strand Magazine* (December 1898), and Warren Earle's "In Re State vs. Forbes" from *The Black Cat* (July 1906). Moskowitz also cited Edwin Balmer and William B. MacHarg's *Luther Trant, Psychological Detective* and Arthur B. Reeve's Craig Kennedy. But none of those stories was like *The Caves of Steel*, in which the murder mystery and the subsequent attempt to unravel the mystery and discover the murderer function as the central structure around which all the other events arrange themselves.

Baley is assigned to the case by an old friend, Julius Enderby, the Commissioner of Police, because the situation with the Spacers is so delicate and Enderby can trust Baley's discretion. Moreover, Baley's loyalty and sense of duty register so high that he can be relied upon to work with a robot.

The case is complicated by the fact that entry to Spacetown is controlled by the Spacers, who put every entering Earthman through a decontamination process that Earthmen consider demeaning. No weapon can be sneaked into Spacetown. Daneel, however, has a possible solution: the Spacer was killed by a group of conservatives called the Medievalists, who want Earthmen to return to a simpler way of life and who resist the introduction of robots. Daneel points out that one of them, with a weapon, could have left New York from one of the hundreds of ancient exits and reached Spacetown by crossing open country. Baley says that is impossible for an Earthman; conditioned by life within the City, he could not cross open country for any reason. A robot, on the other hand, could cross open country but could not kill because of the First Law.

As in every well-made murder mystery, Baley considers a number of suspects and possible explanations. Because Daneel has been constructed to resemble his maker, the murdered Spacer Roj Nemennuh Sarton, Baley at first accuses Daneel of being Sarton, but Daneel proves he is a robot by opening his arm to reveal his mechanical workings. Later, still desperate to put the blame on the Spacers, Baley accuses Daneel of committing the murder and hiding the blaster in his food sac, but Earth's leading robot expert, Dr. Gerrigel, by questioning Daneel, finds that his First Law is intact.

Sammy, the office robot who replaced one young office worker, is found by Dr. Gerrigel with his brain destroyed. Baley is likely to be accused of Sammy's destruction because Baley complained about him and had access to the "alpha-sprayer" that did the destruction. Baley has only an hour or so before the Spacers terminate the case. He confronts Enderby with evidence that the Commissioner himself is guilty both of Sarton's death and of Sammy's destruction. Enderby had planned to destroy Daneel and had Sammy carry the blaster across open country to Spacetown. Enderby shot Sarton thinking he was Daneel and returned the weapon to Sammy before the crime was discovered.

The murder and its detection, though ingenious, are not the primary interest of the novel. No one ever gets worked up about Sarton's death. The Commissioner is agitated—and later this becomes one clue to his guilt—but the Spacers are calm. The possible consequences are more important than the murder itself, and the consequences are science fictional. First, the Spacers have the power to inflict indemnities on Earth if they are offended; and second, the entire New York police force will be humiliated and Baley may lose his job, his hard-won status, and his privileges.

There are even larger consequences: a group among the Spacers, for instance, is forcing the introduction of robots on Earth in order to upset the Cities' economy and to create a group of displaced men who eventually will want to emigrate to unsettled planets. That group believes that the fifty Spacer worlds are too stable and have lost their desire to colonize new planets. Earthmen may be able to develop a new, more desirable collaboration of humans and machines that the Spacers call C/Fe (pronounced "see fee"), for carbon and iron, which are the basic elements for the two kinds of human and robot existences. But other Spacers oppose the plan and may be able to seize upon Sarton's murder as an excuse to stop the effort.

Even this conflict does not reach the heart of the appeal of

The Caves of Steel for the science-fiction reader. That resides in something more basic that is not even in the human-robot collaboration, reluctant as it is on Baley's part, attractive as it is to the reader in the contrast it presents between Baley's emotionalism and Daneel's unmoved intellectualism. The basic concern is the Cities themselves and the people who live in them.

Dr. Han Fastolfe, spokesman for the Spacers who want to break Earthmen free of the home planet to settle some of the hundred million uninhabited planets in the Galaxy, presents the overriding image of the novel: ". . . Earthmen are all so coddled, so enwombed in their imprisoning caves of steel, that they are caught forever. . . . Civism is ruining Earth."

The Cities . . . civism . . . these concepts are what *The Caves of Steel* is about. Asimov alternates exposition about the City and its culture with narrative about the murder investigation, complicating events, and character development. His writing skills have developed to the point that he is able to allow each of these elements to fall naturally and unobtrusively into place. The first extensive discussion of the development of the Cities, for instance, occurs as Baley is riding the expressway toward Spacetown to meet his robot partner for the first time and thinking about the differences between Spacetown and New York, between Spacers and Earthmen.

> Efficiency had been forced on Earth with increasing population. Two billion people, three billion, even five billion could be supported by the planet by progressive lowering of the standard of living. When the population reaches eight billion, however, semistarvation becomes too much like the real thing. . . .
> The radical change had been the gradual formation of the Cities over a thousand years of Earth's history. Efficiency implied bigness. . . .
> Think of the inefficiency of a hundred thousand houses for a hundred thousand families as compared with a hundred-thousand-unit Section; a book-film collection in each house as compared with a Section film concentrate; independent video for each family as compared with video-piping systems.
> For that matter, take the simple folly of endless duplication of kitchens and bathrooms as compared with the thoroughly

efficient diners and shower rooms made possible by City culture. . . .

City culture meant optimum distribution of food, increasing utilization of yeasts and hydroponics. New York City spread over two thousand square miles and at the last census its population was well over twenty million. There were some eight hundred Cities on Earth, average population, ten million.

Each City became a semiautonomous unit, economically all but self-sufficient. It could roof itself in, gird itself about, burrow itself under. It became a steel cave, a tremendous, self-contained cave of steel and concrete.

It could lay itself out scientifically. At the center was the enormous complex of administrative offices. In careful orientation to one another and to the whole were the large residential Sections connected and interlaced by the expressway and the localways. Toward the outskirts were the factories, the hydroponic plants, the yeast-culture vats, the power plants. Through all the melee were the water pipes and sewage ducts, schools, prisons and shops, power lines and communication beams.

There was no doubt about it: the City was the culmination of man's mastery over the environment. Not space travel, not the fifty colonized worlds that were now so haughtily independent, but the City. . . .

The Cities were good.

The techniques that science-fiction writers had been developing to fictionalize issues, to dramatize future societies in the process of telling the story, were tools that had been invented and perfected and that lay at hand for anyone capable of using them. The Kuttners, Henry and C. L. Moore, had used them well in the early and mid-1940s, Heinlein had mastered them, A. E. van Vogt had adapted them to his own magical purposes, and Frederik Pohl and Cyril Kornbluth were beginning to bring them to the ends of satire. But Asimov, who had participated in their development, displayed his skill in their use particularly well in the robot novels.

He provides a host of corroborating details, both psychological and social. Codes of behavior have developed naturally around the major institutions of the Cities. The Personals, for instance, centralize bathroom facilities except for the occasional "activated" washbowl, such as Baley has in his "spacious" three-room apartment. So "by strong custom men disregarded one another's presence entirely either within or just outside the Personals," though women used them for social purposes. The "bright cheerfulness" of the Personals contrasts with the "busy utilitarianism" of the rest of the City. The moving strips of roadway, the expressway and the localways, are places where behavior has become traditional and where juveniles break the traditions and the laws by playing on them such dangerous follow-the-leader games as "running the strips." Ways of behaving in the communal kitchens have become standardized to avoid annoying others and letting others annoy you ("the first problem of living is to minimize friction with the crowds that surround you on all sides"). "When you're young, mealtimes are the bright spot of the day," but "there is no one so uncomfortable . . . as the man eating out-of-Section" and "be it ever so humble . . . there's no place like home-kitchen." It might be noted that the novel contains a concern with food and persistent scenes of eating seldom found in Asimov fiction. Baley, for instance, is constantly worried about missing meals, and he is constantly eating, once in company with Daneel. The flavor and texture of the food is specified in significant detail, which, of course, reinforces the obsessional qualities of subsistence living.

Civism, the philosophy that supports the way of life created by the Cities, combines two elements: a basic level of security ("the mere fact of living in a modern city insured the bare possibility of existence, even for those entirely declassified") and a life enclosed, crowded, and conducted at levels of existence made bearable only by evolved attitudes of Earthmen, the folkways developed to cope with the problems, and certain small privileges that accompany increasing classification. Enderby, for instance, earns the right to a window in his office (this detail also emphasizes his medievalism); Baley has earned the activation of his washbowl and the privilege of eating in his home. Although "it was considered the height of ill form to parade 'status,' the loss of such small privileges would make life unbearable." Modern civism has minimized the competitive struggle for existence that had been the rule during the "fiscalism" of medieval times, but it has not completely eliminated the struggle for status.

All is perceived—and to good effect—through the filter of Baley's consciousness. Asimov shows us his world—or as much of it as his art tells him to show us—not in the first person but in the third, through Baley. The reader is with Baley constantly through the novel: Baley's goals, to solve the mystery and to get rid of the threat of the Spacers, are the reader's goals; his perceptions are all the reader gets; and his thoughts (with such exceptions as are acceptable in third-person narration) are shared with the reader. It is Baley who perceives the Cities as good, and it is his changing attitude toward Daneel (and robots in general), the Spacers, and the Cities that the novel really is about.

The Caves of Steel is that rarity in science fiction, a novel of character. Character is not supposed to concern science-fiction authors very much. Asimov, as a writer who specializes more than most in ideas and rationality, might be expected to care even less. Lije Baley, however, is the key factor in the novel, not merely because he is the detective who must solve the mystery but because of what he is in addition to being a detective.

Unlike other Asimov characters, Baley has a past. His father had been a nuclear physicist with a rating in the top percentile, who was declassified because of an accident in the nuclear plant where he worked. Baley's mother died early, and his father died when Baley was eight. Baley remembers him as sodden, morose, lost, speaking sometimes of the past in hoarse, broken sentences. Baley and his two older sisters went into the Section orphanage. Baley knows the horror of declassification, and that knowledge motivates his desperation to solve the mystery rather than go through what his father suffered. Also unlike other Asimov characters, who are individuals isolated by job or temperament, Baley has a family: a wife, Jessie, who had enjoyed a small, wicked pride in the name Jezebel until Baley told her that Jezebel was not a painted hussy, and a son, Bentley ("Ben"). Baley also has experiences that keep flooding into his mind: the childhood games of running the strips and hide-and-seek with guide rods (whose gradual warming leads visitors toward their destinations), an uncle who worked in Yeast-town (once Newark, New Brunswick, and Trenton) and gave him illegal yeast treats when he was a child.

The changes that the reader perceives in Baley mirror the changes in the basic theme of urging Earthmen into a relationship with robots (C/Fe) that would make possible the colonization of uninhabited worlds. Baley begins vigorously opposed to robots (but not so opposed that his intense feelings of duty and loyalty cannot persuade him to work with a robot). He is gloomy and sardonic as well as a thoughtful man whose fascination with history (like Asimov's) leads him into a variety of historic comparisons and reflections. But his first impulses, to prove that there has been no murder or that if there has, it was committed by a Spacer or by Daneel himself, push him into blind alleys and near disaster. He is not, as he himself reflects, the cool, intellectual detective of fiction; his disturbance at bringing Daneel home makes him forget the murder for a while.

Gradually, Baley begins to change. He listens to Dr. Fastolfe's idealistic plea for the future of humanity. He first rejects the notion of Earthmen going to other worlds and then begins to consider it. He notices the smells of the City for perhaps the first time. He grows used to the presence of Daneel and wonders whether it would be possible to work beside robots to colonize another world. He finds himself echoing Fastolfe's arguments to a Medievalist leader. He begins to confide in Daneel and even to think well of him. "Whatever the creature was," he thinks, "he was strong and faithful, animated by no selfishness. What more could you ask of any friend? Baley needed a friend and he was in no mood to cavil at the fact that a gear replaced a blood vessel in this particular one."

Finally, at the end of the novel, Baley's conversion to Fastolfe's goals is more important than the discovery of the murderer. Enderby is persuaded, on the promise that his crime will not be revealed, to throw his efforts and the strength of the Medievalists behind the attempt to move Earthmen toward extraterrestrial colonization. And Baley finally says to Daneel, "I didn't think I would ever say anything like this to anyone like you, Daneel, but I trust you. I even—admire you." And although Baley considers himself too old to leave Earth (*The*

Naked Sun refutes that assumption), he hopes that Daneel might help Ben to do so some day. At the end, suddenly smiling, Baley takes Daneel's elbow, and they walk out the door, arm in arm.

That final image, more than anything else, speaks to Asimov's own perception of the novel's heart. And, as if to reinforce image with motivation, Daneel has already revealed that the whole Spacer concern had been to try to persuade at least a segment of Earth's population that Sarton's and Fastolfe's goals were their own. Daneel's work with Baley had been an experiment not in whether robots can solve crimes but in whether Earthmen can be persuaded to accept robots and the goal of extraterrestrial emigration. The Spacers conclude that their only hope is the romantics, and the romantics are all Medievalists, actual or potential.

The other characters are drawn with greater care than is customary in science-fiction novels: Enderby, first as the harried Commissioner with his Medievalist affections and then reinterpreted as a Medievalist leader who has been trapped by accident into the role of murderer; Jessie, whose loss of name pushes her into a harmless but misleading flirtation with the Medievalists; and Daneel himself, the polite, deferential, and literal-minded robot detective, with the built-in sense of justice, who provides the ideal foil for Baley's emotionalism, and is, no doubt, the author's reason for making Baley emotional.

Daneel allows Asimov to reexplore the problems of robots that he had covered so thoroughly in *I, Robot*: the First Law, for instance, which eliminates robots as suspects, and the literal aspect of robot minds, such as Asimov dealt with two years later in "Risk." Baley is suspicious of Daneel's statement that a final adjustment of his circuits impressed into his motivation banks a particularly strong drive, a desire for justice. Justice, Baley says, is an abstraction; only a human being can understand it. But Daneel defines justice in pragmatic terms as the condition that exists when all the laws are enforced.

Asimov reverses the situation of "Evidence" when Baley accuses Daneel of being human, but it is not as difficult for a robot to prove that he is not human as vice versa. Like Byerley, however, Daneel can eat; he reveals a food sac from which he must later remove the food. Daneel is asked not to forget something, and he comments that robots are not capable of forgetting. Daneel's humanoid appearance and demeanor make even more effective the scene in which he is slapped by the Medievalist Clousarr. Daneel responds, "That was a dangerous action, Francis. Had I not moved backward you might easily have damaged your hand. As it is, I regret that I must have caused you pain."

Baley refers to Daneel's "queer mixture of ability and submissiveness" at one point. At another, he thinks bitterly about the ambiguities of the First Law: "A robot must not hurt a human being, unless he can think of a way to prove it is for the human being's ultimate good after all." Asimov also has the opportunity to cast a backward glance at Campbell's 1934 story, "Twilight": "He [Baley] had known well enough . . . the qualities that marked off a man from a machine. Curiosity had to be one of them. A six-week-old kitten was curious, but how could there be a curious machine, be it ever so humanoid?"

Asimov also rationalizes the humanoid shape for robots, which he did not do in *I, Robot*. Dr. Gerrigel points out that "the human form is the most successful generalized form in all nature." Therefore, rather than buying "a tractor with a positronic brain, a reaper, a harrow, a milker, an automobile, and so on," it makes more sense to buy "ordinary unbrained machinery with a single positronic robot to run them all" at "a fiftieth or a hundredth the expense."

Asimov supports his vision of the future with a sprinkling of technical details other than those that describe robots or the Cities or the expressways. His Cities are powered by atomic energy (he uses the older term, "atomic pile") and were made possible by force shields, which lessened the threat of atomic war. Asimov foresaw the problem of the disposal of radioactive wastes and had the "so-called 'hot ash' . . . forced by air pressure through leaden pipes to distant caverns ten miles out in the ocean and a half mile below the ocean floor." But "Baley sometimes wondered what would happen when the caverns were filled." The force shield also is present in the form of a force barrier that separates Spacetown from New York City.

There are other details: subetheric hand disruptors, somno

vapor and retch gas (prophetic!) that help police control crowds, blasters (presumably different from subetheric hand disruptors), keratofiber (made out of some kind of horn?), one-way glass transparency at the flick of a switch, trimension that projects images in three dimensions, focused duo-beam for spying, hyposlivers of medication that dissolve into the body, shielded subether communications, no-stick fluorocarbon coatings on cookware, motospirals (a kind of escalator), natural solariums at the top of buildings so the rich can enjoy the sun when they wish, spray-on cosmetics, wire film (a kind of videotape) and a microfilm projector for projection in three dimensions with a film record in the form of a fixed atomic pattern in an aluminum block, and an alpha-sprayer. These are not predictions in the way that Hugo Gernsback's *Ralph 124C41+* was largely a compilation of predictions. They function to reinforce the narrative.

The expressways, for instance, not only provide the flavor of a distant and more efficient future and serve as the means to deal with mass transportation, they also are used later in the story for the escape of Baley and Daneel from the Medievalists. The guide sticks, which lead Baley and Daneel to the laboratory of Clousarr, the Medievalist "zymologist" (yeast expert), later become part of the explanation for the "murder" of Sammy, when Baley speculates that Enderby mis-set the guide stick for Dr. Gerrigel so that the robotocist would discover Sammy's dead body. Similarly, the escape from the Medievalists that takes Baley and Daneel to the atomic power plant provides the opportunity to reveal that gamma radiation can destroy the delicate balance of Daneel's positronic brain and gave Enderby the idea not only of stealing the alpha-sprayer that he ordered Sammy to clap to his head but of framing Baley for the crime.

Some of these details are less persuasive than others, to be sure. Their importance is the way they are worked into the fabric of the novel. They become part of the perfected Asimov style, in a way mainstream critics seldom use the term, or have to. A science-fiction writer must create a convincing milieu for events that have not happened yet or have not happened that we know of.

Asimov developed his style gradually. Campbell helped him, no doubt, by suggesting the value of reinforcing details. Asimov also learned from reading other writers, such as Clifford Simak, and from participation in several Bread Loaf Writers' Conferences. By *The Caves of Steel,* Asimov's style had settled into simple words (except for an occasional technical term) arranged in short sentences, and those sentences arranged in short paragraphs, sometimes only a sentence or two long. Rudolph Flesch would have loved it.

In *The Caves of Steel,* though Asimov's style is limited by the matter-of-fact perceptions of his viewpoint character, his writing does rise to eloquence (usually in his descriptions of the City and its ways) and to sensitive depictions of human nature, as in the following paragraphs, reminiscent of Proust in their observations:

> Every time he [Baley] smelled raw yeast, the alchemy of sense perception threw him more than three decades into the past. He was a ten-year-old again, visiting his Uncle Boris, who was a yeast farmer. Uncle Boris always had a little supply of yeast delectables: small cookies, chocolaty things filled with sweet liquid, hard confections in the shape of cats and dogs. Young as he was, he knew that Uncle Boris shouldn't really have had them to give away and he always ate them quietly, sitting in a corner with his back to the center of the room. He would eat them quickly for fear of being caught.
>
> They tasted all the better for that.

There is, in addition, a sense of place in *The Caves of Steel* (and in *The Naked Sun*) that does not exist in *The Foundation Trilogy* and the robot stories, and for good reason. *The Caves of Steel* is not only a title but a place, a place that is important to the murder investigation, the psychology of the City's citizens, and the theme of the Spacers trying to induce them to leave its protection. Everywhere Baley goes he is conscious of his surroundings: Enderby's office, the expressway, the Personals, his apartment (contrasted later on with a "grim, lower-class apartment"), Spacetown, the motorways, a kitchen, a power plant, and Yeast-town. The presence of an outsider, Daneel, brings everything freshly to Baley's awareness. A sense of place is as necessary to *The Caves of Steel* as it is unnecessary in *The Foundation Trilogy.*

There are other stylistic elements peculiar to science fiction that the mainstream reader might not recognize. Samuel R. Delany commented in a 1979 Modern Language Association meeting that the problem with non-science-fiction readers and critics is that they must be taught to read science fiction sentence by sentence and word by word. In science fiction, he says, the metaphorical may become literal, language has implications that must be understood before the reader is aware of what is going on, and often judgment must be suspended until further information clarifies the situation.

In some senses these elements are part of *The Caves of Steel*. Although Asimov's style, as always, is simple and straightforward, he allows himself the occasional telling metaphor that illuminates the environment and times of the novel. "Medieval," for instance, is that kind of metaphor: it stands for us, our times, our ways. Windows are Medieval. Spectacles are Medieval. The (King James) Bible is Medieval, and it is written in Middle English. The reader is intended to understand not only the passage of three thousand years but the false perspective that lumps centuries and millennia together in categories that are too broad for accuracy.

The Commissioner calls Baley "a modernist" and goes on to describe a romanticized and false version of life before the Cities:

> "In Medieval times, people lived in the open. I don't mean on the farms only. I mean in the cities, too. Even in New York. When it rained, they didn't think of it as waste. They gloried in it. They lived close to nature. It's healthier, better. The troubles of modern life come from being divorced from nature. Read up on the Coal Century sometimes."

In these references, of course, Asimov is talking as well about our own attitudes toward the past, as Poe was in "Mellonta Tauta."

In *The Caves of Steel*, as in well-written science fiction of all kinds, language must constantly be inspected for surprises and reinterpretation. Baley notes, for instance, that there are no expressway directions to Spacetown. He explains why almost immediately: "if you've business there, you know the way" and "if you don't know the way, you've no business there." In a related logical process, the novel raises an aspect of Spacer attitudes that infuriates Earthmen. Earthmen are not allowed into Spacetown except singly and then only when thoroughly cleansed and decontaminated as if they were dirty and diseased. Later this business is turned around and inspected from the other side. Earthmen haven't changed, but Spacers have; like Wells's Martians, they have eliminated infectious diseases and contact with Earthmen might be fatal.

The Caves of Steel contains the kind of science-fiction wit that Frederik Pohl and Cyril Kornbluth displayed to such good advantage in their collaborations (beginning with The Space Merchants) and that Pohl continued in his own satires. Novels and short stories are "viewed," for instance, which suggests a reevaluation of the customs and literacy of a society and linguistic development in general. A reference is made in The Caves of Steel to "whole yeast bread," and Baley remembers when he took his son to the zoo and they saw cats, dogs, and the wonder of sparrows flying.

At one point Asimov describes the natural solariums at the uppermost levels of some of the wealthier subsections of the City:

> . . . where a partition of quartz with a movable metal shield excludes the air but lets in the sunlight. There the wives and daughters of the City's highest administrators and executives may tan themselves. There a unique thing happens every evening.
> Night falls.

Asimov moves on from that revelation about a world in which the fall of night can be a unique event (and is, no doubt, a personal allusion to his most famous single story, "Nightfall") to an analysis of those habits of humanity that can be changed and those that cannot.

> Much of the earlier habits of Earthly society have been given up in the interests of that same economy and efficiency: space, privacy, even much of free will. They are the products of civilization, however, and not much more than ten thousand years old.
> The adjustment of sleep to night, however, is as old as man: a million years. The habit is not easy to give up. Although

the evening is unseen, apartment lights dim as the hours of darkness pass and the City's pulse sinks. Though no one can tell noon from midnight by any cosmic phenomenon along the enclosed avenues of the City, mankind follows the mute partitionings of the hour hand.

The expressways empty, the noise of life sinks, the moving mob among the colossal alleys melts away; New York City lies in Earth's unnoticed shadow, and its population sleeps.

The prose of that observation, it might be noted, need not be ashamed anywhere in literary society.

Ultimately, the appeal of *The Caves of Steel* depends upon two major elements: the depiction of an overpopulated society living in what we would consider a claustrophobic environment, and the relationship between an Earthman and a robot. Asimov tries to get the reader interested in the Sarton-Fastolfe goal of pushing Earthmen into space colonization, but because this goal is distant and idealistic, the reader remains unconvinced. And the threat of robots replacing humans matters only insofar as it motivates Baley.

The environment, on the other hand, is virtually a major character in the novel. Some readers interpret *The Caves of Steel* as dystopian. Asimov refers to this in a headnote to "It's Such a Beautiful Day," a story reprinted in *Nightfall and Other Stories:*

I wrote a novel in 1953 which pictured a world in which everyone lived in underground cities, comfortably enclosed away from the open air.

People would say, "How could you imagine such a nightmarish situation?"

And I would answer in astonishment, "What nightmarish situation?"

The Caves of Steel was written by a claustrophiliac (and an acrophobe) for an editor who had a severe case of agoraphobia. Asimov's dislike for travel and his refusal to fly are well known, but he also enjoys being enclosed. In that same headnote he wrote:

. . . my idea of a pleasant time is to go up to my attic, sit at my electric typewriter . . . , and bang away, watching the words take shape like magic before my eyes. To minimize distractions, I keep the window-shades down at all times and work exclusively by artificial light.

Both Asimov and Horace Gold, who could not leave his apartment for many years, would have enjoyed at least some aspects of life in the caves of steel.

But even the attractions or repulsions of the caves of steel are not at the heart of the novel. The reader wants Baley to accept Daneel, and that acceptance, in the final pages, rewards the reader's expectations with the glow of a resolution satisfyingly accomplished.

The Naked Sun is the reverse of The Caves of Steel. Asimov wrote it out of an emotion other than his love for enclosed environments. He concluded his brief essay on his claustrophilia in Nightfall and Other Stories with the comment:

> . . . sometimes twice in one week, when I feel I've put in a good day's work, I go out in the late afternoon and take a walk through the neighborhood.
> But I don't know. That thing you people have up there in the sky. It's got quite a glare to it.

That glare is the sustaining metaphor in The Naked Sun. Where The Caves of Steel has the feeling of enclosure, The Naked Sun has the feeling of wide-open spaces. Where The Caves of Steel is concerned with overpopulation, Solaria in The Naked Sun is almost unpopulated: it has only twenty thousand humans (but also two hundred million robots), and estates can cover ten thousand square miles. Where Earth is concerned with competition from robots, Solaria is overrun by them, specializes in their production, and exports them to all the other Outer Worlds. And where the endemic psychological problem of Earthmen is agoraphobia, the problem of Solarians is agoraphilia. Solarians so love the feeling of virgin space around them that they seldom come into personal contact with each other. On Solaria a culture has developed in which "viewing" by trimension is the custom, where some cannot tolerate contact with other human beings, and where the rest, when contact is unavoidable, clothe every part of the body except the face.

Baley is summoned to Solaria to solve another murder. A Spacer, Rikaine Delmarre, has been murdered. It is the first crime of violence on Solaria in two centuries, which is why an Earth police detective has been requested. It is also a classic "locked-room" murder mystery in a special science-fiction sense. In that too *The Naked Sun* complements *The Caves of Steel.*

In *The Caves of Steel,* Sarton could not have been killed by an Earthman because an Earthman could not have crossed the open spaces between New York City and Spacetown. A robot could have crossed the open spaces but could not have killed Sarton because of the First Law. Asimov solved the puzzle by having Enderby instruct Sammy to bring him the blaster across the open spaces and later give it back to Sammy to return. It was an ironic confirmation of the necessity of C/Fe, the collaboration between humans and robots. The situation is similar in *The Naked Sun.* No murder weapon is found on the scene; Gladia, Delmarre's young wife, discovers the body and is overcome; and a robot who was on the scene and an apparent witness is incoherent and has to be destroyed. The situation is reversed, however, in that an outsider could have come across open country without difficulty, entered the house, and killed Delmarre, but would have experienced major psychological inhibitions in Delmarre's physical presence as well as having had to face Delmarre's neurotic reactions to his presence.

At the end of the novel Baley gathers together the suspects in true formal murder-mystery fashion, though in science-fiction fashion they all are present by trimensic projection: Gladia; Attlebish, the acting head of Solarian Security; Jothan Leebig, Solaria's best roboticist; Anselmo Quemot, a sociologist; Klorissa Cantoro, Delmarre's assistant fetologist (a Solarian expert on the external development of embryos and the rearing of children to be proper, non-gregarious Solarians); and Altim Thool, a physician. And in proper, formal murder-mystery fashion, Baley recounts each of their motives and opportunities for the murder before he accuses Leebig. Leebig, it seems, had been friendly with Gladia by way of frequent "viewing." More importantly, Delmarre had been working with Leebig on robotics and suspected that Leebig had plans to conquer the Galaxy by means of robots. Leebig had planned to build spaceships with positronic brains that could be instructed to attack other ships under the assumption that those ships, too, contained only robotic brains. Delmarre had been about to reveal Leebig's plan. Leebig had murdered him by creating a robot with detachable limbs. One of these limbs had been used as the murder weapon and then reattached. (Another ironic example of C/Fe.)

The Solarians are aghast at this perversion of robot psychology (they are surrounded by robots and their safety and peace of mind is dependent upon the sanctity of the Three Laws of Robotics), and they turn on Leebig. Leebig himself crumples and admits his guilt when Baley tells him that an assistant is present at Leebig's house and is going to put him under restraint. Leebig commits suicide rather than endure someone's physical presence.

On Earth, when Baley reports to Undersecretary Albert Minnim in Washington, Minnim points out that Leebig could not have killed Delmarre because he could not have endured Delmarre's physical proximity; he would rather die than be that close to another person, as, in fact, he did. Baley admits that Gladia actually killed her husband in a fit of anger (and during a temporary blackout of consciousness), but Leebig had arranged it. Leebig knew of Gladia's quarrels and frustrations with her husband, and instructed the robot to hand her one of its detachable limbs at the moment of her full fury.

Here, as in *The Caves of Steel*, the murder is the precipitating event and the structural element holding the novel together, but it is not the chief focus of the reader's interest. No one in the novel either knows or likes Delmarre—at most they respect him as "a good Solarian"—nor does anyone care about his death. The only real motivation behind Baley's desire to solve the murder is to save the only logical suspect, Gladia, from being accused of having committed the act. Motivations other than discovering the murderer—everyone believes that it was Gladia—exist for almost everyone else as well.

Baley (who now has been promoted to C-6) has still other reasons for his presence on Solaria. He has been asked by Minnim to observe conditions on Solaria because Earth sociologists have predicted that Earth is too dangerous to the Outer Worlds for them to allow Earth to survive. The sociologists expect the Outer Worlds virtually to wipe out Earth within a century. But no Earthman has been allowed to visit the Outer Worlds. Consequently, Earth knows the strengths of the Spacers but not their weaknesses. On the other hand, Daneel (who is again Baley's partner, though he plays a lesser part than in *The Caves of Steel*) has been sent to Solaria to provide help for Baley and to give him the prestige of associating with a Spacer (Daneel passes as human). In reality, however, Daneel is there because the Aurorans (who are from a Spacer planet that has established a more rational relationship between humans and robots) are uneasy about political and technological developments on Solaria and concerned that Solaria might threaten not only Earth but other Spacer worlds.

One major focus of reader interest is Solarian living conditions. Where overpopulation and social and psychological adaptations to it were a major aspect of *The Caves of Steel*, underpopulation and adaptations of the Solarians are the focus of *The Naked Sun*. Solaria, which was settled about three hundred years earlier by the well-to-do of a comparatively nearby planet named Nexon (two parsecs or 6.52 light-years away), is fertile, temperate, and without dangerous animals. The settlers, who had felt cramped on Nexon as its population approached two million and a limitation was placed on the number of robots (robot birth control), resolved to limit human population on Solaria to what they considered the optimum number of 20,000 and allow the robot population to grow unrestricted.

The consequence of huge estates, cheap labor, and trimensic viewing was the absence of cities. Solarians had fewer and fewer reasons for personal contact and gradually developed a pride in never seeing anyone directly, which eventually became a neurosis about seeing anyone. Human population is limited by assigning mates according to genetic considerations (some Solarians wear gene-coded rings). Children are licensed according to population needs and gene charts, then removed as month-old fetuses and brought to term in tanks. Some fifteen to twenty of them are received each month at what is called "the farm" and about the same number are graduated to independence after a lengthy period of education and training. They are raised by robots with human supervision and taught, in spite of their instincts for gregariousness, to prefer isolation—to grow up, that is, into proper Solarians who can barely permit personal contact with their own mates.

This world allows Asimov to play with two separate notions: the social customs of the Solarians and a further elaboration of robotics. Because Solarians do not like, and sometimes cannot endure, contact with other humans, they must learn to work with robots, and they have developed an unusual skill at it. They use robots to tend to the children (Solarians can scarcely bring themselves to touch, or even to mention, "the little animals"). Dr. Delmarre had even developed the ability to instruct a robot to spank a child, an action that could ruin a robot's positronic brain. Baley learns from Jothan Leebig the difficulties of building a robot capable of disciplining children. Baley suggests that throughout history the First Law of Robotics has been misquoted. It should read: "A robot may do nothing that, *to its knowledge,* will harm a human being, nor, through inaction, *knowingly* allow a human being to come to harm." The novel explores, as well, ways of using a robot to commit murder: instructing one robot to put poison into water and another to give it to a human; instructing a robot to hand a child a poisoned arrow; and instructing a robot to hand a woman its arm to use as a club when she is overwrought. In one episode, Baley orders Daneel to reveal himself as a robot to the other household robots so that Daneel will not interfere with Baley's plan, which Daneel thinks is too dangerous and cannot permit. Baley wants to go about interviewing people in person.

Asimov's greatest delight, here at least, is in the social customs that have developed to reinforce the physical situation on Solaria. The language reflects the Solarians' personal-contact taboo: terms relating to personal contact (affection, love, children, even touching) are obscene or scandalous, and films of people kissing are pornographic. Liberties may be taken while viewing; nudity is not uncommon, and the beautiful Gladia first appears to Baley like Venus fresh from her bath. Daneel, incidentally, interprets her action, perhaps correctly, as a ploy to gain Baley's sympathy, though Klorissa is equally

ready to bare herself before the trimensional camera. Gladia
excuses it as "only viewing." On the rare occasions when individuals meet, however, they are fully clothed down to gloves
and stand far from each other.

This leads to one of the key scenes in the novel. Early in
1956 Asimov wrote to me that he had just written a pornographic
scene that the postmaster could not touch. (This, of course,
was more than a quarter century ago when the postmaster was
still declaring books obscene.) He was right. After Leebig commits suicide and just before Gladia is about to depart for Aurora, where she can lead a more "normal" life and her more
affectionate nature can be expressed, she asks for one last interview with Baley and arrives in person, fully clothed, of
course. As they are saying goodbye, she asks if she can touch
him. Slowly, she removes her glove. Asimov has invested the
act with such significance that it is more erotic than explicit
sex.

The emotional content of the scene is heightened by the
possibility of romance between Baley and Gladia. It is no more
than a possibility. Baley is approaching middle age and is a
man of honor. The two recognize the gulf between their cul-
tures—but they also recognize their mutual attraction. When
Baley dreams about his wife, Jessie, she looks a lot like Gladia.
He and Gladia have a meeting at which Gladia overcomes her
Solarian neurosis to allow Baley to get closer and closer, even
to sit on the same garden bench, and to hand him a flower,
their fingers almost touching. And at their final meeting Gladia
not only removes her glove but takes Baley's hand and then
touches his cheek, and Baley feels a sense of loss as she leaves.

Finally, however, *The Naked Sun* is about Elijah Baley and
his battle against agoraphobia. *The Caves of Steel* was concerned mostly with Baley's acceptance of friendship with a
robot. Daneel plays a smaller part in *The Naked Sun*, however. For some chapters, after Baley exposes him as a robot in
order to get freedom to act, Daneel is out of sight entirely. And
although he comes up with some speculations about the murder that Baley knocks down ("Logical but not reasonable.
Wasn't that the definition of a robot?"), he does not participate
in the murder's resolution, being on his way to Leebig's house

(a final irony that Baley himself notes: Leebig committed suicide rather than meet one of the robots he loved).

The key image of the novel after the naked sun is "walls." The first sentence speaks of Baley's panic at the thought of leaving the protection of his New York City walls and of flying to Washington, even though the trip itself would never expose Baley to the open air—"The New York Runway Number 2 . . . was decently enclosed, with a lock opening to the unprotected atmosphere only after air speed had been achieved." The airplane has no windows and a news-strip unrolls constantly at eye level with news and short fiction to distract travelers. Baley even tells himself:

> I'm enclosed. This plane is just a little City.
> But he didn't fool himself. There was an inch of steel at his left; he could feel it with his elbow. Past that, nothing—
> Well, air! But that was nothing, really.
> A thousand miles of it in one direction. A thousand in another. One mile of it, maybe two, straight down.
> He almost wished he could see straight down, glimpse the top of the buried Cities he was passing over; New York, Philadelphia, Baltimore, Washington. He imagined the rolling, low-slung cluster complexes of domes he had never seen but knew to be there. And under them, for a mile underground and dozens of miles in every direction, would be the Cities.
> The endless, living corridors of the Cities, he thought, alive with people; apartments, community kitchens, factories, Expressways, all comfortable and warm with the evidence of man.

From Washington, Baley goes to a spaceship and experiences an Earth night ("Baley shivered spasmodically in the raw, open air"), but it is not so bad because "the night closed in . . . like dark black walls melting into a black ceiling overhead." Then he must travel by Spacer vessel, by Jump through hyperspace, to Solaria. That is not so bad either because the spaceship is all enclosed like a small city and even larger than an airplane. The first crisis comes when the spaceship is scheduled to land on Solaria, and Baley is told it will land in daylight. He will "have to step out onto the unprotected surface of a planet in daytime." He is fighting panic again as the first chapter ends.

Baley tries to tell himself that being in the open is natural;

men had done it all their lives, and the Spacers did it now. "There is no real harm in wall-lessness." But reason alone is not enough. "Something above and beyond reason cried out for walls and would have none of space." Daneel, however, anticipates Baley's neurosis and arranges for an air-tube, commonly used in space between vessels, to be connected to a ground-transport vehicle. Daneel speaks of Baley's "peculiarities," a term Baley doesn't like. He resents Daneel's concern about his neurosis and feels "a sudden need to see," motivated partly by Daneel's oversolicitude and partly by Minnim's instructions to observe. But Daneel will not retract the top of the vehicle for fear of the harm that Baley might suffer. Baley has to trick the robot driver into opening the top and exposing him to Solaria's naked sun: "Blue, green, air, noise, motion—and over it all, beating down, furiously, relentlessly, frighteningly, was the white light that came from a ball in the sky." Daneel has to pull Baley down to keep him from injuring his eyes by staring too long at the sun, and Baley loses consciousness.

Asimov makes Baley's neurosis convincingly crippling but also presents Baley as a man with a stubborn need to face his fear and conquer it.

> What he really wanted was an inner knowledge that he could take care of himself and fulfill his assignment. The sight and fear of the open had been hard to take. It might be that when the time came he would lack the hardihood to dare face it again, at the cost of his self-respect and, conceivably, of Earth's safety. All over a small matter of emptiness.
>
> His face grew grim even at the glancing touch of that thought. He would face air, sun, and empty space yet!

When Baley tries to sleep, however, he pictures the house that has been built for him and Daneel (and will be torn down when he leaves because only one house is allowed per estate and labor is cheap), "balanced precariously at the outer skin of the world, with emptiness waiting just outside like a monster." And he thinks of Jessie, a thousand light-years away, and he wishes there were a tunnel from Solaria to Earth so he could walk back to Earth, back to Jessie, back to comfort and security. . . .

Baley and the reader are continually reminded of Baley's insecurity and his determination to resist it. He reflects that the topmost levels in New York are low-rent (this seems inconsistent with his description in *The Caves of Steel* of the solariums of the wealthy). His dream of Jessie includes a sun shining down on them through the caves of steel. Daneel continues his efforts to protect Baley from his own weaknesses, trying to persuade him on several occasions to stay within the house prepared for them and to do his interviewing by trimensional projection.

Baley finds himself in an airborne vessel for a second time on his way to see the sociologist Anselmo Quemot, but this vessel has windows and the windows are transparent. Baley fights his distress, which Asimov reveals through understatement: "he buried his head in his knees only when he could absolutely no longer help it." But, a bit earlier, Baley "had begun by stepping across open ground to the waiting plane with a kind of lightheaded dizziness that was almost enjoyable, and he had ordered the windows left unblanked in a kind of manic self-confidence." Baley's will begins to master his fears. In the interview with Quemot, opposing fears are neatly balanced as Baley's initial concern about blanking out the windows is matched by Quemot's growing neurosis about Baley's physical presence.

In the next scene, Baley goes to see Delmarre's assistant, Klorissa Cantoro. He scarcely minds the plane trip this time, but he expresses a desire to get indoors quickly—again this is contrasted with Klorissa's concern that he come no closer to her than some twenty-five feet. But Baley asks to go outside again ("I'm trying to grow accustomed to the outdoors") in order to observe the children at play. He has a physical reaction to the outdoors—his body feels chilled, his teeth chatter, his eyes hurt from looking "so far at a horizon so hazy green and blue"—"and yet he could fight off the urge to run, to return to enclosure." He marvels at "a living tree!" A bit later he walks under a group of three trees and finds it "almost like being surrounded by imperfect walls. The sun was only a wavering series of glitters through the leaves, so disconnected as almost to be robbed of horror." But when Klorissa calls to

him "watch out!" his taut emotions "snapped wide and he
flamed into panic. All the terror of the open air and the endless vaults of heaven broke in upon him."

On his way to an interview with Gladia, "for the first time
Baley found himself not minding a plane flight through open
space. . . . It was almost as though he were in his own element. . . . How fast could a man adapt to nightmare? Or was
it Gladia? He would be seeing her soon, not viewing her. Was
that what gave him confidence and this odd feeling of mixed
apprehension and anticipation?"

During the interview, the image of walls reappears in a
light-form portrait Gladia does of him. She encloses it all in
"a flat, lusterless hollow cube of slate gray . . ." and "the light
within shone through it, but dimmer; imprisoned, somehow."
She identifies it as "the wall about you, the way you can't go
outside, the way you have to be inside. You are inside there.
Don't you see?" Baley's disapproval of the image leads him to
agree to walk outside with Gladia, hoping that if he goes in
spite of his impulse to refuse she will agree "to take away the
gray." But as they leave, the structure of light "stayed behind,
holding Baley's imprisoned soul fast in the gray of the Cities."

The walk is the ultimate trial not only for Gladia, who enjoys "seeing" and proximity to a man in spite of her upbringing, but for Baley. He finds that space draws him, but he wants
"Earth and the warmth and companionship of the man-
crammed Cities." But he no longer can summon up an image
of New York to sustain him. The time is late afternoon, and
Baley faces the movement of the sun. Finally, he finds himself
staring directly at the sun as it rests nearly at the horizon, and
he has a vision.

> The sun was moving down to the horizon because the planet's
> surface was moving away from it, a thousand miles an hour,
> spinning under that naked sun, spinning with nothing to
> guard the microbes called men that scurried over its spinning
> surface, spinning madly forever, spinning—spinning . . .

The experience overcomes him; he faints again, from what Daneel later calls the cumulative effects of being exposed to the
open.

Baley's successful fight against his neurosis comes to a resolution when, still weak from his sunset experience, he walks to the window and starts to lift the curtain. Daneel takes it out of his fingers. "In the split fraction of a moment in which Baley watched the robot's hand take the curtain away from him with the loving caution of a mother protecting her child from the fire, a revolution took place within him." Just as Delmarre's nursery robots cannot match long-term good against the short-term discipline of their charges, so Daneel cannot understand Baley's need to face his terror.

> He [Baley] snatched the curtain back, yanking it out of Daneel's grasp. Throwing his full weight against it, he tore it away from the window, leaving shreds behind.
> "Partner Elijah!" said Daneel softly. "Surely you know now what the open will do to you."
> "I know," said Baley, "what it will do *for* me." . . .
> And for the first time he faced it freely. It was no longer bravado, or perverse curiosity, or the pathway to a solution of a murder. He faced it because he knew he wanted to and because he needed to. That made all the difference.
> Walls were crutches! Darkness and crowds were crutches! He must have thought so, unconsciously, and hated them even when he most thought he loved and needed them. . . .
> He felt himself filling with a sense of victory, and as though victory were contagious, a new thought came, bursting like an inner shout. . . .

That thought is the solution to the murder. One good thing leads to another. Asimov has shown Baley passing through successive stages of his agoraphobia and the consequences of his attempts to conquer it, growing more able to control his fear with each incident, until at last he masters his deepest apprehensions and becomes a better person at the same time that he solves the murder that brought him to Solaria.

Only Baley's return to Earth remains to bring the movement of the novel full circle. The theme of *The Caves of Steel* was the need for Earthmen to emigrate to the unsettled planets, as a means not so much of relieving population pressure (an impractical notion) but of resuming humanity's march to the stars so that it can accept its heritage: the uninhabited Galaxy. The theme did not seem to be taken particularly seriously in the first novel, for the possibility of Earthmen going to other planets without their enclosed environment seemed so un-

likely as to be virtually impossible: at best it might be left to
their children or their children's children. But in The Naked
Sun Baley faced his fears for all Earthmen; what he can do,
others can do. Baley thinks of his son Bentley "standing on
some empty world, building a spacious life. It was a frighten-
ing thought. Baley still feared the open. [Asimov is a realist
about human psychology and does not believe that he can work
a miracle and change Baley completely.] But he no longer feared
the fear! It was not something to run from, that fear, but something to fight."

Baley goes through a few paragraphs of reverie, retracing
his experiences with the open spaces and the naked sun on
Solaria, and realizes not only that others can do it but that it
has changed him. He no longer fits in on Earth. "He had told
Minnim that Cities were wombs, and so they were. And what
was the first thing a man must do before he can be a man? He
must be born. He must leave the womb. And once left, it could
not be re-entered." For Baley the caves of steel now are alien.

The novel ends as it began, with Baley facing his fear. But
now he can handle it. He also has been changed by his experience and he understands his dream on Solaria. The last words
of the novel are:

> He lifted his head and he could see through all the steel and
> concrete and humanity above him. He could see the beacon
> set in space to lure men outward. He could see it shining
> down. The naked sun!

The Naked Sun was the last science-fiction novel Asimov
was to write until The Gods Themselves fifteen years later (aside
from a couple of his juvenile novels and his novelization of
the film "Fantastic Voyage"). Why not a third robot novel to
make the series a trilogy? After all, the trilogy is the natural
science-fiction series unless the series continues interminably.
In the second decade of the century there were the George
Allan England Darkness and Dawn trilogy, the Charles B. Stil-
son Polaris trilogy, and J. U. Giesy's "Dog Star" trilogy; more
recently have come J. R. R. Tolkien's The Lord of the Rings
trilogy (1954–55), Frank Herbert's Dune trilogy (1965, 1969,
1976), though now a tetralogy, and so many fantasy trilogies

that one loses track. And, of course, *The Foundation Trilogy.*

Asimov answers the question himself in *The Rest of the Robots,* which in the Doubleday edition included the robot novels.

> While I was writing *The Naked Sun,* it became perfectly clear to me that what I was working on was the second novel of a trilogy.
>
> In *The Caves of Steel* I had a society heavily overweighted in favor of humanity, with the robots unwelcome intruders. In *The Naked Sun,* on the other hand, I had an almost pure robot society with only a thin leaven of humanity barely holding it together.
>
> What I needed to do next was to form the perfect topper to my vision of the future by setting the third novel of the trilogy in Aurora, and depicting the complete fusion of man and robot into a society that was more than both and better than either.
>
> In the summer of 1958 I even started the novel, and then, somewhere in the fourth chapter, between one page and the next, something happened.

What had happened was Sputnik. By the summer of 1958 Asimov had decided that "the American public deserved un-derstanding of science and that it was the burning duty of writing scientists to try to give them that understanding." He turned to the subsequent science popularizations that brought him fame and fortune and that make up the majority of his two hundred plus books.

The explanation of the decision is neat and no doubt true as far as it goes. But there were other reasons. Asimov may have gone as far in science fiction as his talent would carry him. He mentioned this in his autobiography:

> As to my other career, science fiction, there, too, I had gone as far as I could. I might do things that were better than "Nightfall," *The Foundation Trilogy, I, Robot,* or *The Caves of Steel,* but surely not much better. These were already rec-ognized as classics, and I had been writing for fifteen years and I had yet to make more than ten or eleven thousand dol-lars a year as a writer.

Moreover, the third novel in the prospective trilogy was prob-ably not going well. Asimov would not abandon what he con-sidered to be his best writing in the midst of what he considered his best novels—and never return. A third factor in his decision may have been that the first two novels lead to a third only if one considers them to be about C/Fe, the blend of humanity and robots into a better-working culture. Even from that perspective, a novel placed on Aurora would have been the most difficult to bring off successfully, and out of keeping with the utopian forms of the two earlier novels. And C/Fe is only a small part of what *The Caves of Steel* and *The Naked Sun* are about. More engrossing and more vital are Earth and Solaria as cultural mirror images; in this sense a third novel would seem at best only a middle ground and at worst unnecessary.

Finally, if one reads the novels as being about Baley's education—as examples of the type of plot Heinlein has called "the man-who-learned-better"—then that education has been completed. Anything more is simply elaboration. Unlike *The Foundation Trilogy*, which seemed to cry out for a fourth volume. *The Robot Novels* are complete with two. I would be surprised if there ever were another.

6

THE OTHER NOVELS

Asimov's other science-fiction novels do not fall into any series but do fit into the same future history. With the exception of *The Gods Themselves* and the novelization of the screenplay for *Fantastic Voyage*, they began at the start of the fifties and were all published before that decade was over.

Asimov became a science-fiction writer by design, but he became a novelist by accident. It was one of those accidents that seems like ill fortune at the time but turns out to be great good luck in the long run. At least that is how Asimov perceived it in his autobiography, where—as may be natural in a work intended to make sense out of the miscellaneous occurrences of a life that started in obscurity and ended in national treasurehood—everything happened for the best.

No doubt Asimov eventually would have written novels. The time was right, and Asimov himself had worked up to longer lengths. "The Mule," completed May 5, 1945, was fifty thousand words long, just ten thousand short of the standard genre novel. But he might not have begun so soon nor been so successful.

It began with a request from Sam Merwin, Jr., editor of *Thrilling Wonder Stories* and *Startling Stories*. Merwin, or possibly his superior at the magazine publishing house, Leo Margulies, had decided that the magazines should begin to publish *Astounding*-type stories. By this time Asimov was recognized as perhaps not the greatest but the most typical *Astounding* author, and when he dropped in at the magazine office on May 26, 1947, Merwin suggested that Asimov write a lead novel for *Startling Stories*.

Lead novels for science-fiction adventure magazines such as *Amazing Stories*, *Fantastic Adventures*, *Planet Stories*, and Merwin's two magazines ran about forty thousand words, and suitable stories of this length were difficult to find. Some novels could be cut, but not many novels were being written except those intended for serialization. The time for the publishing of original science-fiction novels had not yet arrived. The fan presses were being created—in fact Thomas P. Hadley of Boston had announced the publication of E. E. "Doc" Smith's *The Skylark of Space* in the August 1946 issue of *Astounding*—but they were mostly interested in putting the magazine serials (primarily those of Doc Smith) into more enduring form. Mainstream publishers were publishing anthologies of short fiction, such as Raymond J. Healy and J. Francis McComas's *Adventures in Time and Space* and Groff Conklin's *The Best of Science Fiction* and their annual sequels, and were beginning to show interest in reprinting serials of authors with broader appeal, such as A. E. van Vogt at Simon & Schuster. Robert A. Heinlein was getting the science-fiction juvenile started with Scribner's 1947 publication of *Rocket Ship Galileo*. But, with all the wealth of the untouched science-fiction magazines waiting to be mined for anthologies and novels, no one was actively seeking new novels.

Lead novels usually were written by authors such as Henry Kuttner, Leigh Brackett, and Edmond Hamilton, and by Richard Shaver, Don Wilcox, and Chester S. Geier for the *Amazing-Fantastic* magazines, as a way of making a quick $400 to $800. Asimov was not averse to a quick $800. He also wanted to try other markets. If something happened to Campbell or to *Astounding* he might find himself unable to sell to anybody else. (Almost two years later, on April 9, 1949, Asimov's worst fears seemed to be realized when he read in the newspaper that Street & Smith had suspended all its pulp magazines, only to discover a day or two later that this did not include *Astounding*.) On June 2, then, Asimov began work on a story

dealing with old age. He called it "Grow Old with Me," mis-
quoting the opening line of Robert Browning's panegyric to
old age in "Rabbi ben Ezra":

> Grow old along with me!
> The best is yet to be,
> The last of life, for which the first was made. . . .

Asimov showed twelve thousand words of the story to
Merwin on July 1 and was encouraged to finish it. He began
rewriting on August 3 and completed the forty-eight-thousand-
word novella on September 22. The next day he took it to
Merwin's office. As Merwin took the manuscript he told Asimov that Margulies had decided the attempt to publish
Astounding-type stories had been a failure. He now wanted
blood-and-thunder *Amazing*-type stories. Asimov was taken
aback but felt no need for concern since Merwin had asked
for the novella and had approved part of it.

On October 15 Asimov called Merwin and was told that
the story would need revision. He went to the office and asked
to see Margulies. Merwin came out instead and described the
extensive revisions necessary. To Asimov it meant starting all
over again, ending not only with a poorer story but still without assurance that it would be accepted. In a rare moment of
anger, Asimov said, "Go to hell!" and stalked from Merwin's
office with his manuscript. Later, he regretted the violence of
his reaction, though not the action itself, particularly when
Merwin kept apologizing every time he saw Asimov. "An editor is entirely within his rights to reject a story, even a story
he has ordered," Asimov wrote in his autobiography. But his
disappointment was compounded when Campbell rejected the
novella as well.

Asimov stuck the manuscript in a drawer, more than half
convinced himself that it was worthless. A few months later,
however, Frederik Pohl, who was returning to the agent business, persuaded Asimov to let him show the novella to Martin
Greenberg, a young man who was going into the publishing
of science-fiction books under the name of Gnome Press. There
wouldn't be much money in it for Asimov, but few science-
fiction novels were being published and not only would the

prestige be great but the publication might lead to more important things. At the end of January Pohl reported that Greenberg wanted the manuscript, but by the end of that year nothing had happened with it or seemed likely to happen.

On February 25, 1949, Pohl suggested to Asimov that he try "Grow Old with Me" on Doubleday. By this time Asimov was thoroughly discouraged with it. "No, Fred, it stinks," he said. "Who cares about *your* opinion?" Pohl replied, and once more the manuscript went out. By the end of March Doubleday had agreed to take an option on the book if Asimov rewrote it and lengthened it to seventy thousand words. The option brought him $150 (of which Pohl, as his agent, kept $15) and the promise of $350 more, as an advance against standard royalties, if Doubleday liked the revisions and agreed to publish the novel.

Asimov completed his revisions on May 20, taking six and a half weeks. He was asked to provide a new title and came up with *Pebble in the Sky,* taken from a statement by one of his characters, a scientist named Shekt, that "Earth is but a pebble in the sky." Pohl picked up the manuscript and delivered it to Doubleday on May 22. A week later Walter Bradbury, the editor in charge of the new science-fiction line at Doubleday, called and told Asimov's wife that Doubleday was accepting the novel and had scheduled it for the following January.

When Asimov returned the corrected proofs to Bradbury on November 4, he described a new novel he might write. Bradbury told him to go ahead and write two chapters and an outline, and on that basis he would judge whether he wanted to offer a contract. Asimov was launched as a novelist and a writer of books. Books were to be the source of his future success and reputation and fortune, and *Pebble in the Sky* was to be number one in a list that would grow past two hundred. Before the year was over, Greenberg had offered Asimov a contract for publication of a collection of his robot stories, and Doubleday, an option on his new novel. Even this early in his book-publishing career, Asimov could look back on the rejection of "Grow Old with Me" by Merwin two and a half years earlier as the best thing that could have happened. "Doubleday," he recalled in his autobiography, "had found [the manuscript] more valuable because it had not been published and they might not have taken it if it had been. Since I wouldn't trade ten magazine appearances for that book, I now realized that Merwin had, all unwittingly, done me an enormous favor by rejecting it."

What was the novel that formed the cornerstone of Asimov's gigantic edifice of books? Asimov described it in these terms:

> It dealt with a tailor who managed to get transferred into a future in which old people underwent euthanasia unless they could prove themselves useful to society. The problem was to work out a way in which an old tailor from the past could prove useful enough to a society of the future to be kept alive.

The plot is more complicated than usual for Asimov fiction. The story develops along several simultaneous lines, beginning with the accidental translation (by means of an unrelated laboratory incident) of a sixty-two-year-old retired tailor named Joseph Schwartz to an Earth thousands of years in the future. That Earth has been turned radioactive by atomic wars so remote that the wars themselves have been forgotten. Earth is a neglected and detested world, poor in resources and populated by only 20 million people. It exists in the early period of Asimov's Galactic Empire, which is described at the time of its fall and disintegration in the Foundation stories. The Empire consists of 200 million inhabited planets. Fifty more each day are achieving provincial status. From the heart of that Empire a distinguished young archeologist named Bel Arvardan has come to Earth to find evidence to support his theory that humanity originated on Earth and radiated to other plants and to disprove the "merger" theory that humanity was the natural climax of evolution on any world with a water-oxygen chemical base and that each independent strain of humanity could intermarry.

Arvardan believes that life could not develop on planets that were naturally radioactive. Since only one radioactive planet is inhabited, Earth must have turned radioactive after life developed. Outsiders are forbidden to read the sacred book of Earthmen, The Book of the Ancients, but Arvardan has obtained parts of it and read statements that support his theory. He hopes to discover evidence of prior human habitation in areas now so intensely radioactive that humans cannot survive in them. His task is complicated by the anti-Terrestrialism that exists everywhere else in the Galaxy. Earthmen are considered dirty and diseased, ignorant and superstitious. Earth has a corresponding anti-Outside prejudice that counters the feelings of the rest of the Galaxy with an equally vehement hatred of everything non-Terrestrial. Arvardan considers himself free of prejudice, but in an episode in which he travels in an airplane with a group of Earthmen his belief is challenged.

Earth is so poor that everyone, with a few exceptions for unusual service or distinction, must submit to euthanasia at the age of sixty or when no longer productive. The law is called "the Sixties" and is so much a part of Earth culture that though it might be evaded, like taxes, acceptance is universal.

In another plot line, an Earth scientist named Affret Shekt has invented a Synapsifier, which reduces the resistance of non-nervous tissue between adjoining nerve cells and improves the quickness and effectiveness of thought. The process by which people undergo the treatment, however, is believed to be dangerous, often fatal. A farm family with whom Schwartz finds himself volunteer Schwartz, who is considered feebleminded, for the Synapsifier in the hope of rendering him capable of helping meet their farm quota for produce, for they are sheltering from euthanasia the wife's father, Grew, who has suffered a paralysis of the legs. The process makes Schwartz weak and confused, but as he recovers he learns the language quickly and then slowly develops the Mind Touch, the ability to read minds and then to kill with the mind, and finally the ability to immobilize others and even to control their gross physical movements.

Meanwhile, Arvardan, Schwartz, Shekt, and Shekt's daughter Pola find themselves enmeshed in a plot by the Society of Ancients to revenge themselves upon the rest of the Galaxy for the long history of oppression and anti-Terrestrial prejudice, and perhaps even to win control of the Galaxy and its riches for Earth. The plan is to send off toward a number of the planets in the Galaxy automatically guided missiles loaded with a mutated virus called Common Fever that is prevalent among Earthmen but fatal to Outsiders. The virus has been isolated and prepared in quantity by biological scientists treated secretly by Shekt's Synapsifier. The virus will sweep the Galaxy, destroying almost everyone within months unless the Empire surrenders and begs for the antitoxin. In the beginning, as the virus is spread to untouched planets by infected Outsiders, no one will even know that Earth is responsible.

The person in charge of the plot and the police state, with its spies and informers, is the secretary to the High Minister, a Machiavellian character named Balkis who looks for hidden motives behind every action. As in the Foundation stories, an assistant without real authority manipulates the High Minister, who is a figurehead. Balkis even has visions not simply of Earth's revenge but of himself as the new ruler of the Galaxy.

In a final subplot, Arvardan and Pola Shekt meet by accident and fall in love, although their romance is disrupted for a time by Pola's discovery that Arvardan is an Outsider.

All of these elements entwine themselves in a complicated series of events that ends with Schwartz setting off for the nearby city of Chica (Chicago) in order to avoid the Census and death, and being captured because of his lack of familiarity with the society in spite of the Mind Touch; Pola and her father revealing to Arvardan the plot against the Galaxy; and all of them captured and imprisoned together by Balkis, who has linked them all in his mind in a twisted but purely imaginary plot of agents and deceit. Although Balkis intends to kill them, Schwartz identifies with the Earthmen and their desire for revenge and does not want to interfere. But the others finally persuade him to use his strange mental powers to help them escape and reach a nearby Imperial garrison where they can reveal the impending attack.

In a climactic scene Arvardan is humiliated by an officer of the garrison and challenges the authority of the commanding officer. Eventually, he and the others are not believed even by Ennius, the Procurator, who finds Balkis's story more credible. Only after Schwartz has escaped and the time of the missiles' firing has passed does Balkis boast of his success and Ennius shamefacedly admit his error. At this point, Schwartz enters to reveal that he Mind-Touched an Imperial officer to fly him to Senloo (St. Louis) and bomb the building where the missiles and virus were ready to be sent off.

In the final chapter, the Galaxy is sending vast loads of soil to restore Earth. Schwartz has been decorated by the Empire and is about to leave with the newly married Arvardan and Pola Shekt on a tour of the Galaxy after which the Arvardans plan to return to Earth to work. Arvardan has become a naturalized citizen.

The novel has three major strengths. The first is the historical development of the Galactic Empire, a background that Asimov built with convincing detail through the Foundation stories and in other works. The Empire is ready-made for his use, and the lowly estate of the birthplace of humanity, which has been part of other stories (in the Foundation stories, the birthplace has been lost), serves as a satisfying irony. The second strength is the use of an elderly tailor as hero (at sixty-two, Schwartz must have seemed ancient to the twenty-nine-year-old Asimov and his by-and-large youthful readers). It was an act of daring in a genre that specialized in young men for action and older men for inventions. The choice of hero that may have put off Merwin and perhaps Campbell was ultimately rewarding: Schwartz is reasonably convincing and his development into a man of understanding and strange abilities turns the novel into something of a novel of character. The third strength is in its historical parallel: just as the Empire in *The Foundation Trilogy* is comparable to the Roman Empire when it began its long fall, so Earth in *Pebble in the Sky* is comparable to Judea under the rule of the Romans, when it was awaiting the Messiah.

Asimov's choice of the historical parallel is deliberate. As proof, one can point to his successful use of the same technique in the *Trilogy* and to his fascination with history. There is internal evidence as well: 1) Earthmen clearly represent the Jews; 2) the Empire's representative on Earth is called a Procurator, as was Pontius Pilate, the Roman administrator of Judea who condemned Jesus to the Cross; 3) Earthmen are bloodthirsty, always asking for the death penalty for one of themselves, as did the Jews when they were asked whether to spare Jesus (the High Minister says, ". . . my people are an obstinate and stiff-necked race . . ."); 4) Earth's extremists are called Zealots, as was the radical group that advocated the overthrow of Roman rule; and 5) at one point a troubled Ennius, like Pilate, says of Balkis, "I find no fault with this man." Though Ennius might double for Pilate, the Machiavellian Balkis as Christ stretches the parallel a bit. Perhaps it is not intended to be carried that far.

Asimov may have intended the comparison of Christ and Balkis to point up the significant fact that he is not simply rewriting history. Balkis is not Christ, just as *Pebble in the Sky* is not a simple retelling of the Judea story. Earth is a Judea with special characteristics; it is a Judea with radiation poisoning and institutionalized euthanasia, and it is a Judea given an opportunity to avenge its wrongs and regain its freedom. Asimov's critics (Damon Knight among them) who dismiss his historically inspired science fiction as merely the rewriting of history overlook the fact that the Galactic Empire in the Foundation stories is not the Roman Empire at the time of its fall but a Galactic Empire with foresight—psychohistory—to shorten the Dark Ages and with the Foundations not simply to preserve knowledge, as the monasteries did, but to add to it, disseminate it, and use it as the basis for a newer and more rational Galactic civilization.

Typically, however, Asimov does not allow Judea (Earth) to get its revenge and its freedom. Such short-sighted triumphs are foreign to Asimov's philosophy. He is not religious and dislikes Judaism as a form of "particularly pernicious nationalism. . . ." In *Pebble in the Sky* Asimov opts for civilization and sanity and understanding, which eventually will lead to the restoration of an Earth that was ravaged by the insanities of the little groups firmly convinced, each one, that it was better than the others.

Pebble in the Sky also has its weaknesses. The plot against the Galaxy is an isolated act intended to reverse the balance of power at one blow, unlike the more convincing context of actions in the Foundation stories, each one moving the Galaxy in some small way close to Hari Seldon's vision. Schwartz's bombing of the missile site, which occurs offstage like the violence in the Foundation stories, is a cutting of the Gordian knot that lacks the subtlety with which Asimov unravels his better works. Balkis's insistence on perceiving complicated plots in accidental relationships may be credible considering his own machinations but seems more an authorial convenience in light of the fact that his own conniving rather than someone else's determination brings about his downfall.

In fact, weakness of motivation is the major flaw of the novel. Events happen for the novel's reasons—to keep it going—rather than the characters' reasons. Schwartz just happens to be projected into the future and just happens to stumple into the home of the one family that has reason to take him in. Shekt just happens to have advertised for volunteers on which to test the Synapsifier just before Schwartz arrives from the past (why did Shekt need to test the Synapsifier, since he already had used it on a number of the Society of Ancients' biologists, and why did the Society allow him to advertise?). The crippled Grew just happens to read about it, and the family just happens to decide to volunteer Schwartz for it to cure his mental deficiencies. Later on, Schwartz just happens to escape from the Institute (he has no reason) as Arvardan is passing by, and Pola, going in search of him, just happens to meet Arvardan. Natter, Balkis's agent, just happens to decide to save Schwartz from being captured by Imperial soldiers, and even that decision seems inadequately motivated. Fortunate incidents accumulate. Few of them happen because they must, but all of them are necessary to the manipulations of the story. This leads Asimov to various kinds of shoring-up processes of which Balkis's conspiracy mania is the grossest example. Without it, none of the rest of the events would have mattered: the missiles would have gone off as scheduled and Earth would have had its will of the Galaxy.

Perhaps a simpler explanation for the weakness of *Pebble in the Sky* is that it lacked Asimov's basic method, the puzzle or the mystery. The puzzle or mystery approach provides not only a reasonable and convincing structure for a story, as an individual or a group tries to find a solution to the puzzle or mystery, it also supplies credible motivation.

Asimov's next novel, the one that he described to Bradbury after he had handed him the corrected proofs to *Pebble in the Sky*, had the Asimov method but was weakened by its unsatisfactory solution to the mystery. As a consequence, *The Stars, Like Dust* is Asimov's least favorite novel, although he ascribes his feelings to his attempt to use an outline when writing the book, the last time he did so. Possibly it also suffered from second-novel problems. Asimov recounts in his autobiography that the first two chapters and outline that he turned over to Bradbury on Christmas 1949 were not well received. Bradbury gave him a $250 option to keep working but threw out the chapters Asimov had submitted. "I had apparently committed the customary sin of the sophomore novel," Asimov wrote. "The first novel was fine since I was writing as a novice and had no reputation to uphold. Once it was accepted, however, I was a 'novelist' and had to write the second novel while keeping that reputation secure, which meant to write deeply and poetically and wittily and so on."

Bradbury provided some necessary guidance. He rejected a new version of the first third of *The Stars, Like Dust*, sending it back "copiously red-penciled," but he liked the third try and authorized Asimov to complete the novel. Asimov also got advice from Horace Gold, who had been shown part of the novel by Pohl. Gold wanted to serialize the novel in *Galaxy*, which was good news. Gold's suggestions, however, were not as welcome as Bradbury's.

Eventually, the novel was serialized in *Galaxy* under Gold's title, *Tyrann*, which Asimov disliked. "An absolutely silly title," he called it, and added that "Gold was a good editor, but his taste in titles was execrable." That too contributed to Asimov's feelings about the novel.

The Stars, Like Dust is an adventure story without any meaningful theme or concept. The story is set in Asimov's future history considerably before *Pebble in the Sky*, perhaps one thousand years in our future. (Early in the novel, one character reflects on the "Earthman's habit of building structures of reinforced concrete, squat, thick, and windowless. It was a thousand-year-old tradition dating from the days when the primitive nuclear bomb had not yet been countered by the force-shield defense.") Mankind is still spreading out to the stars, but the Galactic Empire is not yet even a dream; rather, various kinds of governmental systems are being tried. At one point in the novel, Gillbret oth Hinriad describes the four stages of development of a new planet: 1) agriculture or ranching to feed itself; 2) mining and exportation of agricultural surpluses; 3) beginnings of industrialization; 4) mechanization, importation of food, exportation of machinery, investment in development of more primitive worlds. Certain kinds of government are appropriate to each stage, he suggests. Most governments are autocracies, either hereditary or elective, but one planet, because it was initially barren, directed its inhabitants outward for conquest. The Tyranni have conquered fifty worlds with their advanced spaceships, their Spartan culture, and their military skills.

Earth, which is dangerously radioactive in many spots, still is recognized as the birthplace of humanity, and to its university, the University of Earth, come students from many other planets. One of them is Biron Farrill, son of the ruler called the Rancher of Widemos of the agricultural planet Nephelos. Farrill is within a few days of graduation when he is awakened in the night by a visiphone call from a fellow student, Sandor Jonti. But the sending part of the visiphone does not work. Neither do the lights, ventilation, or door when Farrill tries to escape a "radiation bomb" building toward explosion in his closet. Then Jonti blasts the lock, releases him, and tells him his life is in danger; his father has been arrested by the Tyranni and may have been executed. Biron under an alias, should go to the planet of Rhodia and the court of the Director of Rhodia, Hinrik, who has influence with the Tyranni and may be able to get Biron reinstated as his father's successor. Biron reflects that he has not found the Earth document his father had asked him to locate but decides to leave as Jonti suggests. In a personal-beam transmission from the planet Lingane, Jonti learns that the Rancher of Widemos has indeed been executed. Jonti says that Farrill is expendable. A bit later he learns from Rizzett, his agent, that the document both he and Farrill had been seeking has been missing for twenty years.

Meanwhile, Farrill has had his stateroom changed and his

luggage moved on board the spaceship to Rhodia. He learns
that papers revealing his identity have been removed. When
he arrives on Rhodia he is hauled before Simok Aratap, the
Tyranni in charge of the Rhodian sector. Farrill, however,
denies that he is Farrill and the Rancher's son and is allowed
to go to the court of the Director, although Aratap recognizes
that Farrill is lying and, as is revealed in the next chapter,
Farrill realizes that Aratap knows it.

The Director of Rhodia is selected from its own family
members by the ruling house, the Hinriads. Able rulers have
been selected; even adoptions are encouraged. But Tyrannian
conquest brought in different ideas. The conquerors helped to
select Hinrik, who is a terrorized fool. Hinrik tries to persuade
his daughter Artemesia (Arta) to agree to marry an aged noble-
man of the Tyrannian court, but she refuses. When Farrill is
brought to Hinrik, and says he has information that Hinrik's
life is in danger, Hinrik leaves Farrill with Arta. Hinrik's cousin
Gillbret also talks to Farrill and later that evening invites Farrill to his laboratory, where Gillbret reveals that his foolish
chatter is just a pose. He works with spy beams and has invented a new musical and visual instrument that works on the
nerve endings. He calls it a "visisonor." (In *The Foundation
Trilogy* the Mule plays a visisonor—there spelled Visi-Sonor—
an instrument, resurrected from a museum, that no one else
knows how to play properly.) Gillbret wants Farrill to take
Arta and him away from Rhodia in a visiting spaceship.
Spaceship piloting is a forbidden art in Tyranni-controlled
areas, but Farrill has learned it at the University of Earth. Before Farrill can act, however, palace guards invade the laboratory to arrest him. With the aid of Gillbret's visisonor, Farrill
breaks free and gets to Arta's room before the search catches
up. Arta conceals him, and they and Gillbret escape, with Farrill in the uniform of a Rhodian palace guard.

Aratap has arrived, however, in a Tyrannian spaceship to
answer Hinrik's call, and the spaceport is lighted. Farrill and
the Hinriads escape in Aratap's Tyrannian ship. This turns out
to be a mistake, for Tyrannian ships can be traced. They have
other secret abilities as well, such as being able to program a
series of Jumps through hyperspace. Gillbret reveals that more

than twenty years before he had attended the coronation of the present Khan of Tyrann. On his way back to Rhodia the Tyrannian spaceship in which he was traveling was hit by a meteorite, the two crew members were killed, and the control board possibly was damaged as well. But the ship made several automatic Jumps, and at the end of the last Jump men came from a planet in answer to Gillbret's radio message and took him and the ship into underground areas where men from all parts of the Kingdoms were preparing for rebellion against Tyrann. Gillbret was rendered unconscious and woke up in the Tyrannian spaceship floating in space off Rhodia. He has never told this story to anyone before except the Autarch of Lingane, whose name and position in the conspiracy he learned from conversations overheard by spy beam between Farrill's father and Hinrik six months before. But the Autarch had been unwilling to discuss any conspiracy.

Gillbret, Farrill, and Arta resolve to seek out the Autarch and to find the rebellion world. En route, Farrill and Arta fall in love. The Autarch turns out to be Jonti. After Farrill accuses Jonti of using him as a pawn, which the Autarch frankly admits, the Autarch speculates that the rebellion world may be located in the Horsehead Nebula. On Earth he found the coordinates of five stars inside the Nebula that Gillbret's course could have taken him near. The Autarch also accuses Hinrik of having been instrumental in the Rancher's death. This leads to a growing coldness between Farrill and Arta and a growing involvement of Arta with the Autarch as they Jump toward the Nebula and begin exploring the five stars.

The first three are without planets. The group lands to explore a planet of the fourth sun; it has an oxygen atmosphere but no carbon dioxide and is cold and barren besides. Farrill and the Autarch go out to set up a radio transmitter with which to try to contact the rebels, who have not responded to messages from space. But they could be underground or in a hidden valley. Arta sees Rizzett following Farrill and the Autarch with a long-range blasting rifle and follows Rizzett. Farrill reveals that he has accompanied the Autarch knowing that the Autarch planned to kill him and that the Autarch was guilty of his father's death. As the Autarch pulls a blaster out of the radio equipment, he admits his intentions and his guilt. But the blaster has no charge, and the radio communicator switch was shorted so that everyone, including the Autarch's crew, heard his admissions. Rizzett, it turns out, had been on Farrill's side because he had begun to suspect his leader of treachery, including the killing of the Rancher of Widemos.

Farrill helps Arta back to the ship (she had blacked out when running toward Rizzett to stop him, she thinks, from shooting Farrill from the exertion and from failure to breathe properly because of the absence of carbon dioxide). He confesses to her that he had feigned coldness in order to set up the Autarch. Arta forgives him. But as Farrill is addressing the Autarch's crew members in order to obtain their allegiance, Aratap and his soldiers surround them and take them prisoner. They also had heard the conversation between Farrill and the Autarch.

Aratap tries to persuade the prisoners, one at a time, to betray the location of the rebellion world, but they remain silent, all except the Autarch, who is willing to provide the coordinates of the fifth Nebular star if Aratap will kill Farrill. Rizzett is furious in spite of Farrill's attempts to calm him and when the Autarch reveals the coordinates Rizzett grabs a blaster and kills him. Farrill says that this is what Aratap wanted to have happen.

In the confusion, however, Gillbret escaped. He is found in the engine room. Later, his mind and body failing, he reveals to Farrill that he has shorted the hyperatomics so that the ship will blow up when it tries to make a Jump. Farrill, unable to convince the guard of his improvised prison cell, escapes and finally is brought to Aratap, who has the Jump delayed until the short is found. Gillbret dies.

The ship reaches the fifth sun, and Aratap discovers that the star went nova less than a million years before. Aratap says that he now believes, as Farrill has insisted, that there is no rebellion world. Aratap releases the four captives (including Hinrik, who accompanied him from Rhodia) and sends them back to Rhodia. Since there is no rebellion world, he says, it is politically expedient to keep the situation as it is and not reveal in a public trial the rumors of a rebellion world that might trouble Tyrannian rule for a century.

On their own ship, Farrill reveals that Gillbret must have been taken to Rhodia in the Tyrannian ship's final Jump. That was his original destination, and the possibility of a random Jump arriving near a star when space is so large and stars so comparatively few is so unlikely as to be unbelievable. The rebellion world, then, is within the Rhodia system. Arta exclaims that this would mean her father is in terrible danger, but Farrill reveals that Hinrik has known about it for twenty years, indeed, has been the head of it and has been playing the part of a fool so that he can organize rebellion without interference. It was the valuable life of Hinrik that Farrill was trying to save from Gillbret's shorting of the hyperatomics.

Hinrik confesses his deception, marries Arta and Farrill, and reveals that he knows what Earth document the Rancher had asked Farrill to find because he has had it for twenty years: the Constitution of the United States of America. This blueprint, which dealt with a small section of one planet, can be adapted to all the Galaxy and will mean the end of such feudal despotisms as that of the Tyranni but also of the more enlightened rules of the Director of Rhodia and the Rancher of Widemos. Democracy will be the new governmental system.

The Constitution being the valuable document was forced on Asimov by Gold and accepted gleefully by Bradbury. Asimov, in his autobiography, objected to it as "corny and unbelievable. No one could suppose that an instrument of government suitable for a primitive nation forming a small part of a single world would be suitable for a stellar federation." But Asimov managed to make the document as plausible as anything else, which may not be saying a great deal.

Almost everything in the novel lacks the conviction and credibility that distinguish typical Asimov fiction. Farrill has no good reason to go to Rhodia from Earth, nor does the Autarch have any convincing reason for wanting him to go there. Aratap's allowing Farrill to go to Hinrik and Farrill's pursuing that original plan in spite of his knowledge that Aratap is onto him are equally unconvincing. Gillbret and Arta's need to escape is flimsy. Gillbret's story of his encounter with the rebellion world is strewn with coincidences that are only partially justified by the revelation that he arrived in the Rhodian system. Even then there is no good explanation for the fact that his first radio messages are picked up by the rebels but not the Rhodians or the Tyranni. The Autarch's reasons for believing that the rebellion world is inside the Horsehead Nebula are finally exposed as even flimsier than anyone had suspected. If Gillbret overheard Hinrik and the Rancher discussing the Autarch, he must have heard Hinrik not playing the fool, but he betrays no knowledge of Hinrik's act. And Aratap's reasons for letting them go at the end, even though Hinrik plants the thought that Aratap is as intelligent as Farrill and has followed the same line of reasoning and will continue to watch them with the hope that they will lead him to the rebels, are more convenient than plausible.

The major problem of the novel is that it proceeds by concealment of information from the reader and by misunderstanding. In the best Asimov fiction, characters may try to deceive others, but their own motives are clear. In The Stars, Like Dust nobody has sound motivation for what they do, with the possible exceptions of Aratap and the Autarch, both of whom intend to repress or use to their own advantage whatever is going on, and both of whom lose. The novel is a mystery. It offers three questions: 1) what is the mysterious document for which Farrill and the Autarch are searching, why is it missing, where is it, and why is it important? 2) who betrayed the Rancher of Widemos? and 3) where is the rebellion world? The answers to some of these questions, such as the name of the mysterious document, are known to the characters but concealed from the reader; other answers are known by some characters, who are never asked the right questions; and still other answers are known by Farrill long before they are revealed.

Lack of a clear narrative focus leads to false climaxes. The phony attempt on Farrill's life is typical: it leads to Jonti's warning that Farrill's life is in danger (but mostly from Jonti); to the statement by Jonti that Farrill is expendable and to the kind of Mary Roberts Rinehart school of foreshadowing that ends Chapter Two with "Nothing had been left to chance" and Chapter Six with "then he knew what he had to do"; to the statement at the end of Chapter Three that "the ship was carrying him politely, but surely, to his death"; and to Aratap's revelation that his concealed knowledge of Farrill's identity had been "careful maneuvering" that was "cruel" and yet "necessary," while the reader learns, the next time Farrill is encountered, that Farrill knew Aratap was not deceived. Who is maneuvering whom? Asimov and the reader seem to fit best into that equation.

The novel has rewards. The characters are interesting—particularly those of Aratap and the Autarch, and, in a lesser sense because more derivative, those of Hinrik and Gillbret. Aratap is a kind of Balkis (of Pebble in the Sky) without Balkis's weaknesses. Aratap too is a manipulator. He too suspects plots and conspiracies. He too believes he has everything under control. The difference between the two is that Aratap does not act rashly or foolishly, and in the case of The Stars, Like Dust a conspiracy of sorts actually exists. Moreover, Aratap is not vindictive, and at the end he is not certainly defeated.

Farrill, the juvenile lead, grows in a way that resembles Schwartz more than Arvardan. At the end, Farrill's insights bring the novel to a satisfying conclusion, though at the sacrifice of some credibility because the reader cannot see Farrill grow as he or she can see Schwartz do so.

The novel has a few other redeeming aspects, particularly the explanations of physical and social phenomena that may foreshadow the science popularizer to come: a good explanation of hyperspace; a justification of government; a description of the difficulties of stellar navigation; and a discussion of how a plutocracy becomes an autocracy. Finally, the novel offers an effective climactic scene in which Farrill resists Aratap's manipulations.

The Currents of Space led Asimov back to the theme and substance that he was to celebrate in his two robot novels. He described his next novel as "a complicated story of interstellar intrigue and racism." It too began as a novel for Doubleday, which Bradbury approved in idea form on December 28, 1950. On April 4, 1951, he offered Asimov a contract on the basis of the material he had seen, skipping the option phase. It was another step forward for Asimov. Asimov decided to offer the serialization right to Campbell, since he felt guilty about the frequent appearance of his work in *Galaxy*.

The novel took Asimov more than a year to write. He was also busy with his first textbook, a collaboration with two Boston University School of Medicine colleagues, William C. Boyd and Burnham S. Walker, that soured him on collaborating but whetted his appetite for science writing; the first of the juvenile novels he would write under the name Paul French, *David Starr: Space Ranger;* and various shorter projects. He finished *The Currents of Space* on March 30, 1952, and learned on April 17 that Campbell had accepted it for serialization.

The Currents of Space is also a novel that conceals information from the reader. In the Prolog, a character identified as "the man from Earth," who works for the Interstellar Spatio-analytic Bureau (I.S.B.), is being detained by an unnamed man. The Earthman wants to broadcast information that a planet named Florina is to be destroyed. The other man thinks that would cause panic and do no good. The second man says he will remove the Earthman's anxiety with a psychic probe, but darkness comes over the Earthman's mind. "Some of it never lifted again. It took years for even parts of it to lift."

Rik, a mentally incapacitated man known to others as "Crazy Rik," has turned up on a planet that the reader soon learns is Florina. He has been adopted by a childless woman named Valona March, who has nursed him back to health and to some awareness of what is going on around him. She knows Rik's mind has been "turned off," that he once was an educated man. She gets him a job in the kyrt mills, where a kind of miracle fiber is made into cloth. Gradually he begins to remember things from the past: first, that he had a job analyzing "Nothing," and second, that everybody on Florina is going to die. Valona wants him for forget and to stay where he is because she has found out from a doctor she took him to see (who died a week later in a gyro-crash) that Rik had been psycho-probed; she is afraid of losing him. But Rik insists that he must leave the mill and the village and find out more about himself.

Valona goes for help to Myrlyn Terens, the Townman who is the local representative of the absentee landlords, the Squires of Sark. Terens takes Rik to the City. All other cities on Florina have names, but this one is simply the "City" and is shadowed by Upper City, "a horizontal layer of fifty square miles of cementalloy resting upon some twenty thousand steel-girdered pillars" where the citizens of Sark live while on Florina, along with a sprinkling of mercenary "patrollers." Terens is a Florinian native who was educated on Sark, the home planet of the Squires. He hates them and plans to use Rik to get revenge on them. He takes Rik to the Upper City library where Rik, with help, discovers the *Encyclopedia of Sark* article on Spatio-analysis. The article mentions that the Spatio-analyst is "an introverted and, often enough, malajusted individual." The official slogan of the Spatio-analyst Institute is "We Analyze Nothing." Rik realizes that he was a Spatio-analyst. But when he tries to consult other books, instructions direct him to the Librarian. The Librarian accosts him and Terens, and they are confronted by an overage patroller before Valona shows up and knocks out the patroller with his own neuronic whip.

The three escape from Upper City by elevator but are pursued by patrollers. A passerby tells them to seek help at Khorov's bakery, where they slip through a dummy radar furnace (a forecast of the microwave oven) into a hidden room. The baker, Khorov, seems to know a great deal about the situation. He leaves a door open so Terens can leave and tells Valona she can leave but that Rik must stay.

Meanwhile, on Sark, Dr. Selim Junz, a Spatio-analyst from Libair (a planet perhaps originally settled by blacks fleeing Liberia), has been searching for a Spatio-analyst who disappeared nearly a year before, who was last reported in space near Sark. A message had been received from a field man that "the life of every human being on Florina was in danger" and "All Galaxy affected," but field men are considered strange, if not psychopathic. The Sarkites, however, insist that the Spatio-analyst did not land on Sark. In past consultation with the old Trantorian ambassador, Ludigan Abel, Junz revealed his

conviction that the Spatio-analyst landed on Sark and was imprisoned and probably killed because the Sarkites could not
stand to have the whole dirty mess of Sark-Florina political
relationships exposed to the Galaxy. Junz had asked Abel to
find out if the Spatio-analyst was killed. Junz asked the Sarkites to place standard works about Spatio-analysis on reserve
in libraries and to report non-Sarkites who ask for them. If the
Spatio-analyst has become psychotic, the details of his job will
return to his mind first.

More than eleven months later no sign of the missing field
man has been found. Junz is almost ready to quit when he
receives word that someone has requested two standard Spatio-analysis texts at the Florinian branch of the Public Library
of Sark. In discussion with the clerk who reveals this information, Junz learns that the fugitives have been traced to the
Khorov bakery and have been allowed to remain there because
Khorov is a well-known agent of Trantor.

Terens, during his escape from the bakery shop, reflects on
his experience of being taken to Sark as a boy and being so
disillusioned by discriminations against Florinians that he
learned to hate the Sarkites. He also learned to shun Sarkite
agents provocateurs and the conspiracies of Trantor, the gigantic Empire that has expanded to encompass half the inhabited worlds of the Galaxy. Then Rik, the Spatio-analyst, fell
into his hands as the ultimate weapon against Sark.

As Junz goes to see Abel again, Abel reflects on the progress of the Trantorian Empire, which has grown from a republic of five worlds five hundred years earlier to a Trantorian
Confederation and now a Trantorian Empire trembling on the
verge of becoming a Galactic Empire. Abel is uncertain what
to do about Junz and the I.S.B. and the missing Spatio-analyst.
Even if Sark could be proven to be guilty of killing or imprisoning the Spatio-analyst, Abel does not want to provide an
occasion for the remaining non-Trantorian half of the Galaxy
to unite against the Empire. He is upset about Junz's obsession
with exposing and destroying the relationship between Sark
and Florina rather than the larger Galactic issues of unifica-
tion or war. Junz feels so strongly about Sark's tyranny over
Florina because he is dark-skinned and Florinians are un-

usually pale. When faced with Junz's anger, Abel reveals that Khorov is dead, and the fugitives are apparently in the hands of the Sarkites. But in an Asimov novel not everything is what it seems: Khorov had helped Rik and Valona on their way to the spaceport by giving them identification documents. Khorov is killed by a patroller, and Rik and Valona get away in the crowd. Rik persuades Valona to sneak aboard a spaceship with him, but not the one to which Khorov had directed them because he does not trust Khorov and patrollers might be waiting there. Rik's returning memory about spaceship construction and procedures allows them to stow away. After take-off Rik explains to Valona that his job used to be analyzing "the currents of space," the small differences in trace elements that pervade space. He gathered information that is important to ships in calculating their Jumps and is also of possible help in explaining the creation of the universe and its evolution. In the midst of his explanation, Rik remembers the face of the patroller who shot Khorov; it was Terens. They had made a mistake stowing away on a ship.

Meanwhile, on the spaceship Captain Racety has relayed to Lady Samia of Fife an order from her father, the Great Squire of Fife, to return to Sark. She is reluctant to interrupt her research on kyrt. Kyrt is a variety of cotton that on Florina becomes a shining miracle fiber stronger than steel alloys that is used mostly for luxury fabrics. It provides the source of Sark's wealth and the reason for Florina's subjugation. No one knows why kyrt seeds grow into kyrt on Florina and into an inferior grade of cotton anywhere else. Captain Racety discovers the two stowaways.

Back on Florina, Terens learns that Rik and Valona have stowed away on board the ship belonging to the Squire of Fife, one of the five Great Squires, each of whom has his own continent. They have grown powerful in the kyrt trade in a way that Trantor cannot match. They will risk Galactic war rather than give up Florina. Fife is the most powerful of the five. Almost a year ago he had called a meeting by trimensic personification (a process used again later in *The Naked Sun*), in which he shared a blackmail note containing information about the impending destruction of Florina. Fife also told the Squires that a Spatio-analyst had disappeared and sent a message mentioning the destruction of Florina. Fife suggested that Trantor was trying to blackmail them, that they should try to find the Spatio-analyst, and that they should await a second message. It never came. Now Fife calls them together again and speaks of high treason.

Meanwhile (there are many "meanwhiles" as the point of view shifts chapter by chapter and even within chapters to pick up another part of the action), Terens has taken an elevator to Upper City, goes to City Park, stuns a Squire with his neuronic whip, dresses himself in the Squire's clothing, and then incinerates the Squire to delay pursuit.

Lady Samia, on board the spaceship, insists on talking to Rik and Valona. Under questioning, Rik remembers that he is from Earth. Lady Samia and the Captain have never heard of Earth, but the Captain has heard of the Sirius Sector and subsequently remembers that Earth is the planet that claims to be the birthplace of humanity. Rik also remembers being a Spatio-analyst, that Florina and possibly the Milky Way are in danger, and the interview on Sark described in the Prolog. He doesn't remember, however, what was done to him or by whom. Before he can be questioned again, Captain Racety receives a message to hold the two for the Department of Security (DepSec).

Meanwhile, the Squire of Fife tells the other Great Squires about the recent events on Florina and speculates about their meaning and the actions involving the Spatio-analyst that lie behind them. He suggests that one of the Great Squires intercepted the Spatio-analyst, intended to blackmail the other Squires, kept the Spatio-analyst around for further information, and used a psycho-probe on him before transporting him to Florina where he could be kept safely and checked periodically. Fife believes that his earlier conference scared off the blackmailer. He tells them that officers loyal to him have taken over the Navy and that he is taking control of a united Sark. Rik, Valona, and the Townman are in his hands. What he does not know is that the DepSec man bringing in the Townman is a Trantorian agent.

The Great Squire of Steen flees to the Trantorian Embassy

to ask for Trantorian intervention in return for Trantorian participation in the kyrt trade, but Abel refuses, suggesting instead that he will ask to interview the Spatio-analyst, holding possession of the Townman as a threat to Fife. But at the spaceport Terens enters Lady Samia's car at her invitation. In a mad moment he kisses her just as a pursuing car catches up and Trantorian agents take a picture of them embracing before they make off with him.

Abel blackmails Fife into a meeting by threatening to release the picture, a threat that can work only in Sark's sick social system. Steen, who has gone with Abel, accuses Fife of being the guilty Great Squire. Abel questions Rik and asks what he remembers. The only thing Rik can remember is the word "Fife," then a man named Fife looking down at him. Fife, whose legs are much shorter than his torso, gets down from his chair to demonstrate that he could not have looked down at a seated man.

Terens, who is present in trimensic personification, is questioned by Junz about the Squires who might have come to the village where he was Townman to keep track of Rik. Terens cannot remember any Squires or any patrollers who exhibited an undue interest. Then Valona points out that Terens was the only one who knew everything and watched everything. Terens admits that he was the psycho-prober. He had been temporary traffic manager at the spaceport when the Spatio-analyst landed, had identified himself as the Squire of Fife, had sent the blackmail letter, and had used a psychic probe to remove the anxiety from the surface layer of the Spatio-analyst's mind. But because Rik was a Spatio-analyst, the anxiety went much deeper, and the probe dug out most of the conscious mind along with it. Terens then arranged to be transferred to Florina as Townman and took the Spatio-analyst along with him on forged papers. Terens reveals that, according to the Spatio-analyst, Florina's sun is in the pre-nova stage. All he can remember about the details is "the carbon current of space" and "catalytic effect."

Up to now, no one has been able to predict novas. Junz points out, however, that one of the two stellar nuclear transformations uses carbon as an intermediate stage, or catalyst, in the process of changing hydrogen into helium. He speculates that Rik has traced a carbon current in space and that a star passing through a current containing unusual concentrations of carbon becomes unstable, the star's radiation is boosted tremendously, and the outer layers explode into a nova.

Both Fife and Abel raise doubts about the evacuation of Florina on the basis of such an unsubstantiated theory. Junz points out, however, that the matter concerns the whole Galaxy, since twenty full novas occur every year and another two thousand stars shift their radiation characteristics sufficiently to render their planets uninhabitable. Every fifty years, then, an inhabited planet becomes too hot for life, and every five thousand years some inhabited planet has a fifty-fifty chance of being puffed to gas by a nova. If Trantor does nothing for Florina, the other people in the Galaxy will feel that nothing will be done for them either if help is in the way of the economic convenience of a few powerful men.

Abel still is not convinced until Junz points out that Florina produces kyrt because its sun is in the pre-nova stage. With this information, it will be possible to produce kyrt anywhere. Junz suggests that Trantor buy Florina from Sark and evacuate it. Terens is put in charge of the evacuation.

In an Epilog, a year later, Florina has been almost completely evacuated. Rik and Valona are married, and Rik is content to go back to Earth and work there, unfit any longer to be a Spatio-analyst because the anxiety that made him one is gone but able to live once more on the radioactive Earth that had made him anxious. Terens, going down with his planet, has been granted permission to stay on Florina until the end.

In spite of the obvious improvements of *The Currents of Space* over *The Stars, Like Dust*, the book also has some clear weaknesses. The apparent hero and heroine, Rik and Valona, are more acted upon that actors, and they develop little during the progress of the novel. The role of the real hero, Terens, who precipitates the events of the novel out of his rage at the Squires and love for Florina, is obscured because of plot necessities.

Shifts between actors in the complex situation artificially conceals information from the reader that might naturally be revealed, from the Prolog almost to the end. This is particularly artificial when the viewpoint is Terens's and reveals some of his thoughts and memories but not all. Asimov's best novels—the robot novels and *The End of Eternity*—follow a single character throughout. The reader learns only what the character learns in search of a solution to a mystery. At this relatively early period in his experience as a writer of novels, Asimov may have felt uneasy about his ability to sustain a prolonged narrative while focusing on a single character. Shifting to other characters and other actions allowed him to put the novel together like a series of alternating stories.

The sequence of flashbacks required by the concern about events of the previous year seems both a weakness and a strength. The continual shifts in time create a certain amount of confusion and a grasping for tenses, but the relationship between past and present, once the rhythm has been established, creates effective juxtapositions that have relevance to the theme.

The characterizations are a strength of the novel. Unlike *The Stars, Like Dust*, the characters in *The Currents of Space* are less stereotyped and more lifelike, from the memory-damaged Rik and the loyal Valona to the angry Terens, the pragmatic Abel, and the powerful dwarf, Fife. They are better drawn, no doubt, because they are better motivated. In addition, Asimov's language is groping its way toward the economy of the robot novels. The social commentary on racial prejudice, developed through the counterpoint of the white-skinned cotton-pickers of Florina, makes the statements that slavery is economic, not racial, and that racial prejudice can be applied to any color of skin and be equally reprehensible and repugnant.

Most important, the subject of the novels, the coming destruction of a planet and ultimately the discovery of a process for identifying incipient novas, is momentous. Readers feel that the twists and turns of the plot are not simply manipulations. The suspense is not built artificially, in spite of the withholding of the psycho-prober's identity, but has a natural momentum. Events finally justify themselves. The novel also shows another stage in the development of the Galactic Empire, which then falls in *The Foundation Trilogy.*

Moreover, the novel unfolds as a mystery. It offers three important questions to be answered. At one point Lady Samia lists them:

> The three points were therefore these. (1) What was the danger that threatened Florina, or, rather, the entire Galaxy? (2) Who was the person who had psycho-probed the Earthman? (3) Why had the person used the psycho-probe?

Asimov's method works best when he offers a mystery to be solved, questions to be answered that clearly must be answered and whose answers justify the concern raised about them.

In 1961 *The Currents of Space, Pebble in the Sky,* and *The Stars, Like Dust* were reprinted in an omnibus volume under the title *Triangle.*

The Asimov juveniles originated March 22, 1951, at lunch with Bradbury and Pohl. Asimov considered the suggestion that he write a juvenile science-fiction novel modeled after radio's long-running series, *The Lone Ranger.* It might lead to a television series featuring a Space Ranger that would make millions for all concerned. No one present—science-fiction editor, agent, or writer—dreamed that television, then in its early years, would have few long-running series. Asimov speculated in his autobiography that the reason for this was that "the addition of the sense of vision enormously hastened a sense of satiation." No one knew, either, that a juvenile television series, *Rocky Jones, Space Ranger,* already was in the works.

What bothered Asimov, rather, was the uniform awfulness of everything on television (with the single exception of the Sid Caesar-Imogene Coca *Your Show of Shows*). He did not want his name associated with the medium. (Television people, if they had known Asimov's opinion, might well have smiled at the veteran of pulps with garish covers and untrimmed edges, but Asimov would have defended the intrinsic value of the contents.) Bradbury said, "Use a pseudonym," and Asimov agreed to do it. Following the example of Cornell Woolrich, who chose a nationality for his pseudonym William Irish, Asimov selected the name "Paul French." When it became apparent that the Space Ranger would not end up on television, Asimov dropped the Space Ranger paraphernalia and put the juveniles under his real name as soon as possible.

He wrote *David Starr: Space Ranger* quickly; it was completed on July 29. (His juveniles are no longer than 50,000 words compared to the 60,000 to 70,000 of his adult novels.) Doubleday got it into print in near-record time, and Asimov had an advance copy by January 15, 1952. By the time it was published, Asimov's relationship with Doubleday had changed. He had only to say he would do another and Doubleday produced a contract and advance. The second juvenile, *Lucky Starr and the Pirates of the Asteroids,* was written between July 5 and October 24, 1952. (Starr had been named David, after his son, and was nicknamed Lucky in the second and subsequent books because Asimov decided David was too pedestrian for a space adventurer.) Within little more than a month Asimov began work on *The Caves of Steel.*

The third novel in the juvenile series, *Lucky Starr and the Oceans of Venus,* required some revision that Asimov thought justified. (Doubleday objected to Starr's being so close-mouthed that his loyal partner thinks he is "an utter bastard"). The final manuscript was submitted on March 17, 1953, and published in 1954. A year went by without a Lucky Starr novel. Asimov was busy with *The End of Eternity* and a series of science books he had begun to write for Abelard-Schuman (*The Chemicals of Life,* 1954; *Races and People,* 1955; and *Inside the Atom,* 1956) and for McGraw-Hill (*Chemistry and Human Health,* 1956). He also was busy with short stories and with the cares of a homeowner, for he and his wife had bought their first house. *Lucky Starr and the Big Sun of Mercury* appeared in 1956, *Lucky Starr and the Moons of Jupiter* in 1957, and *Lucky Starr and the Rings of Saturn* in 1958.

The juveniles were in the older style of the science-fiction adventure story that Jules Verne had pioneered, H. G. Wells had stooped to upon occasion (notably for a good part of *The*

First Men in the Moon), and E. E. "Doc" Smith and John W. Campbell (in his earlier writing) had adapted to the new science-fiction magazines. The formula that evolved requires two (or sometimes more) continuing characters, usually a hero and his best friend. The hero usually is a scientist and the best friend does not understand much science but is loyal and good in a fight. A great deal of conversation takes place between the hero and his friend in which the science of the story is explained, and a certain amount of byplay is involved that substitutes for characterization and stage action, created by the difficulties the hero's friend gets into through his hot temper and rash actions. One might note a certain resemblance of the hero and his friend to the Lone Ranger and his loyal Indian sidekick, Tonto.

In the Asimov juveniles, the scientist hero is David "Lucky" Starr, a member of Earth's Council of Science at an astonishingly youthful age. The friend is John "Bigman" Jones, who is five feet two but strong and sensitive about his height. In the first book, Starr picks up Jones on Mars. With humanity flying about among the planets and even among the stars, science has become of constantly increasing importance, for solving both internal problems of health and energy and external problems of scientific and alien threats to Earth. So the Council of Science has become a major political force on Earth, and Starr is its best roving investigator.

He roves first to Mars, then to the Asteroids, third to Venus, fourth to Mercury, fifth to Jupiter, and sixth to Saturn. It is clear that Asimov intended to visit each of the planets [1] and possibly expand his arena to other star systems, but Starr (and Asimov) ran out of gas at Saturn, with Neptune, Uranus, and Pluto still to go.

Asimov's juvenile novels added little to the development of science fiction, or to Asimov's reputation, or even to the development of the science-fiction juvenile. They were largely scientific exposition with a frosting of narrative to keep the youthful reader involved between discussions. In contrast, Robert A. Heinlein's juveniles, once he developed his skills at

1. In Volume Two of his autobiography Asimov wrote that the next book, if he had written it, would have been *Lucky Starr and the Snows of Pluto*.

the genre beginning with *Red Planet* in 1949, were so thoroughly science-fiction novels that most were serialized in adult magazines. One might speculate that the Heinlein juveniles lead young readers to read more science fiction; those by Asimov, to read more science. Nevertheless, the Lucky Starr books were successful juveniles and have remained in print.

The typical Asimov juvenile opens with a scientific mystery that Starr and Jones are sent to investigate. At their best the novels develop with the skill of Asimov's mysteries: the puzzles are fascinating and the solutions are ingenious. In between, the reader is presented with a great deal of information about the nature of the universe and the laws that govern its behavior. It is ironic that the facts known about several of the planets have changed since the novels were written. In *Opus 100* (1969) Asimov noted this fact with embarrassment and speculated that the novels, then out of print, might have to stay out of print. The Mars book might be reprinted (all that had then been discovered was that Mars was cratered, and craters were not difficult to insert), but the Venus and Mercury books "cannot be patched; they can only be scrapped." Nevertheless, at least the latter two were put back into print with 1970 Asimov forewords explaining that Venus has no oceans and that Mercury does not keep one side perpetually toward the sun so that there is a bright side and a dark side. Typically, Asimov used the forewords to explain how the new information was obtained and what the new understanding revealed.

The novels probably did for their young readers what they were intended to do: made the readers think and value the intellectual process and sometimes made them marvel at the wonders of the universe and even sometimes experience what is still beyond our abilities to experience. Those things all are important to Asimov. In *Opus 100* he recounted how some people tease him about his refusal to get into an airplane and tell him, "You don't know what you're missing." "Hah!" he wrote. "I've floated in Saturn's rings. They don't know what they're missing."

But the scientific emphases of the juvenile novels, with sizable chunks (attractive and digestable chunks) of scientific description dropped into the middle of them, were leading Asimov out of science fiction into science writing. He wrote in *Opus 100*:

> One of the special delights of writing science fiction is mastering the art of interweaving science and fiction; in keeping the science accurate and comprehensible without unduly stalling the plot. This is by no means easy to do, and it is as easy to ruin everything by loving science too much as by understanding it too little.
>
> In my case, I loved science too much. I kept getting the urge to explain science without having to worry about plots and characterization.

First, however, Asimov finished *The End of Eternity* (1955). This novel and *The Naked Sun* (1957) were the last novels of his nearly twenty-year career as a science-fiction writer. His two later novels were to be surrounded by oceans of non-fiction books. *Fantastic Voyage* (1966) was a better-than-competent novelization of a screenplay, but the creative act was the screenplay, and even that was a collaboration. It was written by Harry Kleiner, based on a story by Otto Klement and sometime science-fiction writer and editor of *Planet Stories* Jerome Bixby and adapted by sometime science-fiction writer David Duncan. *The Gods Themselves* (1972) was an important afterthought that will be taken up in Chapter 7.

The End of Eternity had its origin in an advertisement in a pre-1945 *Time* magazine. Typically, Asimov had been checking out bound copies of the magazine from the Boston University library and leafing through them nostalgically. In one he noticed an advertisement that for a moment looked like "the familiar mushroom cloud of the nuclear bomb." Then, as he looked closer, he recognized it as Old Faithful geyser in Yellowstone National Park. Asimov began to wonder under what circumstances a drawing of a nuclear bomb might be published in a magazine many years before 1945.

On December 7, 1953, he began work on a novelette titled "The End of Eternity." He finished it on February 6, 1954, and sent the 25,000-word story off to Horace Gold at *Galaxy*. Three days later Gold called him and wanted a complete revision. Asimov refused, and on March 17 he left the manuscript with

Bradbury at Doubleday to see if it had possibilities as a novel. On April 7 Bradbury offered a contract. By now, the advance had climbed to $1,250.

The End of Eternity is about reality manipulation. In the 24th century Vikkor Mallansohn discovered the Temporal Field that made possible existence outside time and travel between times. In the 27th century, an organization was created to travel outside of time, in what was called "Eternity." At first, the organization existed mostly to handle trade between Centuries, but gradually it began to alter Reality by changing key events that were calculated to improve the general good of humanity. "The greatest good of the greatest number" became the working principle of Eternity.

Asimov imagined the system in thorough detail. He peopled Eternity with maintenance personnel, who keep physical facilities operating, and administrators. The emphasis of the novel, however, is upon a third group, those Eternals, as they are called, who actually operate upon Reality: Observers, who gather data about the various Times; Sociologists, who calculate the effects of change on society; Life-Plotters, who calculate the effects of change on individuals; Computers, who analyze the individual acts that will produce the desired changes; and Technicians, who effect the changes in Reality. The ideal is the Minimum Necessary Change (MNC) for the Maximum Desired Response (MDR). The Technicians are the scapegoats of Eternity. Reality-changing results in guilt feelings among the Eternals, and they displace this onto the Technicians who actually accomplish the changes.

Eternals are recruited from various Centuries after the creation of Eternity. They are men, always men because women have ten times the impact on Reality and men's absence from Reality will cause the least effect. They are recruited into Eternity as fifteen-year-olds, educated for ten years, spend an indefinite period of time as Observers (physiotime it is called, to distinguish it from Time in Reality), and then, if successful, become Specialists. If they are not successful, they become maintenance men. As Andrew Harlan reflects at one point, "The life of an Eternal may be divided into four parts: Timer . . . Cub . . . Observer . . . Specialist."

Eternity started with only a few Centuries. Maintenance of its existence outside Time requires great expenditures of power; it became possible only by tapping the nova that the sun eventually becomes. Gradually, Eternity expanded "upwhen" until it discovered in one Century, later altered, a matter duplicator that allowed it to re-create itself throughout upwhen. From 70,000 to 150,000 upwhen Eternity, for reasons it cannot discover, cannot enter Time. These are called the Hidden Centuries. After 150,000 Earth still has living creatures, but humanity has disappeared. Eternity cannot discover why this is so, nor can it do anything about the situation until it can enter the Hidden Centuries.

All this background is revealed gradually through the tightly controlled viewpoint of Andrew Harlan. After serving his ten-year stint as Cub and four years as Observer, Harlan became Senior Observer to Assistant Computer Hobbe Finge in the 482nd. They do not get along, but Harlan's reports are good and within three months he becomes a Technician, the personal Technician of Senior Computer Laban Twissell, an important member of the Allwhen Council. One of Harlan's first assignments is to teach a Cub, Brinsley Sheridan Cooper, about Primitive history, that period before the creation of Eternity. Primitive history is Harlan's hobby, and he has assembled a number of references, including a complete bound set of a news magazine of the 20th. Cooper is an unusual Cub: he was taken into Eternity at the age of twenty-three and after he already was married.

After two physioyears, Harlan once more is assigned to Finge at the 482nd and meets Finge's secretary Noÿs Lambent, who has been recruited from the permissive society of the 482nd to fill a minor position. Harlan suspects that she is involved in a sexual liaison with Finge and dislikes her. Thus, a bit later, he finds himself in a difficult situation when he is assigned to her estate to make some observations of her time. When they are alone, Noÿs gives him an intoxicating drink, whispers to him, and they make love. Harlan discovers that he not only enjoys the experience, but that he is in love with Noÿs.

On his return, however, Harlan is forced to reveal to Finge

all that has happened. Finge taunts him with the information
that aristocratic women of the 482nd believe that Eternals are
immortal (which isn't true) and that intercourse with an Eternal will make them immortal. But Harlan persuades himself
that it doesn't matter why Noÿs loves him. He searches until
he finds a proposed Reality Change that is inexpertly com-
puted; with this as blackmail, he persuades the Sociologist responsible and a Life-Plotter to perform a Life-Plot for Noÿs in
the Reality Change planned for the 482nd. To his joy he discovers that Noÿs doesn't exist in the new Reality (and thus
can be removed from the present one without notice). The Life-
Plotter doesn't quite see how she fit in the old one.

Harlan smuggles Noÿs into Eternity and hides her far upwhen in the untenanted 111,394th. He does mathematical research on an aspect of Eternity that came to him during his
sexual experience with Noÿs. In going back several times to
her estate in the 482nd to obtain clothes and books (films) for
her, he is shaken to hear someone in the same house with him
and then, on a second occasion, to see himself. It is the kind
of paradox that some Eternals believe Time cannot endure. On
his return to his room, Twissell relays a message from Finge
that the 482nd Reality Change has been completed, and then
Twissell tells Harlan that he has something to tell him the
next day. Harlan tries to rejoin Noÿs but finds a block at the
100,000th that he cannot go beyond.

Harlan obtains a neuronic whip and makes Finge confess
that he has known about Harlan and Noÿs's activities and has
sent a report about them to the Allwhen Council. Harlan is
willing to bargain with Eternity for Noÿs and thinks he has secret knowledge that will protect them. The next day he meets
at lunch with a subcommittee of the Allwhen Council and
believes he is being taunted by one member. Afterward he faces
Twissell with his supposition about what has been happening: Vikkor Mallansohn, he says, could not have built a Temporal Field without equations that were not invented until the
27th. Cooper, he thinks, had been educated to go back to the
24th and teach Mallansohn the equations so that Eternity can
be invented. Twissell says that he knows about Harlan and the

girl and that everything will work out all right. Twissell has more important matters on his mind.

Harlan is partly right, Twissell says. Mallansohn left a record of his life in a Time-stasis. It was opened by the first of the great Eternals and passed along in strictest security until it reached Twissell. The memoir reveals that Cooper did go back to teach Mallansohn the equations, but Mallansohn died; Cooper took his place. At the end of his life, Cooper realized that he *was* Mallansohn. All the preparations described in the memoir have been carried out so that Cooper can go back, do what Mallansohn was said to have done, and write his memoir so that it can be found and the cycle renewed.

Twissell takes Harlan to a room in which a time-travel machine stands. It is like the kettles used by all Eternals but enclosed and double-walled to contain its own Temporal Field. It must take Cooper back to the 24th, to Primitive history before Eternity. While Harlan is inspecting the control room, Twissell locks him in because Cooper's memoirs mention that Harlan was at the controls. If Harlan does not pull the switch, someone outside the control room will pull it.

Harlan feels that he is being tricked but cannot think of anything he can do. After Cooper has been told everything he recounted in his memoirs that he was told, Harlan is given the countdown and pulls the switch. But when Twissell comes in to congratulate him, Harlan says that the plan did not work. He used the energy cell of the neuronic whip to melt the locking mechanism on the time-gauge, moved it down blindly, and brought it back blindly when the time-thrust was over. Cooper is lost in the Primitive Era. Harlan waits for Eternity to blink out of existence.

Twissell says that they still can restore Eternity as long as they can undo the damage, by going back, for instance, to find Cooper and restore him to the right spot in Time. They must discover when that spot was through research in Harlan's Primitive history materials, where Cooper might have left a message. An advertisement in the news magazine that Cooper knows Harlan possesses would be a good possibility, Harlan suggests.

Harlan finally discovers the message but will not tell Twissell what it is until he recovers Noÿs. Twissell does not know about the barrier at the 100,000th but thinks it is impossible. When they go to find Nöys, no barrier stops them. En route Twissell speculates about the possibility that Reality Changes might conceal a fear among Eternals of meeting supermen and that the Hidden Centuries might hide such people. Harlan shows him Cooper's message: an advertisement for a market newsletter in front of a drawing of a mushroom cloud. The drawing would mean nothing to 1932. To reinforce the message, the newsletter is called

> All the
> Talk
> Of the
> Market

The first letters vertically spell "ATOM."

Harlan insists that Noÿs accompany him in the kettle to 1932 (or 19.32, as the Eternals think of it). In a cave there he confronts her with the accusation that she is from the Hidden Centuries. Perhaps she is one of the supermen that Twissell was talking about. Harlan believes that he has been manipulated from his first meeting with Noÿs. He believes that she whispered to him, just before they made love, the clues that led him to suspect Twissell's plans for Cooper. He suspects that the barrier at the 100,000th had been set up by Noÿs and her confederates to lead him into the acts of rebellion that resulted in Cooper's being cast away in Time. He threatens to kill her with a blaster, then to take Cooper back to his correct destination and save Eternity.

Noÿs admits she is from the Hidden Centuries. People there had learned of Eternity's existence before it reached them, even before it had reached the 10,000th. The Hidden Centuries had time travel, but it was based on a different set of postulates. They viewed rather than shifted masses and were able to perceive alternate Realities. They discovered that they were in a Reality of low probability, traced their way down to Eternity and up to the 125,000th, where humanity at last had discovered the secret of the interstellar drive and the Jump through hyperspace. But humanity found the Galaxy occupied by other intelligent races. Humanity returned to Earth and died out.

Noÿs says that Eternity must be destroyed. It has persistently eliminated spaceflight from humanity's Realities. The Hidden Centuries have discovered what they call the Basic State. In this Reality, humanity discovers spaceflight early, goes out to the stars, and builds a human Galactic Empire (one might call this *The Foundation Trilogy* Reality). If Eternity had not been established, Noÿs says, the energies that went into temporal engineering would have gone into nucleonics, the interstellar drive would have been invented, and humanity would have reached the stars more than a hundred thousand centuries earlier. At that time the stars would have been untenanted, and mankind would have established itself throughout the Galaxy.

"Any system like Eternity," Noÿs says, "which allows men to choose their own future will end by choosing safety and mediocrity, and in such a Reality the stars are out of reach." Noÿs wants to send a letter to an Italian scientist (Enrico Fermi?) so that the first nuclear explosion will take place in 1945, not in the 30th century. There is a chance that Earth will end up with a radioactive crust (the *Pebble in the Sky* Reality), but before that there can be a Galactic Empire, an actual intensification of the Basic State. Noÿs says, "Cooper will disappear along with his advertisement; Eternity will go and the Reality of my Century, but *we* will remain to have children and grandchildren, and mankind will remain to reach the stars."

Before Harlan himself knows whether he will carry out his threat to kill Noÿs and rescue Cooper or do as Noÿs asks, the kettle disappears, signaling the final end of Eternity . . . "and the beginning of Infinity."

The plot, thus outlined, is reasonably straightforward. Its time sequence has been realigned into linear form here, but as written, the novel is told in various kinds of flashbacks. A pattern of confusion about time results that is appropriate to the theme of the novel and even pleasing, though this may not be why Asimov chose to narrate in that fashion. Contemporary literary critics using theories of structuralism and semiotics, who find themselves concerned about time, among other matters, might find interesting the varieties of time that exist within this novel, which deals with time, discusses time, swears by time ("Time!" and "Father Time!"), and was inspired by *Time*.

The End of Eternity deals with all sorts of time, from the time involved in the procession of the Centuries within Eternity (which is traveled spatially by kettle, although the kettles never move), the time that passes for the Eternals (physiotime), the times of entry into Time, the sequence of events within Time (our temporally bound definition), and the artifacts of Time that never was (that Eternity has altered out of Reality) that still are preserved within Eternity (such as the matter duplicator, the neuronic whip, and the dozens of variations of the works of a writer named Eric Linkollew). One person's time is not another person's time, of course, unless they may accidentally come together for a brief period, but each can describe it to others.

In the following outline, subdivided by chapters, the kinds of time within the narrative are identified in brackets by character initials and a sequence number. A minus (−) before the initial or number means that this sequence has been eliminated in at least one Reality.

Chapter 1. Harlan goes upwhen from the 575th to the 2456th to blackmail Sociologist Kantor Voy into calculating Noÿs's Life-Plot [H 19]. While there, he looks some twenty-five Centuries into the future to the time of electro-gravity space travel [-2481st 1].

Chapter 2. Harlan, standing at the gateway to Time in the 2456th [H 20], recalls his experience as a Cub, after having spent fifteen years in Time (the 95th): his graduation, his four plus years as Observer and assignment to Finge at the 482nd, and the invitation from Twissell to be his personal Technician [H 2].

Chapter 3. Harlan, still standing at the gateway to Time in the 2456th [H 21] and still recalling his earlier experience, recalls his meeting with Cooper and a year or so of experience as Twissell's Technician in the 575th [H 3]. He remembers Cooper telling him what he was as a Timer in the 78th [C 1]. One alteration of Reality for Twissell in the 223rd [223rd 1] resulted in the elimination of a war in the 224th [-224th 1]. Then Harlan dreams of his mother [H 1].

Chapter 4. Harlan, still standing at the gateway of Time in the 2456th [H 22] and still recalling his earlier experience, recalls his temporary assignment to Finge at the 482nd [H 4]. Finge is from an energy-centered culture in the 600s [F 1]. Harlan meets Noÿs [N 3] and is assigned an Observer task in the 482nd where he is to live in Noÿs's house [H 5].

Chapter 5. Harlan, still standing at the gateway to Time in the 2456th [H 23] and still recalling his earlier experience, recalls his first sexual experience with Noÿs. She mentions a discrepancy in time in which she went into Eternity [N 2] and came out [N 4]. She has lost three months of Time but not three months of physiotime [H 6].

Chapter 6. Harlan, still standing at the gateway to Time in the 2456th, recalls that a month has passed since the night he made love to Noÿs [H 6]. Now he enters the 2456th from Eternity, moves a small container, and returns [H 24]. Sociologist Voy is studying the 2481st, where a rusty spaceship sits at a deserted spaceport [2481st 1]. During his talk with the Life-Plotter, Harlan thinks of Noÿs and the morning after their lovemaking [H 7]. Then the Life-Plotter tells him that Noÿs does not exist in the new Reality planned for the 482nd [H 25].

Chapter 7. Harlan leaves the 2456th [H 26] and recalls sending his report to Finge [H 8] on his observations in the 482nd and going back to his room [H 9]. There Finge contacts him by vision plate and then comes to see him in person [H 10].

Chapter 8. Harlan goes back to the 482nd to take Noÿs upwhen to the 111,394th [H 11]. While there, Harlan remembers his early Cubhood when he learned that his Hometime and even his family might not exist as he remembered them [H 2]. Then he tells Noÿs about Reality [H 12].

Chapter 9. Harlan moves his effects from the 482nd to the 575th where he picks up his duties with Cooper and Twissel. He shuttles back and forth to spend time with Noÿs in the 111,394th [H 13]. He goes back to Noÿs's house in the 482nd to pick up some books [H 14] and recalls [H 16] having been there before [H 15] to get some clothing and feeling that someone else was in the house, hearing a loud noise, and feeling that a door had closed behind him. Now [H 16] he hears someone laugh and drops his knapsack.

Chapter 10. Harlan opens a door, sees a man's back and the man starting to turn. As Harlan closes the door, he realizes that the man is himself. He had accidentally misadjusted the contols into the 482nd [H 14] to almost the previous time [H 15]. (This experience then can be identified as just after H 11 in the 482nd, but in Harlan's physiotime as H 14, H 15, and H 16; or, since H 15 and H 16 are identical times, they could be identified as H^1 15 and H^2 15.) Harlan returns to Eternity and studies scheduled Reality Changes until he comes up with the faulty one planned for the 2456th [H 17]. Twissell tells him by vision plate that the Reality Change in the 482nd was entirely successful and that he will see Harlan tomorrow in the Computing Room [H 18]. Harlan goes to the 2456th [H 19]. to have Noÿs's existence Life-Plotted [H 20–26]. He goes racing upwhen to tell Noÿs and slams into the barrier at the 100,000th [H 27]. He returns, with the neuronic whip, to confront Finge.

Chapter 11. Harlan returns to his quarters in the 575th, tries to see Twissell and fails, finally goes to sleep and is awakened the next morning for lunch with the subcommittee of the Allwhen Council. Finally, he confronts Twissell with his conclusion that Cooper is returning to the 24th to teach the Lefebvre equations to Mallansohn. Twissell tells him that Cooper is Mallansohn [H 28].

Chapter 12. Harlan expresses his concerns about Noÿs, and Twissell tries to reassure him [H 29]. Then Twissell tells Harlan about the memoir Mallansohn left behind [E (for Eternity) 1] and its description of how Cooper was inducted into Eternity [C 3], trained in mathematics by Twissell and in Primitive sociology by Harlan [H 3], and sent back to teach Mallansohn [C 4] but became Mallansohn and left the memoir [C 5, M 1]. Twissell tells Harlan how the memoir passed down through Eternity until it reached him when he became a Senior Computer [T 3]. He leads Harlan into the room with the enclosed kettle and then into the control room where Harlan finds himself locked in [H 30.].

Chapter 13. Twissell tells Cooper [C 6] what Cooper later

[C 7] will write in his memoir in the 24th [C 2] as Harlan watches [H 31]. Twissell also describes what his experimental group did to calibrate the energy thrust necessary to transport Cooper [T 4.]. With Harlan's hands at the controls, Cooper is sent back [H 32] and Harlan awaits the end of eternity. Then Harlan tells Twissell [H 33] what he did with the controls [H 32].

Chapter 14. Twissell and Harlan [H 34] discuss the causes of Harlan's actions and the reasons for their misunderstanding [H 28–29]. Twissell also tells of Finge's request for Harlan's services and Finge's communication about Harlan to the All-when Council that came automatically to Twissell [T 5]. He also recalls a liaison he once enjoyed with a woman when he was a Junior Computer [T 1] and the child she bore before her death. He watched the child grow and even visited him when the son was 34 [T 2¹], and he describes the Reality Change he agreed to that as a side effect turned his son into a paraplegic at the age of four [T 2²].

Chapter 15. Harlan tries to duplicate his spastic movement of the thrust control and then searches his news magazines for a message from Cooper [H 35]. After discovering the advertisement, he tells Twissell about the barrier at the 100,000th and what happened to him [H 27].

Chapter 16. While Twissell and Harlan are going upwhen to Noÿs [H 36], Twissell talks about the history of Eternity [E 2] and the possibility of supermen in the Hidden Centuries. After their return with Noÿs, Harlan shows Twissell the advertisement from a 1932 magazine [C 1]. Harlan agrees to go back for Cooper if Noÿs accompanies him [H 37].

Chapter 17. Harlan and Noÿs prepare to go [H 38] on an exploratory trip to determine Cooper's exact time of arrival, then return and travel again to a point in time fifteen minutes after Cooper's arrival, pick him up, and deliver him to 2317. As that is done, Cooper's experience in 1932 will disappear (except for fifteen minutes) as will the advertisement [-C 1]. But when Harlan and Noÿs arrive in 1932 and Noÿs confronts Harlan and his coldness, he recalls [H 39] the barrier at the 100,000th [H 27] and its consequences [H 28–32]. He accuses Noÿs of being from the Hidden Centuries. He also recalls the night she whispered to him before their first sexual experience

[H 7] and the comment of the Life-Plotter about Noÿs not fitting into the old Reality of the 482nd [H 25], their first trip to the 111,394th when Noÿs stopped the kettle [H 11]. He says he is going to kill Noÿs [H 40].

Chapter 18. Noÿs admits she is from the Hidden Centuries and challenges Harlan to kill her [H 41]. When he is willing to listen to her explanation, she talks about the future of humanity and Eternity's effect upon it [E 3]. She also describes the actions of the Hidden Centuries when their residents discovered time travel and Eternity and the Basic State. During this, Harlan remembers the reactions of Voy to the elimination of electro-gravity spaceflight [H 24; -2481st 1] and Life-Plotter Neron Feruque to ease his guilt railing at Eternity's handling of anti-cancer serums [H 25]. Noÿs talks about the reaction of humanity to the discovery that the Galaxy already was in alien hands [HC (Hidden Centuries) 2] and about the alternate reality in which Eternity is not found and humanity reaches the stars more than a hundred thousand Centuries earlier [BS (Basic State) 1]. She also tells Harlan that she was educated for her job to destroy Eternity [N 1] but had a choice of five Realities that seemed least complex. She chose the one in which she went back to the 482nd [N 2], met Finge and then Harlan [N 3], in which Harlan loved her, misdirected Cooper, and returned with her to the Primitive where they lived out their lives together [N 4]. But Harlan, holding her at gunpoint, is in a slightly different Reality, just as Twissell accompanying him in his last trip to the 111,394th [H 36] was not part of that Reality [N 4²]. When Harlan asks why it was not enough just to misdirect Cooper, Noÿs says that the probability of the creation of Eternity must be reduced to nearly zero. The Minimum Necessary Change to achieve that is for her to send a letter to " a man of Italy" who will begin experimenting with the neutronic bombardment of uranium. Harlan is horrified at the prospect of destroying Eternity [H 42] but responds to her accusation that Eternals are psychopaths by recalling his group of Cubs learning about Reality [H 2] and recalling the abnormal life led by Eternals [H 2–37]. His decision [H 43] is signaled by the disappearance of the kettle [-E 1–3]. (Of course, almost everything else turns to minuses as well, for now no Reality exists except the Basic State strengthened by the results of Noÿs's letter.

Asimov probably did not plan this labyrinthine complex of time relationships as a way of providing a stylistic counterpoint to the theme. Certainly he was aware of the complexities of the subject. Heinlein had already exploited the paradoxes of time travel in "By His Bootstraps," although the solipsism of "All You Zombies—"was still in the future. Reality-changing was not as thoroughly explored as it would be after Fritz Leiber's Change War stories culminating in "The Big Time" (*Galaxy*, March-April 1958) and Philip K. Dick's reality-questioning stories and novels of the fifties and sixties, but H. Beam Piper's Paratime Police stories began running in *Astounding* in July 1948 and his "Time Crime" was serialized beginning February 1955. The ideas were not new even then, but Asimov considered in detail the complications of a systematic effort to change reality.

When Twissell is instructing Cooper, Harlan thinks:

> Remember that, Cooper! Remember the 13th Reality of the 222nd so that you can put it into the Mallansohn memoir so that the Eternals will know where to look so they will know what to tell you so you can put it. . . . Round and round the circle goes . . . ."

After Harlan sends Cooper off to the wrong time, Twissell brings up the question of why Reality changes immediately after an alteration in Time; a Technician, he says, could go back and reverse the Change he has made. It must, he says, have to do with intention: the Technician has no intention of reversing his alteration, so Reality changes. But Eternity has not yet vanished, so Harlan must intend to reverse his action with Cooper. As a concluding nicety in Asimov's toying with the nature of reality and an action carefully prepared by Twissell's previous theorizing, the kettle disappears at the end even before Harlan is aware he has reached a decision: the kettle knows before he does.

These are only two examples among many that might be cited in support of Asimov's understanding of the complexities with which he was dealing and the thoroughness with which he dealt with them. *The End of Eternity* lacks the inspired madness of Dick's explorations of reality, but Dick's purpose was to raise doubts about reality. Asimov's was to understand it and to work his way through the difficulties to a reasonable basis for action.

The flashback technique, appropriate as it is, probably was the result of Campbell's early advice to Asimov, given while Asimov was working on his second published robot story, "Reason":

> Asimov, when you have trouble with the beginning of a story, that is because you are starting in the wrong place, and almost certainly too soon. Pick out a later point in the story and begin again.

In his autobiography Asimov writes, "Ever since then, I have always started my stories as late in the game as I thought I could manage." That, no doubt, is the case with *The End of Eternity* and explains why Harlan is left standing at the gateway of Time for five chapters and why readers must pick their ways gingerly through a minefield of past tenses.

In *The End of Eternity* Asimov tackles sex for the first time (the titillation of the moment in *The Naked Sun* in which Gladia removes her glove and touches Baley on the cheek still lies a year ahead). Doubleday raised a brief question about it—Asimov, like Verne before him, was known for the purity of his writing—but Asimov's wife read through the chapter, looked up, and asked, "Where was it?" For Asimov it was a breakthrough. Not so his characterization. The minor characters have some vitality—Finge, Twissell, even Cooper—but Harlan is so subordinated to his role that Noÿs's love for him seems incredible. Harlan is stiff, cold, unyielding, and unlikable, and Noÿs gets no chance to exist as an individual until the final chapter. The novel is dominated by its theme.

The theme of *The End of Eternity* is as significant as anything Asimov ever touched. Since it was virtually Asimov's last extended thought about science fiction until unusual circumstances produced *The Gods Themselves*, the 1955 novel may define the values Asimov was upholding after nearly twenty years of writing science fiction. It may also provide clues to his decision to leave the fantasy world of fiction writing for the real world of science writing.

The End of Eternity shares with other Asimov fiction his basic concern for intelligent choice. Although Harlan begins as a cold and withdrawn Eternal, apparently moved only by intellectual concerns and sharing the values of a group that can change other people's Realities and lives at will, and although Harlan changes only because of his love for Noÿs, reason still wins out over emotion. In the final chapter, Harlan is persuaded by Noÿs's rational arguments, not by his love for her. Out of resentment that his love has been manipulated, Harlan has made up his mind to kill Noÿs, but when he matches his own experience with Noÿs's accusations, he is persuaded.

In another sense, perhaps, Asimov's old science-fiction enthusiasms may have emerged victorious over his rationality. After her comments on Eternity's choosing safety and mediocrity, Noÿs says, "The real solutions . . . come from conquering difficulty, not avoiding it." Carried to their ultimate conclusion, these statements, which Asimov implicitly accepts for the sake of the novel, imply that humanity cannot improve its lot by rational choice. Or perhaps, if Asimov is given credit for dealing with a special case, they mean only that humanity cannot change the past.

If one wished to personalize the message of the novel, one might speculate that Asimov, looking back over his own past, has concluded that no amount of tinkering will change it for the better. This is, indeed, one of the messages of his autobiographical writings. Everything happened for the best: Campbell's early rejections, Sam Merwin's rejection of "Grow Old with Me," the change of administration at the Boston University School of Medicine that led to his full-time writing (which still awaited him). . . . If he had had the opportunity to make things happen differently, he would have made the wrong choice, he might be saying, would have chosen safety and mediocrity over risk and greatness. In The End of Eternity, at least, Asimov chose, as rationally as he could, uncertainty over certainty and infinity over not eternity but Eternity, that is,

over the limitation of man's possibilities by too much tinkering with them. Asimov is not denying humanity's potential
for rationality or the need for considering choices rationally
but humanity's capacity to play God. Humanity will not consciously choose the uncertainty of adventure, or the adventure
of uncertainty.

Within two years Asimov was to turn away from the certainty of science fiction to the uncertainty of science writing.
But he is by nature a cautious man: he had already pretested
the market and had five science books behind him before he
cast himself adrift from the science fiction he had lived with,
suffered with, triumphed with, and profited from for twenty
years.

7

THE STUFF ITSELF

By mid-1970 Asimov had returned to New York—alone. Talk of divorce had increased in frequency in recent years. "After 1969," Asimov reported in his autobiography, "which seemed to consist, in retrospect, of one long slide toward divorce, there had been an upturn, a kind of pleasant Indian summer, a glimmering twilight that had lasted six weeks. . . ." Then he (and his wife, apparently) accepted the fact that the marriage was beyond saving.

At first, Asimov was going to take an apartment in nearby Wellesley while the divorce went forward. Then he learned that his wife would allow only a separation. Divorce in Massachusetts without his wife's cooperation was virtually impossible for a man with Asimov's stern ethical imperatives, so he moved to New York where he could institute no-fault proceedings.

His future second wife, Dr. Janet Jeppson, whom he had met earlier on a few occasions, helped him to find an apartment and adjust to life as a single man after nearly thirty years of marriage. Once more he was back in the city where he had grown from a child of three to a young man of twenty-nine who was a successful but not financially well-rewarded science-fiction author. Now he was fifty years old. His hundredth book had been celebrated in 1969 with *Opus 100* and numerous interviews, some on television. He was becoming known as the most prolific man of letters of his time, and his reputation as a child prodigy had been supplanted by the image, however exaggerated, of an authority on almost everything.

Asimov was much in demand as a public speaker commanding substantial fees. He could find a publisher for almost anything he wished to write—and for some books he did not. He was wealthy; in spite of the impending divorce settlement he would never have to worry about money again, even if he never wrote another word. But that, of course, was unthinkable. Writing was his life, even if it was no longer his livelihood. He accepted small advances so publishers would let him write what he wanted to write.

A couple of questions, however, disturbed him. He was not sure he could write in new surroundings: radical changes always brought this terrible possibility into his mind. Each time, however, the fears had been unnecessary, and this time was no different. One question remained to be answered: would he ever write serious science fiction again? In spite of his statement at the end of his collection, The Bicentennial Man, that he had never stopped writing science fiction, the intensity with which he had written his early stories, the amount of himself that he had poured into those hopeful works, had been missing for a number of years.

If anything, Asimov's social life improved in New York. He soon was seeing his editors more regularly than ever and, in addition, his old science-fiction friends, Lester del Rey, Judy-Lynn Benjamin (who became Mrs. del Rey), Robert Silverberg, and others, including John Campbell. And he attended various local science-fiction conventions. At one of them on January 23, 1971, Robert Silverberg and Lester del Rey participated in a dialogue about "the ins and outs of science fiction." At one point Silverberg illustrated the greater importance of the human aspects of a science-fiction story over the scientific detail by asking why anyone should be overly concerned with some trivial matter concerning, say, plutonium-186.

In the audience Asimov laughed because he knew there was no plutonium-186 and could not be. After the dialogue he told Silverberg this, and Silverberg shrugged it off. Asimov said, "But just to show you what a real science-fiction writer can do, I'll write a story about plutonium-186."

"Go ahead," Silverberg said. He was putting together the first issue of an anthology of original fiction to be entitled *New Dimensions*. "If you write one that meets my minimum standard of literacy, I'll publish it."

This kind of banter is exchanged among Asimov, del Rey, Silverberg, Ellison (see Asimov's two introductions to Ellison's *Dangerous Visions*), and a few others. In his autobiography Asimov described an exchange of insults with an editor and added, "You can't fool around that way if you don't like a guy." He also described how he was always getting "wiped out" by his friends. Occasionally, however, these exchanges get under the skin. When Asimov described the above conversation with Silverberg in his autobiography, he inserted the phrase "who knew that very well" between "Silverberg" and "shrugged it off," but in an early introduction to his novel that followed Asimov told the story differently. Silverberg did not remember it that way, however, and Asimov, no doubt feeling that the introduction might damage their friendship, had it removed.

The incident, nevertheless, may have provided the inspiration for what would turn out to be Asimov's last science-fiction novel for at least a decade. The novel that became *The Gods Themselves* might never have been started if Asimov had conceived it as a novel from the beginning.

Asimov described his attitude toward science-fiction writing in the mid-1960s when Harlan Ellison asked him to write a story for *Dangerous Visions*. Asimov begged off, offering instead to write an introduction because, he said, he lacked the time for a story. (He ended up writing two introductions, one describing the changes in science fiction and why he did not write a story for the collection, the second recounting his first put-down meeting with Ellison.) His real reason was, he wrote in his autobiography, "I couldn't face trying to write a story that could pass muster in the 1960s, when such talent as I had suited only the 1950s. I felt that I couldn't measure up any longer and I didn't want to prove it."

Evelyn del Rey helped to dispel some of this feeling when she asked him why he didn't write science fiction anymore. Asimov replied sadly, "Evelyn, you know as well as I do that the field has moved beyond me." And she replied, "Isaac, you're crazy. When you write, you *are* the field." He returned to writing short stories.

A novel, nevertheless, was something different; it may have been well that this one sneaked up on him. His story kept growing beyond the five thousand words that he had promised Silverberg until it reached twenty thousand. That was a short novel. Thinking that Doubleday, which was to publish *New Dimensions,* might expand the volume to include the extra length of the story, Asimov took it to Larry Ashmead, Doubleday's current science-fiction editor. Ashmead telephoned to say that anthologization was out; he wanted the story expanded into a novel.

Asimov did not want to expand it. On the spot, however, he offered to write two more sections of equal length: "The story involves an energy source that depends on communication between ourselves and another universe, and it ends downbeat. What I can do is retell the story from the standpoint of the other universe and still leave it downbeat. Then I can take it up a third time in still a third setting, and this time make it upbeat."

"Are you sure you can do this?" Ashmead asked.

"Absolutely positive," Asimov responded, although he had just made up the idea on the spur of the moment. But as he added in his autobiography, "If I couldn't, I wasn't Isaac Asimov." On March 8, 1971, he dropped in at Doubleday and signed a contract to write the novel. He also set to work on a different story for Silverberg's anthology, a short story titled "Take a Match" that appeared in *New Dimensions II* (1972).

Asimov might have been reluctant at first to tackle a new science-fiction novel not only because of his feeling that he belonged to another, perhaps outmoded, generation of science-fiction writers—he had divided science fiction into periods he called "adventure-dominant, science-dominant, sociology-dominant, and style-dominant," and it was not difficult to perceive that he thought style-dominance was a perversion of Campbell's vision—but because he had not written an adult science-fiction novel for more than fifteen years (or any kind of science-fiction novel, including juvenile, for thirteen).

In addition, he had more writing projects than he could handle, and he was involved in a lengthy and disturbing divorce negotiation with his wife. He also found writing science fiction more difficult than anything else.

In the introduction to *Nebula Award Stories Eight*, which he edited for the Science Fiction Writers of America the year after the publication of *The Gods Themselves*, he compared science fiction to other kinds of writing and wrote, "A good science-fiction writer can, very probably, write anything else he wishes (and for more money), if he decides to take the trouble to do so. . . . It is uphill to science fiction; downhill to everything else."

He goes on to offer himself as the world authority on this subject:

> I began by writing science fiction, yes, and for over thirty years I've found that my training in science fiction made it possible for me to write anything. I have written mysteries, both novels and short stories, for instance. I have also written nonfiction books on every branch of science, both popularizations for the general public and textbooks at both the graduate level and the grade-school level. I have written history books, discussions of the Bible, Shakespeare, Byron, and Milton. I have written satires and jokebooks. I have written about 150 books as of now, and I tell you, that of all the different things I write, science fiction is by far the hardest thing to do.

The introduction was entitled "So Why Aren't We Rich?" It was a bit ironic, since Asimov was one of the few science-fiction writers who was rich—probably he was a millionaire by that time. In his autobiography he totaled his income at the end of each year. It reveals increasing financial success that brought him from the uncertainty of the early days when he waited anxiously for a check from Campbell to a growing bank account and growing confidence that he could leave his salaried position at Boston University with scarcely a thought about financial insecurity. He stopped revealing his annual income with the year 1962: 1961 had amounted to $69,000; 1962 to $72,000. In 1970, his divorce trial revealed his income was $205,000.

By almost any measure (and certainly his own, since he did not have expensive habits), he was financially secure, even though some of his savings were invested in New York City bonds and a generous settlement with his wife was ahead. His income came mostly from books other than his science fiction. None of his books was a best-seller—though his science fiction continued to sell well—but the sheer volume of the non-fiction had brought him to his present status. Only about 30 of those first 150 books he wrote or edited were science fiction. Books such as *The Intelligent Man's Guide to Science*, his first major science-popularization success, brought him a single royalty check of $27,600.

So it was that *The Gods Themselves* came to represent a return and a confirmation and a risk that Asimov found himself willing to take. It was an act of daring that deserved the rewards it earned. The novel sold well, was critically well received, and won both Nebula and Hugo Awards. Asimov had received the approval of his fellow fans and his fellow writers.

The novel also has particular merits as a summing-up point. Asimov had told Silverberg that he would show "what a real science-fiction writer can do . . . ." He meant that he would write a science-fiction story in which the science was at least as important as the characters, a story which could not happen without the scientific content. It would conform to the definition he had used about 1951 in an article for *The Writer* and had repeated in his frequently reprinted essay, "Social Science Fiction," in Reginald Bretnor's 1953 collection, *Modern Science Fiction*: "Science fiction is that branch of literature which is concerned with the impact of scientific advance upon human beings." In the *Modern Science Fiction* essay, he inserted the word "Social" before "science fiction."

In spite of the definition, scientific advance was not always at the heart of Asimov's science fiction. Occasionally, a hard scientific datum or development would inspire a short story. But Asimov's novels were more inspired by history than science; they were more speculative than extrapolative.

The Gods Themselves was to be different. The idea had sprung from a scientific anomaly—the impossibility of plutonium-186—and it was to develop into a story whose science was as hard as any conceived by Harry Stubbs, whose carefully extrapolated alien environments had begun to be published in *Astounding* in June 1942 (only three years after Asimov's work), under the pseudonym Hal Clement. The impossibility of plutonium-186 was basic to the story. For the reader to understand this, Asimov had to educate him or her in the complexities of nuclear physics.

One important fact was the structure of the atomic nucleus, which is composed of neutrons and protons, identical in weight but differing in charge. Both are massive as atomic particles go—many times more massive than electrons, for instance, which orbit in "shells" around the nucleus, give the element its chemical properties, and balance, with their negative charge, the positive charge of the nucleus. Ordinarily, like charges repel each other. The protons clustered together in the nucleus ought to push each other away, but they are held together by what is known as the strong nuclear interaction, the strongest known force in the universe. This interaction seems to be exerted by the neutrons because a number of protons in the nucleus need a larger number of neutrons to hold them together.

Elements are placed in the periodic table of elements according to their charge, that is, the number of electrons they possess as well as the corresponding number of protons in the nucleus. Their atomic weights, however, are the total of protons and neutrons in the nucleus; sometimes this is not a simple number when an element has isotopes (different forms of the same element with one neutron more or less in the nucleus), whose natural atomic weights average out as a fraction.

Plutonium-186, then, would have a charge of 94, which makes it plutonium, and its atomic weight would be 186. The number of protons in the nucleus would be 94. If one subtracts 94 from 186, one arrives at the number of neutrons in the nucleus: 92. This is not enough neutrons to keep the protons from repelling each other, and thus plutonium-186 is impossible. The plutonium nucleus that we can analyze in our world has an atomic weight of 242, which means that the 94 protons have 148 neutrons to hold them together.

Asimov was faced with the logical problem of rationalizing the existence of plutonium-186. It could exist, he realized, only in an alternate universe in which the strong nuclear interaction was even stronger than in our universe—perhaps one hundred times stronger—in order to keep the protons together. Asimov could have written a story about such an alternate universe—a place in which plutonium-186 could exist—and eventually he did. But that alone would not have met the challenge. A universe such as that, with no connection to our world, would have been remote from the concerns of the reader. Asimov wanted to bring the plutonium-186 into our universe, and he did—by exchanging it for an isotope of tungsten with an atomic weight of 186. Tungsten-186, which has a charge of 74, has 74 protons in the nucleus but 112 neutrons to hold them together. How could it become plutonium-186? By changing twenty neutrons in its nucleus into twenty protons.

The scientific background of the story must have taken shape in much this way: in an alternate universe that has a much stronger nuclear interaction plutonium-186 would exist, but tungsten-186 would not. It would be unstable because it has too many neutrons (or too few protons). In our universe, tungsten-186 is stable, but plutonium-186 is unstable. If quantities of the two elements were exchanged between the two universes, power would be released in each of them: in our universe plutonium-186 would emit positrons as protons within the nucleus were converted into neutrons, and in the alternate universe tungsten-186 would emit electrons as neutrons were changed into protons. In each universe positrons would annihilate electrons and produce energy. In the process, our universe would lose twenty electrons and the alternate universe would gain twenty. The exchange could mean a clean, inexhaustible power source for both universes.

One question Asimov does not raise (or answer), possibly because it might sabotage the scientific basis for his novel, is the amount of energy required to transfer the materials between the universes. If the laws of nature (and human nature as well) hold true as we have experienced them, it seems likely that the transfer would use up more energy than it would produce. For this reason, perhaps, Asimov has the transfer effected, mysteriously, by aliens in the alternate universe; he thus avoids raising the question of the energy cost of transfer.

The human characters can never know the alien situation, and the aliens have alien concerns.

There is a cost involved, however—entropy may not be violated after all—and that cost becomes the dynamic force behind the narrative. Asimov has commented that when he writes fiction he is delighted to find that an element he inserted into a story simply because it occurred to him, later comes exactly to hand when he needs it. The complication of The Gods Themselves must have delighted him.

All of this interesting, even fascinating, speculation, however, is esoteric and difficult fictional material. Asimov works it into fiction by focusing on the nature of discovery. The process by which plutonium-186 is introduced into our universe becomes the substance of the first half of Part I of the novel.

The Gods Themselves, as Asimov promised Ashmead, is divided into three roughly equal sections. The title of the novel is taken from a line in Friedrich von Schiller's play Jungfrau von Orleans (Joan of Arc), "Against stupidity, the gods themselves contend in vain,"[1] and each of the three parts has a phrase of the quotation as an epigraph. The first part, "Against Stupidity . . . ," describes how Frederick Hallam discovers plutonium-186. An old reagent bottle labeled "Tungsten Metal" that had been on the desk he had inherited when he came to work at the university one day contains a clear iron-gray metal instead of dusty gray pellets. Hallam takes them to be analyzed and discovers that they are the impossible plutonium-186. In subsequent days he discovers that the substance, originally non-radioactive, gradually becomes more radioactive; it emits positrons. For safety, the plutonium-186 is powdered, scattered, and mixed with ordinary tungsten and then, when that grows radioactive, with graphite.

Eventually, at a seminar organized to discuss the problem, the possibility is raised that the plutonium-186 may have come

---

1. The German quotation has been translated by Bartlett's Familiar Quotations as "Against stupidity the very gods themselves contend in vain" and by The Oxford Dictionary of Quotations as "With stupidity the gods themselves struggle in vain." Asimov must have obtained his translation from another source.

from a parallel Universe (which comes to be called the para-Universe) and then that it may have been sent deliberately into our Universe by an intelligent agent. After some experimentation, Earth sets up a power system to make use of the new energy. Apparently, the aliens in the para-Universe do the same thing with the tungsten. The process on Earth comes to be called an Electron Pump, since in effect it pumps electrons from our Universe into the para-Universe; more formally it is called the Inter-Universe Electron Pump. It becomes a major project, associated with a university, and eventually the source of plentiful, non-polluting energy at almost no cost.

This much of the story could be the beginning of a utopian novel that describes how humanity uses the new energy to improve its condition, or a dystopia that shows how humanity misuses the energy to turn a blessing into a curse. Neither would make a particularly different nor particularly promising novel. Asimov turned it into something unique, something with the special substance of hard-core science fiction, by dealing with the scientific consequences of the Electron Pump and the human difficulties of the people in charge to perceive these consequences and to act upon them.

Asimov tells the "Against Stupidity" part from the third-person viewpoint of an antagonist, Peter Lamont, who sets out to write a history of the development of the Pump. Lamont's first approach to Hallam, however, infuriates Hallam and embitters Lamont. Hallam is delighted to cooperate until Lamont innocently suggests that the para-men are more intelligent than humans, since they initiated the exchange and even sent directions on iron foil for building the Pump. Hallam calls such notions "mysticism" and shouts Lamont from the room.

Lamont, determined to pick holes in the project, recruits a new University scholar, Myron Bronowski, a translator of ancient Etruscan writing, to aid him in communicating with the para-men. And Lamont tries to find some unforeseen problem with Pumping. "Everything in history had had a catch," he thinks. "What was the catch to the Electron Pump?"

One possible problem with the Pump lies in what happens during the process of Pumping. The effect of the transmission of electrons had been considered and discarded: the electron supply would last for a trillion trillion trillion years, and the entire Universe wouldn't last a tiny fraction of that. But Lamont perceives that the physical laws of the two Universes are being exchanged as well, and that could mean trouble. Because the significant difference between the two Universes is the strength of the nuclear interaction, nuclear fission is more likely in our Universe, nuclear fusion in the para-Universe. As the nuclear interaction grows stronger in our Universe, the sun may turn nova. And as the reaction weakens in the para-Universe, their small suns will have greater difficulty sustaining the fusion reaction and will cool down.

Bronowski gets a message from the para-Universe. It says: "F-E-E-R." Lamont tries to persuade the influential Senator Burt, head of the Committee on Technology and the Environment, to intervene, but Burt feels that he cannot succeed against Hallam. Lamont also fails with Professor Joshua Chen, who prefers the possibility of immortality implied by the cheap energy of the Pump. Then Bronowski gets another message:

> PUMP NOT STOP NOT STOP WE NOT STOP PUMP WE NOT
> HEAR DANGER NOT HEAR NOT HEAR YOU STOP PLEASE STOP
> YOU STOP SO WE STOP PLEASE YOU STOP DANGER DANGER
> DANGER STOP STOP YOU STOP PUMP.

Bronowski, however, sees the futility of trying to convince the world of the danger. He quotes Schiller and leaves Lamont alone, frustrated, and without hope.

Asimov uses a couple of narrative devices to involve the reader quickly in Part I. Rather than beginning with the discovery of plutonium-186 and working forward to the period thirty years later when Lamont's involvement begins, Asimov, true to Campbell's ancient advice, begins not even with Lamont's entry upon the scene but as Lamont's and Bronowski's efforts to communicate with the para-men are about to succeed. Actually, Bronowski has received the first message and is waiting to tell Lamont.

Asimov starts the novel, in fact, with a segment numbered "6." A note facing the contents page tells the reader that the book begins with section 6. "This is not a mistake. I have my own subtle reasoning. . . ." Then the book picks up section

1, as Lamont learns how the discovery of plutonium-186 occurred. Subsequently, fragments of section 6 alternate with sections in numerical order up to the end of section 5, in which Lamont presents his theory to Hallam in a way he knows Hallam will not be willing to consider. Section 6 then concludes with the "F-E-E-R" message, and Part I continues to its conclusion in straightforward chronological (and numerical) sequence. Asimov has carried the method of The End of Eternity a step farther to a sharing of his flashback methods with the reader.

These devices would not be sufficient to sustain the narrative without the details Asimov supplies on the nature of scientific discovery and the inner workings of the academic and scientific establishments. At last Asimov turned to writing science fiction out of his own experience, which he had not done in earlier stories. His description of the discovery of plutonium-186 draws not only upon his extensive research into and writing about science but surely, for characters as well as events, upon his experiences within the academic world.

Hallam, for instance, pushes his investigation into the metal that has changed within the reagent bottle on his desk because he had said, when he discovered it, "That's not the tungsten," and his colleague across the hall, a more highly regarded young scientist named Benjamin Allan Denison, had challenged him with, "How would you know?" If Hallam had not been pushed, the plutonium might simply have become more radioactive until it exploded with catastrophic results. Later in Lamont's investigation, he discovers that official accounts credit Hallam with speculations about the origin of the plutonium although others had actually made the remarks. Hallam, however, headed the team to investigate the plutonium, and Hallam received the acclaim and the power.

Later Asimov describes a similar sequence of events. Lamont is set in opposition to Hallam by Hallam's reaction to his innocent suggestion about the superiority of the para-men, and again when Lamont reaches his inspiration about the Pump after a colleague remarked that Hallam was untouchable "as long as the Electron Pump is the key to human para-

dise." Still later Asimov describes the process of discovery as
Lamont follows the elusive train of thought that begins with
"what was the catch to the Electron Pump?" and ends with
the gradual equalization of natural law: "within a month he
had that feeling that every scientist recognizes—the endless
click-click as unexpected pieces fall into place, as annoying
anomalies become anomalous no more—It was the feel of
Truth." Asimov seems to be saying that discoveries begin with
accidents, but that those accidents happen to people who are
prepared by education and temperament and ability to recognize them when they occur and to follow them to their ultimate meanings.

The characters are more realistic than Asimov customarily
presents. In fact, the novel offers more anti-heroism than her-
oism, in keeping with the trends in science fiction that began
with the New Wave. Hallam is an ordinary and unlikable man
pushed into a position of power by accident, and Lamont, who
tries to tear him down, is not much better. Lamont simply
happens to be right, and Hallam happens to be wrong. Lamont's motivation is revealed at the end of Part I, however,
when he mourns not for the end of the world but that "no one
on Earth will live to know that I was right."

The characters seem to be drawn, if not from real life as in
Asimov's first mystery novel, The Death Dealers (1958), at least
from observation and combination of characteristics. In Hallam's reaction to Lamont's suggestion about para-men superiority, the reader might sense a hint of John Campbell's reaction to the possibility of alien superiority in the stories
presented to him, some of which were by Asimov himself.

Part II, titled ". . . The Gods Themselves . . . ," is concerned
with the para-men and the para-Universe. Like much that Asimov has done in the second half of his career (the novelization of Fantastic Voyage, The Sensuous Dirty Old Man, Murder at the ABA), Part II was the result of a challenge. Some of
the challenges have been posed by others; some, by Asimov
himself.

A paperback house had expressed interest in the novel after

seeing Part I. The editor asked Ashmead, "Will Asimov be putting sex into the book?" Ashmead responded, "No!" When Ashmead reported the conversation to Asimov, Asimov

> felt contrary enough to want to put sex into the book. I rarely had sex in my stories and I rarely had extraterrestrial creatures in them, either, and I knew there were not lacking those who thought that I did not include them because I lacked the imagination for it.
>
> I determined, therefore, to work up the best extraterrestrials that had ever been seen for the second part of my novel.

The extraterrestrials are among the most fascinating and believable aliens yet imagined in science fiction. Part II also is concerned almost entirely with sex. That it is alien sex must have made it all the more enjoyable for Asimov.

The planet on which the para-men exist in the para-Universe is a barren, rocky place orbiting, as scientists in Part I speculate, around a small, dim sun. The para-people find it congenial, though not as congenial as it once was. Their Universe, which burns its suns more rapidly because of the ease of the fusion reaction, is running down. The para-people are energy-eaters. They "eat" by walking or basking in the sunshine. They also spend much of their time involved with sex or family.

They are not quite gods. They are nebulous creatures, more like ghosts. As infants they can melt into each other, or even into rocks, and one sex retains the ability to melt throughout its lifetime; in fact, their reproduction depends upon it. This sex is called an Emotional or mid. There are two other sexes: a Rational or left-ling, and a Parental or right-ling. When a triad is formed, the Emotional helps the Rational and the Parental to melt together, a state in which they lose consciousness and which may last for ecstatic hours or days. During the melting, if the conditions are right, a seed may be passed from the Rational to the Parental by the Emotional. In the Parental the seed incubates into a new para-child.

Para-children are born in sequence: first a Rational, then a Parental, and finally an Emotional. The creation of an Emotional required a great deal more energy than the others and is thus more difficult. The Parental not only gives birth to the para-children but cares for them until they are mature. Parentals customarily are concerned with procreation and family and are largely motivated by instinct. Emotionals usually are concerned with eating—since they are more tenuous, they require more time to absorb the sun's energy—and with melting. As a consequence, Emotionals usually are flirtatious, social, and foolish. Rationals spend their time learning and thinking. After three children have been born (infrequently after a second three) the Rational determines that the time is right and the triad "passes on."

A second group of alien creatures lives somewhat apart within the para-Universe. They are called Hard Ones because they cannot melt. Indeed, contact with the Soft Ones, those who can melt, causes the Hard Ones pain. The Hard Ones are more rational than the Rationals; they have their own scientific concerns but act as tutors to the Rationals and mentors to the others.

Part II is about a triad that differs in significant ways from the others. Odeen, the Rational, is more intellectual than other Rationals and is the favorite pupil of a Hard One named Losten. Tritt, the Parental, is moved almost entirely by his sense of the fitness of things, but he exercises more initiative than the usual Parental: he pesters Odeen to get them an Emotional so that they can melt properly and is even bold enough to ask Losten. Losten produces Dua, the Emotional, who is relatively unconcerned with eating and thus has difficulty helping the triad produce a baby Emotional. Dua also is overly concerned with thought so that other Emotionals taunt her with the dirty name of "Left-Em," which refers to an Emotional who behaves like a Rational. Odeen enjoys talking to Dua about his ideas, however, and all three enjoy the melting, which Dua does so much better than the others, perhaps because she is different.

Dua is unhappy, and this provides much of the structure of the story. She suffered a trauma when her Parental's triad passed on; she does not want to help to create a baby Emotional because then she too might have to pass on. Odeen, who is happy with Dua and even fonder of Tritt, is unhappy only because Tritt is unhappy. Tritt is unhappy because he does not have a little Emotional to complete his group of children. He keeps after Dua to eat and after Odeen to make her eat.

All of this is gradually complicated by what Odeen and later Dua learn about their world. Thousands of cycles ago, for instance, there were many thousands of Hard Ones and millions of Soft Ones. Now there are only three hundred Hard Ones and fewer than ten thousand Soft Ones. Energy is diminishing; their sun is cooling. All the stars in their Universe are coming to an end. The fusion reaction in the para-Universe works so easily that all the particles are combined after a million lifetimes.

So the Hard Ones, led by an unseen and mysterious Hard One named Estwald, have initiated the plutonium-tungsten exchange with Earth's Universe in order to provide an artificial source of energy to keep their world going. At first, the energy is harsh and bitter to the taste, but Estwald has been working to improve it.

Part II comes to a climax when Tritt, pushed beyond endurance by Dua's unwillingness or inability to cooperate in producing a baby Emotional, goes to the caverns of the Hard Ones to get Estwald's help. When he does not find Estwald, he does something, the results of which are not apparent until later. Dua, meanwhile, in drifting away from Tritt, goes to the caverns of the Hard Ones and senses Tritt's presence. She melts completely into the cavern wall, which she has never done before, and in this state finds herself much more able to understand the Hard ones and what they are doing. She returns in excitement to Odeen and asks him questions while, hungry for once, she eats at the private feeding station that Odeen has installed for her (Dua is hungry because her melting into the rock consumed energy).

While Dua is eating, Odeen discusses with her the differences between the Universe from which they are getting energy and their own. Dua has the feeling that something bad happens in the process. Odeen says that their sun cools down a little faster, but that they do not need the sun anymore. That was not what was bothering Dua. But the discussion ends there. Dua's feeding has made her larger and compacter, and she makes an unusual erotic advance that results in a new and more satisfying melting than ever.

Later, Dua asks Odeen whether their Universe's laws don't get into the other Universe. Odeen says they do, and their suns speed up and get hotter. Dua realizes that this is where she keeps getting the something-bad feeling. Odeen admits that speeding up the nuclear fusion might make the suns in the other Universe explode. Dua is horrified—this might kill the people in the other Universe. Odeen does not understand. They won't need the people in the other Universe to make the exchange, he says, because the explosion of their sun will create such a flood of energy that they can tap it directly; it will be enough to last a million lifetimes.

Hard Ones arrive at this moment to ask if one of the triad stole a food ball (a storage battery charged at the Positron Pump). Tritt confesses that he did to feed Dua, and now he has a baby Emotional growing inside him. Dua flees in anger, feeling that Tritt has tricked her into helping to create a baby Emotional, that Odeen connived with Tritt, and that now they will pass on. She thinks she learns a bit later that the Soft Ones are machines created by the Hard Ones and that when their usefulness is over they are destroyed by the Hard Ones. She also learns that communication with the other Universe is possible. Eventually, after hours spent hiding in the walls of the Hard Ones' caverns, she learns how to send messages herself, first "F-E-E-R" and then the message beginning: "PUMP NOT STOP NOT STOP WE NOT STOP PUMP . . .."

Odeen and Tritt come to find her in the caverns that are the Hard Ones' laboratories, just as she has sent that message. She has used up almost her entire energy doing so. As they restore her from a battery, Odeen tells her she is partly right. The Hard Ones are the only living creatures in their world, but that is because the Soft Ones are the immature forms of the Hard Ones. When the Soft Ones melt, they become a Hard One for the period they do not remember. They must return to being Soft Ones while they keep developing. When the Rational realizes the true state of affairs, all three have developed sufficiently and the Rational can then guide a perfect melt that will form the Hard One forever. The Soft Ones cannot be told about this by the Hard Ones because then the development would be aborted, the time of the perfect melt could not be determined, and the Hard One would form imperfectly.

For generations the Hard Ones have been combining triads with great care to form particularly advanced Hard Ones. The triad of Odeen-Dua-Tritt was the best ever put together. And Dua was the most important addition to the triad. Losten, who brought Dua to Odeen and Tritt, was once the triad that gave birth to Dua; part of Losten was Dua's lost Parental. The Odeen-Dua-Tritt Hard One is destined to be the best ever formed. They melt and form Estwald.

Once more Asimov is not content simply with the problems of the energy exchange, which Hallam has called "the road that is downhill both ways." That part does have its central interest, to be sure, with its twists and turns and logical confirmations. In the para-Universe the Electron Pump is called, of course, the Positron Pump: it pumps positrons, not electrons. The facts of the para-Universe that have been the subject of ingenious speculation in Part I are strikingly confirmed in Part II: the small suns, the relatively short lifespan of the para-Universe (the questions raised about how the para-Universe was created and if it was created at the time our Universe was created why it is still around, or if it was created later by what mechanism, are avoided by Odeen's comment that time may pass differently in the two Universes), and most of all the alien life-patterns. Creatures of diffuse substance are made possible by the stronger nuclear force, and energy-eaters are more probable where energy is made more easily available by the fusion process. Odeen points out that in their Universe "matter doesn't fly apart" because "the tiny particles do manage to cling together across the space that separates them." Melting is not possible in the other Universe, Odeen says, because the particles spread the wave-forms more and need more room. With the transfer of natural law from the other Universe, melting would slowly become more difficult, but the Universe would long be over before it became noticeable. It is even credible that creatures who feed directly on energy might be more likely to recognize the existence of an alternate Universe and be able to transfer material to it. Moreover, the para-people have the motivation to initiate the exchange: their own imminent starvation and racial death.

These details must have delighted Asimov—the "click-click as unexpected pieces fall into place, as annoying anomalies become anomalous no more"—especially the attributes of the Hard Ones. The Hard Ones are most rational and are mostly concerned with the mind and their inquiries into the Universe not only because they are the result of a process guided by a Rational but because they are more dense. Rationals are more dense than Parentals who are more dense than Emotionals; thus Emotionals rarely are capable of thought, Parentals are capable of thought only about family matters, and Rationals devote most of their time to abstract thinking. In the para-Universe to be dense is to be intellectual. (This does not work out completely. Dua, intellectual though she is, has "retained a girlishly rarefied structure.") Thus when Dua merges with the cavern wall and becomes more dense, she can understand many things, including the language of the Hard Ones: they use air vibrations instead of the energy exchange or telepathic communication of the Soft Ones.

All of this, however, including Dua's concern about the people in the other Universe, which leads to the sending of the messages (a consequence, perhaps, of her seldom-used Emotional attributes), is reinforced by the main narrative structure, of which the relationship between the Universes is a subordinate part. The main structure concerns the triad and the working out of its problems: Tritt's desire for an Emotional and then a baby Emotional; Odeen's attempt to keep the triad harmonious, his pleasure with Dua, and his greater love for Tritt; and mostly Dua's difference and her desire to understand her situation and to avoid producing a baby Emotional and passing on. In addition to the narrative conflicts, the reader enjoys the science-fictional delight of the working out of the alien tripartite life form.

Moreover, Part II has a plentiful supply of Asimov's favorite fictional device: the mystery. Several mysteries demand solutions. Who are the Hard Ones, and why do they never talk about themselves? Why do they teach the Rationals, and what is their relation to the Soft Ones? What happens to Soft Ones when they pass on? Who is Estwald, and why does he never appear? Other intriguing questions are raised to be answered by the events of the story.

Beyond this are the philosophical and psychological comments implied by the narrative, and the style in which the narrative is presented. In Part I Asimov drew upon his experience to describe the nature of scientists and the process of science. In Part II he drew upon his experience with people on a more intimate level to describe the relationships between the sexes, even if there are three of them. The tripartite nature of the Soft Ones, who eventually combine into one mature Hard One, allows Asimov to deal with the multiple facets of human psychology.

A psychologist might suspect that Asimov's Emotional, Parental, and Rational represent Freud's Id, Superego, and Ego. Elizabeth Anne Hull in an article published in *Extrapolation* (Summer 1981) analyzes the novel, including Parts I and III, according to Eric Berne's transactional analysis, and its "child," "parent," and "adult." Asimov has denied that he knows anything about transactional analysis or Freud, and has added, a bit disingenuously perhaps (for he has made his fortune out of making obscure material comprehensible), that he probably would not understand them if he did.

No one need accept Asimov's statements about himself as absolute truth. In the afterword to Olander and Greenberg's *Asimov*, for example, Asimov first builds a case for his not having incorporated in his fiction any of the psychological and artistic aspects the essays discovered in his work because he wrote too fast and did not have the special knowledge necessary. He then admits that the parallels discovered by others might have been in his unconscious. His customary posture about literary criticism, and often psychological analysis as well, is to deny conscious intent. In 1950, however, he sat, unannounced, in a classroom in which his story "Nightfall" was analyzed, then introduced himself afterward with the comment that the analysis was all wrong. The professor (Gotthard Guenther) replied, "What makes you think, just because you are the author of 'Nightfall,' that you have the slightest inkling of what is in it?" Ever since, Asimov has been willing to admit that his subconscious may have slipped things into his story that he did not consciously intend.

In *The Gods Themselves*, however, Asimov was not so much dealing with the parts of human psychology as with the nature of men and women. He says that he was convinced at an early age that women were puzzling creatures of mystery and, though he has learned about them as he has matured, he cannot shake his early attitude. Thus Part I of *The Gods Themselves* has no women characters, and Part III has a woman in an important role (and significantly, in terms of sexual differences, as an "Intuitionist") but working as a tour guide.

Part II, however, is focused on Dua, for whom Asimov uses the pronoun "she." Tritt and Odeen are referred to as "he." It is the Emotional who is necessary for sex, who has the power to say "yes" or "no." Most Emotionals are foolish, silly, empty-headed creatures, who are concerned mostly with coquettishness, gossip, and basking in the sun; they are even described as gluttonous. They like the company of other Emotionals: Odeen reflects that "the Rational had his teacher . . . and the Parental his children—but the Emotional had all the other Emotionals." Odeen finds them incomprehensible. "Who could tell what any Emotional thought?" he asks himself. "They were so different they made left and right seem alike in everything but mind."

In the Rational, Asimov surely identifies himself, the rational man, who loves to learn and to teach and who is puzzled by the irrationality of the people around him, by the stubborn parental drives that have created the most serious problem facing the world, and most of all by those emotional responses to situations that cannot be reached by reason. In the novel, Rationals have little understanding of emotional matters. Odeen reflects that "there was almost a perverse pride among Rationals in their relative poverty of perception. Such perception wasn't a thing of the mind; it was most characteristic of Emotionals. Odeen was a Rational of Rationals, proud of reasoning rather than feeling. . . ." Only Rationals too are embarrassed by their feelings. Odeen, for instance, when he first meets Tritt feels embarrassed by an inner warmth and the feeling that there was something Tritt wanted that was utterly divorced from thought.

Rationals are not without flaws. Asimov portrays them as unable to imagine the agony of an Earth destroyed by a nova, or even, in their lack of empathy, being unable to conceive of the humanity of an alien. The final melting of the triad into a Hard One may not be so much the uniting of the parts of the psyche but the blending of flawed humans into a unified whole person combining male and female attributes, as well as jointly shared parental instincts, into one rational being.

The Parentals are less easy to assign sex. Asimov calls them "he," and Dua calls her Parental "Daddy." It would be too easy to assign them female roles; in any case, it rings false. Perhaps the Parental is an amalgam of the male and female impulses to procreation and family building. Asimov himself, according to the evidence of his autobiography, is a concerned and devoted father. The characteristics displayed by Tritt seem relatively unappealing; he is stubborn and uncaring about anything except his own satisfaction, which, to be sure, results in the continuance of the species, which otherwise might well have died out long ago. In the para-Universe, with its falling birthrate, this instinctive behavior seems essential, and Asimov grants it its necessary place.

Finally, Dua, the focus of Part II, is different from other Emotionals. As a female, Dua is concerned with rationality. She finds Odeen more fascinating, much more interesting than Tritt, and her fellow Emotionals are hopeless. "Dua was so non-Emotional an Emotional!" Odeen thinks. She is curious, she wants to find out why things are as they are, and she enjoys having Odeen teach her as much as Odeen enjoys teaching her. Odeen is pleased that she is different, pleased that she wants to share his intellectual life, and pleased that he is pleased. Without going too far into an analysis of Asimov's personal life, one might speculate that he is comparing his first wife and her lack of interest in his work with his second wife (a physician, a psychiatrist, and after their marriage a novelist as well) and her ability to share his interests and intellectual life.

These attitudes may not endear Asimov to feminists. But

if Part II has a human message as well as a novelistic one, it may be in support of the feminist position that traditional sex roles should not keep men from expressing their emotions or women from areas of life traditionally considered closed to them by biology or character.

Asimov always has insisted that he has no style as a writer, that all he wants to do is write clearly. Joe Patrouch (in his 1974 book, *The Science Fiction of Isaac Asimov*) has pointed out, accurately, that simple sentences and clear statements are in themselves a style. Asimov has been a bit critical of writers who seemed to value style over content. His famous categorization of science fiction into periods ending with style-dominance scarcely conceals a note of disappointment; he values the sociology-dominant period into which most of his own work falls.

The first two parts of *The Gods Themselves* seem unusually style-conscious for Asimov. The sentences are straightforward, and, except for the scientific explanations, the vocabulary is unadorned. A sense of place is no more evident than ever (and less than in *The Caves of Steel* and *The Naked Sun*)—even the alien landscape, often the colorful foreground of science fiction, is described simply as rocks and caverns. But the conscious arrangement of narrative elements and the way in which Asimov shares this artfulness with the reader is clearly a matter of style. Part I starts with section 6 and then flashes back to pick up the beginnings of the plutonium-186 story. In Part II, Asimov echoes the tripartite nature of the aliens by dividing the narration into segments labeled "a" for those in which Dua is the viewpoint character, "b" in which it is Odeen, and "c" in which it is Tritt, with numbers to designate the progressing sections as "1a," "1b," "1c," "2a," and so forth. In their individual narratives, Dua, Odeen, and Tritt recall the part of the story that is appropriate to each—Dua, the parting with her Parental; Odeen, the meeting with Tritt; Tritt, the asking for an Emotional who turned out to be Dua—and each subsection moves the basic story forward as well. The logical progression falters only after "6b," at which point it skips Tritt's narrative segment (all three viewpoints are represented at the end of "6b," as the melting into the Hard One occurs) and moves directly to "7abc," in which Estwald steps forward. This is fully as stylist a device as any cast up by the New Wave.

Part III is neither as involving nor as intriguing as Parts I and II. Perhaps it succumbs to Gunn's Law, which asserts that science-fiction novels tend to fall apart at the end. Asimov confronted the novelistic imperative to wind up the threads laid out with such care in the first two parts. But the winding-up process is seldom as exciting as the laying-out, and Asimov has an entire third of the novel devoted to it.

Part III is titled ". . . Contend in Vain?"—with the question mark added to provide a suggestion of hope that is ultimately justified by the resolution. The scene is Earth's Universe about a year after Lamont tried to convince Senator Burt that the Pump should be stopped. The narrative is straightforward. Two people traveling on the same vessel arrive on the moon with a group of tourists. One is described only as a middle-aged tourist. The other is Konrad Gottstein, Commissioner-Appointee to the Moon. He was formerly on the staff of Senator Burt and had been assigned an investigation of the Electron Pump for waste and personal profit-taking. The middle-aged tourist makes friends with the Lunarite tour guide Selene, pronounced SELL-uh-nee (Asimov often makes a point of how his characters' names are pronounced), and arouses her interest by asking to see the Earth-controlled proton synchrotron.

Selene is the sexual partner of Lunarite physicist Barron Neville, who is engaged in research later revealed as involved with creating an Electron Pump, or something like it, on the Moon. The Moon has no Electron Pump because the para-Universe will not accept tungsten made available there. Neville hopes to be able to learn enough to initiate an exchange from Earth's Universe rather than depending upon the para-people to do it. He also believes that Earth is conspiring to keep the Electron Pump from the Moon. He asks Selene to see the middle-aged tourist again, to play up to his growing romantic interest in her, and to find out what he is doing on the Moon and why he is interested in the proton synchrotron.

Later, after Selene has shown the middle-aged tourist something of life in the man-made tunnels of the Moon (there is some resemblance here to the caverns of the para-world) and reported on their conversations to Neville, Gottstein confronts the middle-aged tourist with knowledge of his identity: he is Benjamin Allan Denison, the once-promising radiochemist whose challenge to Hallam (described in Part I) resulted in Hallam's stubborn pursuit of the plutonium-tungsten exchange, the development of the Electron Pump, and Denison's fall from science into male cosmetics as a result of Hallam's enmity. Denison rose to a vice-presidency, which he has given up to immigrate to the Moon, where he hopes to reestablish himself as a physicist.

Gottstein remembers him as a scientist who came to Burt's committee with the theory that Lamont later developed independently. Gottstein obtains Denison's agreement to keep him informed about anything he might discover in his dealings with the Moon scientists. The departing Commissioner has warned Gottstein that something might be going on that needed watching.

Denison tells Neville about himself and is told that he can work in the Lunarite laboratories. In the laboratories Denison is able to use a Pionizer, invented by the Lunarites, which does in a small space what the proton synchrotron does in a large one. With the Pionizer Denison gets results that he feels confirm the dangers he and Lamont have warned about: within a few years or a few decades, the growing strength of the nuclear force will lead to the explosion of the sun, perhaps even the entire arm of the Galaxy. Neville discounts Denison's findings, saying that they are within the limits of error of his process. Denison explains to Selene that people believe what they want to believe. Neville does not like to leave the tunnels in which he was born and raised (like the city-dwellers in *The Caves of Steel,* he suffers from agoraphobia). He wants the Electron Pump so badly because then the Moon will not be dependent upon solar batteries, for which people must go out on the surface. Denison suggests to Selene that Earth will not shut down the Electron Pump because it is dangerous; Earth must be offered something better. He offers a clue: the number two is ridiculous and cannot exist. Selene guesses what he means: if there are two alternate Universes, there must be an infinity of them.

The accuracy of Selene's guess surprises Denison. Selene reveals, in a conversation with Neville and later with Denison, that she is an Intuitionist. Genetic manipulation, some of which was aimed at producing more people with intuitional ability, was discredited on Earth after an (undescribed) time of troubles called the Great Crisis reduced Earth's population from six billion to two billion and left behind a permanent distrust of technology and a reluctance to risk change because of possible side effects. Although Selene is not the result of a genetic experiment, her ancestors might have been. Among other things, Selene's intuition led to the invention of the Pionizer. She functions as Neville's Intuitionist.

Selene speculates to Denison that the para-Universe might not care if the sun explodes, for then they might be able to get energy directly from Earth's Universe. Indeed, para-men might even prefer that the Galactic arm explode into a quasar and would like to keep Earth from stopping the Pump before that happens. In experiments on the surface of the Moon, Denison and Selene, who have grown more intimate, use the Pionizer to tap another Universe and succeed. Gottstein comes upon them while the experiment is going on. Later, Denison explains to Gottstein that they have tapped a Universe, which might be called an anti-para-Universe, in which the strong nuclear reaction is so weak that the entire Universe could consist of a single star. It would be a situation similar to that in Earth's Universe before the explosion of the cosmic egg, or "cosmeg." As humanity taps the cosmeg-Universe for energy, the seepage of natural law will counteract the effect of the Electron Pump and with proper coordination leave a net zero result. The cosmeg-Universe, on the other hand, might eventually explode as the strong nuclear force leaked into it. This explosion, however, would result not in damage but in conditions under which life eventually would be possible. This sequence of actions might, in fact, explain the explosion of the cosmeg in Earth's Universe, as some other Universe tapped it for energy.

Gottstein offers to take this information back to Earth in the form of a paper. Denison wants Lamont and Neville to be listed as co-authors. Lamont accepts (and receives appropriate honors and position, while Hallam is demoted), but Neville refuses. In a final wrap-up, Gottstein brings back from Earth plans for constructing cosmeg pumps on the Moon because they must be operated in a vacuum. Some of the cosmeg pumping will be used for energy, but most, for a while at least, will serve to counteract the changes in field intensities introduced by the Electron Pump. Neville, however, wants to use the cosmeg pumps to convert the Moon into a stellar ship. By transferring momentum to the cosmeg-Universe, the Moon could accelerate at any convenient rate without loss of mass.

Allowing the Moon to leave Earth orbit could create problems in balancing the Electron Pumping. Denison points out, however, that the problems could be solved by constructing space stations with cosmeg pumps attached. But, he says, the Moon won't leave its orbit because there is no sense in it doing so. It would be more efficient to build starships that would be easier to accelerate and require less energy. Neville wants to take the Moon because of his neurosis. It is Neville's prison, Denison says, but it need not be the prison of every other Lunarite.

Neville is adamant even when Selene, who has been waiting in another room and has heard everything, comes in and disagrees with him. Neville is outvoted decisively by the citizens of Luna City, and the novel ends with Selene asking Denison if he would be willing to contribute sperm toward her artificial insemination. A second son for her has just been approved. They end in each other's arms.

Part of the letdown in Part III is due to the speculative intensity of Part II, which is difficult to match. By comparison, Part III seems uninventive. Even the reader's natural curiosity about the fate of Estwald and the triad in which the reader has invested so much concern is unrewarded; one does not know whether the part of Estwald that is Dua ever convinces the composite Hard One that survival should not be bought at the price of destroying the other Universe. One cannot conceive of an effective way in which the reader could be returned to the para-Universe, but this does not lessen the disappointment.

Part III does not even offer the scientific credibility of Part I. The ingenuity with which Asimov rationalized the existence of plutonium-186 and the attention he lavished on the accident-plus-preparation process by which the Electron Pump was created makes the development of energy from the cosmeg-Universe seem unlikely and unconvincing. The solution is ingenious but also convenient.

Without the intrinsic narrative interests that propel Parts I and II, Asimov resorts to artificial suspense in Part III. Instead of the natural mysteries that drive his best work, he offers concealed identities and information (the kind of substitute for the built-in puzzle that weakened *The Stars, Like Dust*). The only reason to conceal Denison's identity until section 6, for instance, is to paper over the lack of suspense with a contrived curiosity about who the middle-aged tourist is. For a while, the reader is tempted to believe and even wants it to be Lamont. In a similar way, the information that Selene is an Intuitionist is hidden from the reader (and from Denison) until section 11, even though Selene and Neville converse privately in alternating chapters. The purpose of the Lunarite physicists is kept secret nearly to the end. Asimov tries to rationalize withholding information from the reader by establishing Neville as suspicious, even paranoid. At one point Selene chides herself for thinking of the secret purpose as "the other," rather than naming it, and she says she has been infected by Neville's chronic suspicions. All of this is weakness rather than strength.

The strengths of Part III are the descriptions of lunar life, the characterization, and the final solution to the Electron Pump problem. Much of Part III is a guided tour of Lunar City and environs. It seems little more than padding in the midst of the more pressing concerns about the Electron Pump, but the scenes are presented so winningly and so thoroughly imagined that they rival the similar presentations in Heinlein's *The Moon Is a Harsh Mistress*. Acrobatic performances and games ("a melee in the giant gymnasium") get almost an entire section as does gliding (with the aid of argon-filled gliders attached to the shoes) on a lunar slope. Asimov describes the food (artificial and mushy, but the Lunarites, who have grown up on it, like it better than natural food), the language of contempt (Earthies, Lunies), the gravity (hard on Earthmen, even harder on anyone who tries to return to Earth), the difficulties of sleeping in one-sixth Earth gravity, and the problems of elimination. More importantly, he describes the social mores of the Lunarites: nudity is accepted as comfortable and natural; population is controlled by rationing the right to children; artificial insemination is the normal method of conception (although disapproved on Earth, it is allowed on the Moon for medical reasons; it is not clear whether artificial insemination is the custom among Lunarites or only between Lunarites and Earthie immigrants); and sex between Lunarite and immigrant or tourist is undesirable because of the possibility of injury to the slighter, less heavily muscled Lunarites as well as the difficulty of coordinating Earth-accustomed muscles to the Moon's gravity. This earns Asimov a pleasant reward at the end of the novel (as in The Naked Sun) when he brings Selene and Denison together.

As in Part I, the characters seem like real people. Denison is not a hero (no doubt he functions as the author's representative: Denison's age is forty-eight; Asimov's, when he wrote the novel, was fifty-one), and Selene is not a heroine. Selene's attachment to the sullen Neville seems perverse, though her later rejection of him seems correspondingly more satisfying. Neville, on the other hand, is a more classic villain (although Asimov can probably understand his attachment to his lunar tunnels and sympathize with his desire to take the solid Moon along with him on his space travels). Gottstein seems a character of convenience. The reader longs a bit for Lamont's intensity or even Bronowski's wit.

Denison, however, who downplays everything, has what is always for Asimov (and for those readers who like Asimov's fiction) the saving grace of rationality. He behaves rationally, understanding the stupidity of others (the stupidity against which the gods themselves, but not Denison in his later years, contend in vain), realizing that one must make people want what is good for them rather than waste effort and time on

trying to make them stop doing what they want to do. He accepts the weaknesses of others as readily as he admits his own.
He has learned (rather like Asimov learned to give up the
smart-aleck quip and become lovable). At the age of twenty-
five, he says, he was still such a child that he had to amuse
himself by insulting a fool for no reason other than that he
was a fool. Since Hallam's folly was not his fault, Denison
admits he was the greater fool to insult him. Since then, he
has learned not to insult others and has learned to accept help
where it is offered without false pride and without illusions
as to why it is offered. He refrains from hurting others. He
wants Neville's name added to the scientific paper as co-
author in order to save Neville's and Lunarite pride. When he
first kisses Selene, he puts his hands behind his back; when
he moves toward her at the end, he moves hesitantly.

The final strength of Part III, the solution to the scientific
problem, justifies—or almost justifies—its weaknesses. The
concept of the cosmeg-Universe seems so neatly implied by
the para-Universe, as the opposite end of the nuclear force
spectrum, that it falls naturally into place as the last piece of
the puzzle. And its existence is reinforced by the cosmological
explanation it implies for the explosion of this Universe's
original cosmic egg.

The entire novel plays itself out on Asimov's traditional bare
stage. Few surroundings are described; even the lunar environment is only referred to by the texture of its food, the lessened influence of gravity, and the presence of Earth in the
lunar sky. Asimov fiction always has had this characteristic,
perhaps reinforced by his first book-editor's criticism of his
attempts at colorful writing in the early drafts of his second
novel, The Stars, Like Dust. More likely, writing goes faster
and more easily for Asimov with limited description, and Asimov always has written swiftly. Moreover, ideas play themselves out most effectively and most clearly in isolation, and
Asimov, in The Gods Themselves as the present example, is
more concerned about the "idea" of lunar life than about its
reality.

The important aspect of The Gods Themselves may be not

so much what it is but what it represents. Though better written, better conceived, and even more greatly honored than earlier Asimov work, The Gods Themselves is not as important as half a dozen of those earlier books. The novel came at a time when science fiction was maturing into individual statements by individual authors; each new novel was considered mostly on its own merits rather than on its context and its contribution to that context. Each, therefore, might be individually superior but less important in terms of the genre of which it was a part. So it was with The Gods Themselves. It was important as a statement by Asimov that science still could be the distinguishing characteristic of science fiction, that the older traditions of science fiction (not always honored in their own time, even by Asimov) could be built upon rather than discarded, that science-important fiction could be recognized as contemporary. And, as a personal statement, the novel demonstrated that Asimov still could write serious science fiction.

Whether Asimov will write another science-fiction novel after the sequel to The Foundation Trilogy may be irrelevant. He is an important writer of our time, a recognized master of the science popularization, a polymath profligate with books in many fields and pursued by opinion-seekers of all kinds on a variety of subjects, a witty, expensive, much-sought-after speaker, a commercial spokesman upon occasion, and only last a science-fiction writer, insofar as his general reputation goes. The occasions of his one hundredth and two hundredth book publications brought him considerable attention from the book world and perhaps even from the book-reading world. He has been reviewed and interviewed and profiled in and on a variety of national media. He is an institution. The delightful part of the man is that, in spite of his fame and wealth and general reputation, he has never forgotten his roots. He still considers himself a science-fiction writer. He was shaped by science fiction and by John Campbell, just as he was shaped by an upbringing in Brooklyn and his servitude in the series of candy stores from which he was liberated only late in his teens, by his precociousness, and by his father's stern ethical principles. Out of all these influences came the Asimov stories in the Golden Age of the magazines and the books published when science fiction first was breaking into the book market. As a consequence, the stories influenced the genre because they led the way in critical times. They retain that importance, but it may exceed their basic value as literature.

If Asimov writes another novel like *The Gods Themselves*, it will be applauded by his readers, who by this time number in the millions. But nothing Asimov can do in the science-fiction field will enhance or detract from his accomplishments. Asimov still has the power to give pleasure through his rational brilliance, to himself as well as to others. If he writes more science fiction, he will write it, as he writes other books these days, for personal satisfaction.

At the end of the first volume of his autobiography, Asimov wrote that in science fiction "I had gone as far as I could. I might do things that were better than "Nightfall," *The Foundation Trilogy, I, Robot,* or *The Caves of Steel,* but surely not much better." That judgment was sound: he may have done better but not much better. What he did in his chosen field, however, was no small thing. Those works, and other Asimov stories and books, helped to shape science fiction just as Asimov himself was shaped by it. Asimov's continuing presence in the field of science fiction has importance as a reminder not only of the past but of the way in which the past is a foundation for the present, and of the way in which the past can renew itself. Rationality still can be relevant.

CHRONOLOGY

1920 Isaac Asimov is born in Petrovichi, U.S.S.R., on January 2 (the date may have been as early as October 4, 1919), first child of Judah Asimov and Anna Rachel Asimov, née Berman.

1923 The Asimovs emigrate to the United States and settle in Brooklyn.

1925 Teaches himself to read and begins his career as a child prodigy.

1926 His father buys the first of a series of candy stores in Brooklyn. His life begins to be shaped by the demands of the store.

1928 Becomes a U.S. citizen.

1929 Discovers science-fiction magazines and becomes a fan.

1931 Attempts his first fiction.

1932 Enters high school.

1935 Enters Seth Low Junior College. His writing increases. Writes a letter to *Astounding* that is published.

1936 Continues his college education at Columbia.

1937 Begins writing letters to *Astounding* again.

1938 Begins to keep a diary and joins the Futurians. Takes his first story to John W. Campbell, Jr., new editor of *Astounding*.

1939 First published story, "Marooned Off Vesta," appears in *Amazing Stories*, "Trends," in *Astounding*. Earns his B.S. degree from Columbia and enters graduate school there, majoring in chemistry.

1940 Begins writing robot stories.

1941 Writes "Nightfall."

1942 Begins the Foundation series with "Foundation." Suspends his graduate studies to be a chemist at the U.S. Navy Yard in Philadelphia. Marries Gertrude Blugerman.

1945 Is drafted after V-J Day (and released less than a year later).

1946 Returns to his studies at Columbia.

1948 Earns his Ph.D. and takes up post-doctorate work at Columbia.

1949 Is hired as an instructor in biochemistry at the Boston University School of Medicine.

1950 Doubleday publishes his first novel, *Pebble in the Sky*; Gnome Press, his first collection, *I, Robot*. His books continue to appear every year.

1951 Son David is born. Is promoted to assistant professor.

1952 First non-fiction book, *Biochemistry and Human Metabolism*, is published. Doubleday publishes first Lucky Starr juvenile. He continues to alternate science fiction with non-fiction books and articles, particularly science popularizations.

1955 Daughter Robyn is born.

1956 Is paid $10 for his first talk and begins a career as a popular speaker.

1957 Begins his first monthly science column for *Venture Science Fiction* (later taken over by *Fantasy and Science Fiction*).

1958 Leaves full-time teaching for full-time freelance writing. After 1958 publishes no new science-fiction novels until the novelization of the screenplay for *Fantastic Voyage* in 1966 and *The Gods Themselves* in 1972. Continues writing an occasional science-fiction short story, but most writing is non-fiction.

1962 Edits *The Hugo Winners*, the first of his anthologies, and begins the autobiographical comments that characterize the rest of his collections and anthologies.

1963 Is awarded a "Special Hugo" by the World Science Fiction Convention for his science articles in *Fantasy & Science Fiction*.

1966 Is guest-of-honor at the World Science Fiction Convention. Foundation series wins a Hugo. A special edition of *Fantasy & Science Fiction* is dedicated to Asimov and his work.

1969 Publishes his 100th book.

1970 Separates from his wife and moves back to New York.

1972 Doubleday publishes *The Gods Themselves*.

1973 Wins a Nebula Award and a Hugo Award for *The Gods Themselves*. Is divorced and marries Dr. Janet Jeppson.

1974 Publishes *Before the Golden Age*.

1976 The first issue of *Isaac Asimov's Science Fiction Magazine* appears.

1977 "The Bicentennial Man" wins both a Nebula and a Hugo.

1979 Publishes his 200th book, including the first volume of his autobiography, *In Memory Yet Green*.

1980 The second volume of his autobiography, *In Joy Still Felt*, is Asimov volume 214.

CHECKLIST OF WORKS
BY ISAAC ASIMOV

In the following list of short stories some of the titles of magazines in which the stories appeared have been shortened. Common designations such as "Stories" or "Science Fiction" have been omitted or abbreviations such as SF for "Science Fiction" have been used. Below is a full listing of abbreviations.

Amazing Amazing Stories
Analog Analog Science Fiction/Science Fact
Asimov's SF Magazine Isaac Asimov's Science Fiction Magazine
Astonishing Astonishing Stories
Astounding Astounding Science Fiction
B.U. Graduate Journal Boston University Graduate Journal
F&SF The Magazine of Fantasy and Science Fiction
Fantastic Universe Fantastic Universe Science Fiction
Future Future Fiction (1940), Future Combined with Science Fiction Stories (1950), Future Science Fiction (after 1952)
Galaxy Galaxy Science Fiction
If If, Worlds of Science Fiction (to 1959), Worlds of If (1959–74)
Infinity Infinity Science Fiction
Marvel Marvel Science Fiction
Planet Planet Stories
Satellite Satellite Science Fiction
SF Quarterly Science Fiction Quarterly
SF Stories Science Fiction Stories
Space Space Science Fiction
Star SF Star Science Fiction
Startling Startling Stories
Stellar Stellar Science Fiction
Super Science Super Science Stories
Super SF Super-Science Fiction
Thrilling Wonder Thrilling Wonder Stories
Universe Universe Science Fiction
Venture Venture Science Fiction

The abbreviation of the Asimov collection in which the short story is reprinted is also given in the following list. Full titles of those collections with their abbreviations following in parentheses can be found under "Science-Fiction Short Stories and Short-Story Collections" (p. 225). The full title of the appropriate *Foundation Trilogy* volume or of *Opus 100* is given following a short story that later appeared as part of that work.

Short Stories

1930s

"Marooned Off Vesta," *Amazing*, March 1939; AM, TBOIA.
"The Weapon too Dreadful To Use," *Amazing*, May 1939; TEA.
"Trends," *Astounding*, July 1939; TEA.

1940s

"Half-Breed," *Astounding*, February 1940; TEA.
"Ring Around the Sun," *Future*, March 1940; TEA.
"The Callistan Menace" ("Stowaway") *Astonishing*, April 1940; TEA.
"The Magnificent Possession," *Future*, July 1940; TEA.
"Robbie" ("Strange Playfellow"), *Super Science*, September 1940; I,R.
"Homo Sol," *Astounding*, September 1940; TEA.
"Half-Breeds on Venus," *Astonishing*, December 1940; TEA.
"The Secret Sense," *Cosmic Stories*, March 1941; TEA.
"History," *Super Science*, March 1941; TEA.
"Heredity," *Astonishing*, April 1941; TEA.
"Reason," *Astounding*, April 1941; I,R.
"Liar!," *Astounding*, May 1941; I,R.
"Super-Neutron," *Astonishing*, September 1941; TEA.
"Nightfall," *Astounding*, September 1941; NAOS, TBOIA.
"Not Final!," *Astounding*, October 1941; TEA.
"Christmas on Ganymede," *Startling*, January 1942; TEA.
"Robot AL-76 Goes Astray," *Amazing*, February 1942; TROTR.
"Black Friar of the Flame," *Planet*, Spring 1942; TEA.
"Runaround," *Astounding*, March 1942; I,R.
"Time Pussy," *Astounding*, April 1942; TEA.
"Foundation" ("The Encyclopedists"), *Astounding*, May 1942; *Foundation*.
"Bridle and Saddle," ("The Mayors"), *Astounding*, June 1942; *Foundation*.
"Victory Unintentional," *Super Science*, August 1942; TROTR.
"The Hazing," *Thrilling Wonder*, October 1942; TEA.
"The Imaginary," *Super Science*, November 1942; TEA.

"Death Sentence," *Astounding*, November 1943; TEA.
— "Catch That Rabbit," *Astounding*, February 1944; I,R.
"The Big and the Little" ("The Traders"), *Astounding*, August 1944; *Foundation*.
"The Wedge" ("The Merchant Princes"), *Astounding*, October 1944; *Foundation*.
"Blind Alley," *Astounding*, March 1945; TEA.
"Dead Hand" ("The General"), *Astounding*, April 1945; *Foundation and Empire*.
— "Escape" ("Paradoxical Escape"), *Astounding*, August 1945; I,R.
"The Mule," *Astounding*, November, December 1945; *Foundation and Empire*.
— "Evidence," *Astounding*, September 1946; I,R.
— "Little Lost Robot," *Astounding*, March 1947; I,R.
"Now You See It" . . . ("Search by the Mule"), *Astounding*, January 1948; *Second Foundation*.
"No Connection," *Astounding*, June 1948; TEA.
"The Red Queen's Race," *Astounding*, January 1949; TEA.
"Mother Earth," *Astounding*, May 1949; TEA.
". . . And Now You Don't" ("Search by the Foundation"), *Astounding*, November, December 1949, January 1950; *Second Foundation*.

1950s

"The Evitable Conflict," *Astounding*, June 1950; I,R.
"Legal Rites," *Weird Tales*, September 1950; TEA.
"Darwinian Pool Room," *Galaxy*, October 1950; BJAOS.
"Green Patches," *Galaxy*, November 1950; NAOS.
"Day of the Hunters" ("Big Game"), *Future*, November 1950; BJAOS.
"The Little Man on the Subway," *Fantasy Book*, Vol. I, No. 6, 1950; TEA.
"Satisfaction Guaranteed," *Amazing*, April 1951; EIRE, TROTR.
"Hostess," *Galaxy*, May 1951; NAOS.
"Breeds There a Man . . . . ?" *Astounding*, June 1951; NAOS, TAGC.
"C-Chute," *Galaxy*, October 1951; NAOS.
"Shah Guido G," *Marvel*, November 1951; BJAOS.
"The Fun They Had," NEA Service, December 1951; EIRE, TBOIA.
" 'In a Good Cause—,' " *New Tales of Space and Time*, 1951; NAOS.
"Youth," *Space*, May 1952; TMWAOS.
"What If—," *Fantastic*, Summer 1952; NAOS.
"The Martian Way," *Galaxy*, November 1952; TMWAOS, TBOIA.
"The Deep," *Galaxy*, December 1952; TMWAOS.
"Button, Button," *Startling*, January 1953; BJAOS.
"The Monkey's Finger," *Startling*, February 1953; BJAOS.
"Sally," *Fantastic*, May–June 1953; NAOS.
"Flies," *F&SF*, June 1953; NAOS.

"Kid Stuff," *Beyond*, September 1953; EIRE.
"Belief," *Astounding*, October 1953; TAGC.
"Everest," *Universe*, December 1953; BJAOS.
" 'Nobody Here But—,' " *Star SF*, 1953; NAOS.
"Christmas on Ganymede," *Wonder Stories Annual*, 1953; TEA.
"Sucker Bait," *Astounding*, February, March 1954; TMWAOS.
"The Immortal Bard," *Universe*, May 1954; EIRE.
"Let's Not," *B.U. Graduate Journal*, December 1954; BJAOS.
"The Pause," *Time To Come*, 1954; BJAOS.
"It's Such a Beautiful Day," *Star SF*, #3, 1954; NAOS, TAGC.
"The Portable Star," *Thrilling Wonder*, Winter 1955.
"The Singing Bell," *F&SF*, January 1955; AM.
"Risk," *Astounding*, May 1955; TROTR.
"The Last Trump," *Fantastic Universe*, June 1955; EIRE.
"Franchise," *If*, August 1955; EIRE.
"The Talking Stone," *F&SF*, October 1955; AM.
"Dreamworld," *F&SF*, November 1955; *Opus 100*.
"Dreaming Is a Private Thing," *F&SF*, December 1955; EIRE.
"The Message," *F&SF*, February 1956; EIRE.
"The Dead Past," *Astounding*, April 1956; EIRE, TBOIA.
"Hell-Fire," *Fantastic Universe*, May 1956; EIRE.
"Living Space," *SF Stories*, May 1956; EIRE.
"What's in a Name?," *The Saint Detective*, May–June 1956; AM.
"The Dying Night," *F&SF*, July 1956; NT, AM, TBOIA.
"Someday," *Infinity*, August 1956; EIRE.
"Pate de Foie Gras," *Astounding*, September 1956; AM.
"The Watery Place," *Satellite*, October 1956; EIRE.
"First Law," *Fantastic Universe*, October 1956; TROTR.
"The Last Question," *SF Quarterly*, November 1956; NT, TBOIA, *Opus 100*.
"Gimmicks Three" ("The Brazen Locked Room"), *F&SF*, November 1956; EIRE.
"Jokester," *Infinity*, December 1956; EIRE.
"Each an Explorer," *Future*, #30, 1956; BJAOS.
"Strikebreaker" ("Male Strikebreaker"), *The Original SF Stories*, January 1957; NAOS.
"The Dust of Death," *Venture*, January 1957; AM.
"Let's Get Together," *Infinity*, February 1957; TROTR.
"A Woman's Heart," *Satellite*, June 1957.
"Blank!," *Infinity*, June 1957; BJAOS.
"Does a Bee Care?" *If*, June 1957; BJAOS.
"Profession," *Astounding*, July 1957; NT.
"It's Such a Beautiful Day," *Authentic SF Series*, July 1957; NAOS.
"A Loint of Paw," *F&SF*, August 1957; AM.
"Ideas Die Hard," *Galaxy*, October 1957.
"I'm in Marsport Without Hilda," *Venture*, November 1957; NT, AM.
"Galley Slave," *Galaxy*, December 1957; TROTR.

"The Gentle Vultures," *Super SF*, December 1957; NT.
"Insert Knob A in Hole B," *F&SF*, December 1957; NAOS.
"Lenny," *Infinity*, January 1958; TROTR.
"Silly Asses," *Future*, February 1958; BJAOS.
"The Feeling of Power," *If*, February 1958; NT, *Opus 100*.
"All the Troubles of the World," *Super SF*, April 1958; NT.
"Buy Jupiter," *Venture*, May 1958; BJAOS.
"The Clash of Cymbals," *Venture*, July 1958.
"The Up-to-Date Sorceror," *F&SF*, July 1958; NAOS.
"The Ugly Little Boy" ("Lastborn"), *Galaxy*, September 1958; NT.
"S, as in Zebatinsky" ("Spell My Name with an S"), *Star SF*, #4, 1958; NT.
"A Statue for Father" ("Benefactor of Humanity"), *Satellite*, February 1959; BJAOS.
"Anniversary," *Amazing*, March 1959; AM, TBOIA.
"Unto the Fourth Generation," *F&SF*, April 1959; NAOS.
"Obituary," *F&SF*, August 1959; AM.
"Rain, Rain, Go Away," *Fantastic Universe*, September 1959; BJAOS.

1960s

"The Covenant," *Fantastic*, July 1960.
"What Is This Thing Called Love?" ("Playboy and the Slime God"), *Amazing*, March 1961; NAOS.
"The Machine That Won the War," *F&SF*, October 1961; NAOS.
"My Son, the Physicist," *Scientific American*, February 1962; NAOS.
"Star Light," *Scientific American*, October 1962; AM.
"Author! Author!," *The Unknown 5*, 1964; TEA.
"Eyes Do More Than See," *F&SF*, April 1965; NAOS.
"Founding Father," *Galaxy*, August 1965; BJAOS.
"The Billiard Ball," *If*, March 1967; AM, TBOIA.
"Segregationist," *Abbottempo*, Book 4, 1967; NAOS.
"Exile to Hell," *Analog*, May 1968; BJAOS.
"Key Item," *F&SF*, July 1968; BJAOS.
"The Proper Study," *Boys' Life*, September 1968; BJAOS.
"The Holmes-Ginsbook Device," *If*, December 1968; *Opus 100*.
"Feminine Intuition," *F&SF*, October 1969; TBMAOS.

1970s

"Waterclap," *Galaxy*, May 1970; TBMAOS.
"2430 A.D.," *IBM Magazine*, October 1970; BJAOS.
"The Greatest Asset," *Analog*, January 1972; BJAOS.
"Mirror Image," *Analog*, April 1972; TBOIA.
"Take a Match," *New Dimensions* II, 1972; BJAOS.
"Light Verse," *Saturday Evening Post*, October 1973; BJAOS.
"Thiotimoline to the Stars," *Astounding, the John W. Campbell Memorial Anthology*, 1973; BJAOS.

"That Thou Art Mindful of Him," *F&SF*, May 1974; TBMAOS.

"Stranger in Paradise," *If*, May–June 1974; TBMAOS.

"Half-Baked Publisher's Delight," *If*, August 1974.

"The Heavenly Host," *Boys' Life*; December 1974.

"The Life and Times of Multivac," *New York Times Magazine*, January 5, 1975; TBMAOS.

"A Boy's Best Friend," *Boys' Life*; March 1975.

"Point of View," *Boys' Life*, July 1975.

"The Winnowing," *Analog*, February 1976; TBMAOS.

"The Bicentennial Man," *Stellar*, #2, February 1976; TBMAOS.

"Old-Fashioned," *Bell Telephone Magazine*, February 1976; TBMAOS.

"Marching In," *High Fidelity*, April 1976; TBMAOS.

"Birth of a Notion," *Amazing*, April 1976; TBMAOS.

"The Tercentennary Incident," *Ellery Queen's Mystery Magazine*, August 1976; TBMAOS.

"To Tell at a Glance," *Saturday Evening Post*, February 1977.

"True Love," *American Way*, February 1977.

"Think!," *Asimov's SF Magazine*, Spring 1977.

"Sure Thing," *Asimov's SF Magazine*, Summer 1977.

"About Nothing," *Asimov's SF Magazine*; Summer 1977.

"Found!," *Omni*, November 1978.

"Nothing for Nothing," *Asimov's SF Magazine*, February 1979.

"Fair Exchange," *Asimov's SF Adventure Magazine*, Fall 1979.

"Josephine and the Space Machine," Field Newspaper Syndicate, 1979.

1980s

"The Last Answer," *Analog*, January 1980.

"For the Birds," *Asimov's SF Magazine*, May 1980.

"Death of a Foy," *F&SF*; October 1980.

"A Perfect Fit," *EDN*, October 14, 1981.

"Ignition Point," *Finding the Right Speaker*, 1981.

"Lest We Remember," *Asimov's SF Magazine*, forthcoming.

"One Night of Song," *F&SF*, forthcoming.

"The Smile that Loses," *F&SF*, forthcoming.

Science-Fiction Novels

Pebble in the Sky. Doubleday, 1950.

The Stars, Like Dust. Doubleday, 1951.

Foundation. Gnome (Doubleday), 1951.

David Starr: Space Ranger. Doubleday, 1952.

Foundation and Empire. Gnome (Doubleday), 1952.

The Currents of Space. Doubleday, 1952.

Second Foundation. Gnome (Doubleday), 1953.

Lucky Starr and the Pirates of the Asteroids. Doubleday, 1953.

The Caves of Steel. Doubleday, 1954.
Lucky Starr and the Oceans of Venus. Doubleday, 1954.
The End of Eternity. Doubleday, 1955.
Lucky Starr and the Big Sun of Mercury. Doubleday, 1956.
The Naked Sun. Doubleday, 1957.
Lucky Starr and the Rings of Saturn. Doubleday, 1958.
Fantastic Voyage. Houghton Mifflin, 1966.
The Gods Themselves. Doubleday, 1972.

Mystery Novels

The Death Dealers. Avon, 1958.
Murder at the ABA. Doubleday, 1976.

Science-Fiction Short Stories and Short-Story Collections

I, Robot (I,R). Gnome (Doubleday), 1950.
The Martian Way and Other Stories. (TMWAOS). Doubleday, 1955.
Earth Is Room Enough (EIRE). Doubleday, 1957.
Nine Tomorrows (NT). Doubleday, 1959.
The Rest of the Robots (TROTR). Doubleday, 1964.
Through a Glass, Clearly (TAGC). New English Library, 1967.
Asimov's Mysteries (AM). Doubleday, 1968.
Nightfall and Other Stories (NAOS). Doubleday, 1969.
The Best New Thing. World Publishing, 1971.
The Early Asimov (TEA). Doubleday, 1972.
The Best of Isaac Asimov (TBOIA). Sphere, 1973.
Have You Seen These? NESRAA, 1974.
Buy Jupiter and Other Stories (BJAOS). Doubleday, 1975.
The Heavenly Host. Walker, 1975.
"The Dream," "Benjamin's Dream," and "Benjamin's Bicentennial
    Blast." Private print., 1976.
Good Taste. Apocalypse, 1976.
The Bicentennial Man and Other Stories (TBMAOS). Doubleday, 1976.
Three by Asimov. Targ, 1981.
The Complete Robot Short Story Book. Doubleday, forthcoming.
A short-story collection including the short stories from 1977 through
    1981 and a few others. Doubleday, forthcoming.

Mystery Short-Story Collections

Tales of the Black Widowers. Doubleday, 1974.
More Tales of the Black Widowers. Doubleday, 1976.

The Key Word and Other Mysteries. Walker, 1977.
Casebook of the Black Widowers. Doubleday, 1980.

Science-Fiction Anthologies (Edited by Asimov)

The Hugo Winners. Doubleday, 1962.
Fifty Short Science-fiction Tales (with Groff Conklin). Collier, 1963.
Tomorrow's Children. Doubleday, 1966.
Where Do We Go From Here? Doubleday, 1971.
The Hugo Winners, Volume II. Doubleday, 1971.
Nebula Award Stories Eight. Harper & Row, 1973.
Before the Golden Age. Doubleday, 1974.
The Hugo Winners, Volume III. Doubleday, 1977.
One Hundred Great Science-fiction Short-short Stories (with Martin
    H. Greenberg and Joseph D. Olander). Doubleday, 1978.
Isaac Asimov Presents the Great SF Stories, 1: 1939 (with Martin H.
    Greenberg). DAW Books, 1979.
Isaac Asimov Presents the Great SF Stories, 2: 1940 (with Martin H.
    Greenberg). DAW Books, 1979.
The Science Fictional Solar System (with Martin H. Greenberg and
    Charles G. Waugh). Harper & Row, 1979.
The Thirteen Crimes of Science Fiction (with Martin H. Greenberg
    and Charles G. Waugh). Doubleday, 1979.
Microcosmic Tales (with Martin H. Greenberg and Joseph D. Olan-
    der). Taplinger, 1980.
Isaac Asimov Presents the Great SF Stories, 3: 1941 (with Martin H.
    Greenberg). DAW Books, 1980.
The Future in Question (with others). Fawcett, 1980.
Who Dun It?. Houghton Mifflin, 1980.
Space Mail. Fawcett, 1980.
Microcosmic Tales (with others). Taplinger, 1980.
The Seven Deadly Sins of Science Fiction (with Charles G. Waugh
    and Martin H. Greenberg). Fawcett, 1980.
The Future I (with Martin H. Greenberg and Joseph D. Olander).
    Fawcett, 1980.
Isaac Asimov Presents the Great SF Stories, 4: 1942 (with Martin H.
    Greenberg). DAW Books, 1980.
Isaac Asimov Presents the Best Science Fiction of the 19th Century
    (with Martin H. Greenberg and Charles G. Waugh). Beaufort, 1981.
The Seven Cardinal Virtues of Science Fiction (with Charles G. Waugh
    and Martin H. Greenberg). Fawcett, 1981.
Fantastic Creatures. Franklin Watts, 1981.
Miniature Mysteries. Taplinger, 1981.
The Twelve Crimes of Christmas. Avon, 1981.
Isaac Asimov Presents the Great SF Stories, 5: 1943 (with Martin H.
    Greenberg). DAW Books, 1981.

Catastrophes (with Martin H. Greenberg and Charles G. Waugh).
    Fawcett, 1981.
Isaac Asimov Presents the Great SF Stories, 6: 1944 (with Martin H.
    Greenberg). DAW Books, 1981.

Autobiography

In Memory Yet Green. Doubleday, 1979.
In Joy Still Felt. Doubleday, 1980.

Other Works

Opus 100. Houghton Mifflin, 1969.
Opus 200. Houghton Mifflin, 1979.
Asimov on Science Fiction. Doubleday, 1981.

SELECT LIST OF WORKS
ABOUT ISAAC ASIMOV

Allen, L. David, *Asimov's Foundation Trilogy and Other Works* (Lincoln, Neb.: Cliff's Notes, 1977). A follow-up by a University of Nebraska English department faculty member to his Cliff's Notes *Science Fiction: An Introduction* (1973), in which he analyzes *I, Robot.* Some valuable comments about how Asimov's works function as fiction.

Goble, Neil, *Asimov Analyzed* (Baltimore: Mirage, 1972). This is a fascinating study of Asimov's writing strategies and style in non-fiction and fiction, with word-frequency counts and sentence and paragraph analysis.

Miller, Marjorie M., *Isaac Asimov: A Checklist of Works Published in the United States, March 1939–May 1972* (Kent: Kent State University Press, 1972). The basic checklist, though now dated.

Moskowitz, Sam, "Isaac Asimov" in *Seekers of Tomorrow: Masters of Modern Science Fiction* (Cleveland: World, 1966). A beginning look at Asimov's life and work even before Asimov himself had started writing about it.

Olander, Joseph D., and Martin H. Greenberg, eds., *Isaac Asimov* (New York: Taplinger, 1977). One of a series of collections of essays on a single author edited by Olander and Greenberg, this volume brings together a variety of views about various aspects of Asimov's work, concluding with Asimov's unusual reaction to all the analysis.

Patrouch, Joseph F., *The Science Fiction of Isaac Asimov* (Garden City, N.Y.: Doubleday, 1974). An analysis of Asimov's works that considers their narrative success or failure. The author teaches English literature at the University of Dayton and in the late 1970s published science fiction of his own.

Tepper, Matthew B., *Asimov Science Fiction Bibliography* (Chinese Ducked Press, 1970). An early bibliography.

Wollheim, Donald A., *The Universe Makers* (New York: Harper & Row, 1971). A personal view of the development of science fiction by a pioneer author and editor, now a publisher, in which Asimov, and particularly his Foundation series, plays a key role, especially in establishing a consensus future history.

INDEX